Financing Transportation Networks

For Roslyn and Trinh

Financing Transportation Networks

David M. Levinson

Assistant Professor of Civil Engineering, University of Minnesota, USA

TRANSPORT ECONOMICS, MANAGEMENT AND POLICY

Edward Elgar
Cheltenham, UK • Northampton, MA, USA

© David M. Levinson 2002

Published by
Edward Elgar Publishing Limited
Glensanda House
Montpellier Parade
Cheltenham
Glos GL50 1UA
UK

Edward Elgar Publishing, Inc.
136 West Street
Suite 202
Northampton
Massachusetts 01060
USA

A catalogue record for this book
is available from the British Library

Library of Congress Cataloguing in Publication Data
Levinson, David, 1967-
    Financing transportation networks / David Levinson.
        p.cm. – (Transport economics, management, and policy)
    Includes bibliographical references and index.
    1. Toll roads. 2. Roads–Finance. I. Title. II. Series.

HE336.T64 L48 2002
388.1'14–dc21   2001040976

ISBN 1 84064 594 6

Printed and bound in Great Britain by Biddles Ltd, *www.biddles.co.uk*

Contents

Acknowledgements

This book is based in part on my doctoral dissertation *On Whom the Toll Falls* completed in 1998. That work was greatly aided by my committee, ably chaired by Mark Hansen, and including Carlos Daganzo, David Gillen, and Betty Deakin. In addition, Adib Kanafani (along with David Gillen) was a co-author on the "full costs" research on which Chapter 3 is based, and Elva Chang was a co-author on the electronic toll collection report on which Chapter 12 is based.

In addition to those named above, the book was further informed by helpful comments from numerous individuals who read previous drafts of parts of this work, or listened to presentations. I would like to thank the following individuals for their comments and ideas: Gary Barnes, Marcus Berliant, Ken Button, Trinh Carpenter, Joy Dahlgren, Robert Forsythe, Todd Goldman, Phil Goetz, Kingsley Haynes, Yuanlin Huang, Shara Lynn Kelsey, Daniel Klein, John Lalos, Robin Lindsey, Lars Lundquist, Adrian Moore, John Quigley, Gabriel Roth, Steve Shladover, Steve Schmanske, Bill Stone, Roger Stough, Erik Verhoef, Marty Wachs, Mel Webber, Tara Weidner, and Stein Weissenberger.

I also want to thank students of my Transportation Economics and Transportation Systems Analysis classes who helped discuss earlier drafts of the book, in particular: Ravi-Praveen Ambadipudi, Rabinder Bains, Shantanu Das, Sujay Davuluri, John Hourdakis, Sesh Kanchi, Ramachandra Karamalaputi, Jiji Kottommannil, Satyanarayana Muthuswamy, Sreemannarayan Nanduri, Pavithra Parthasarathi, Peter Rafferty, Ravi Rajamani, Kate Sanderson, Adarsh Sekhar, Atif Sheikh, Prasoon Sinha, Vijay Subramaniam, Bhanu Yerra, Lei Zhang, and Xi Zou.

The congestion pricing email list administered by the Humphrey Institute of the University of Minnesota engendered some stimulating discussions reflected in Chapters 10 and 11, suggesting there is some signal amidst the noise.

Various parts of this research were presented at the Conference on External Costs of Transportation, Montreal, October 1996; North American Meeting of the Regional Science Association International, in Arlington, Virginia, November 1996; University of California at Davis Conference on the Social Costs of Highway Transportation, May 1997; Transportation Research Board Conferences in Washington DC in January 1998, 2000, and

2001; Western Regional Science Association Meetings in February 1998 in Monterey and 1999 in Ojai California; and the 14th International Symposium on Transportation and Traffic Theory, July 1999 in Jerusalem. It has also been presented at seminars at Portland State University, George Mason University, Massachusetts Institute of Technology, University of Iowa, University of Illinois at Urbana-Champaign, Purdue University, Florida International University, and the University of California at Berkeley. Comments and questions from the audiences of those sessions helped shape the final work

This research was funded in part by the California High Speed Rail Commission and California Department of Transportation as part of a study on The Full Cost of Intercity Transportation: An Intermodal Comparison; a Dissertation Fellowship from the University of California Transportation Center, University of California at Berkeley's PATH program, the Value Pricing Project at the Humphrey Institute of the University of Minnesota, and the Department of Civil Engineering at the University of Minnesota.

Parts of this book have been previously published, and are used with permission of the respective publishers. The introduction and conclusions are drawn from "Taxing Foreigners Living Abroad", Access #13; (1998) pp. 16-21. Chapter 2 previously appeared as "Road Pricing in Practice", Chapter 2 of *Road Pricing, Traffic Congestion and the Environment*, (ed.) Ken Button, Erik Verhoef. Edward Elgar Publishers. Chapter 3 includes part of "A Comparison of the Social Costs of Air and Highway", *Transport Reviews* 18:3 (1998) pp. 215-240, and "The Full Cost of Intercity Highway Transportation", *Transportation Research -D* 3:4 (1997) pp. 207-223. Chapter 4 appeared as "Why States Toll: An Empirical Model of Finance Choice", *Journal of Transport Economics and Policy* 35(2) (2001) pp. 223-238. Part of Chapter 6 was previously published as "Financing Infrastructure Over Time", *American Society of Civil Engineers Journal of Urban Planning and Development*, 127(4) (2001) pp. 146-157. Chapter 8 appeared as "Revenue Choice on a Serial Network", *Journal of Transport Economics and Policy* 34(1) (2000) pp. 69-98.

1. Introduction

'To improve the British economy, I'd tax all foreigners living abroad'
(Chapman et al. 1989).

Will toll roads ever be the norm and 'free' roads a distant memory? Today's electronic toll collection technology can assess tolls from vehicles traveling at full speed on toll roads, bridges, and tunnels, permitting us to take seriously the notion that direct financing of roads might again become widespread. Transportation economists advocate tolls that vary by time of day to finance highways, mitigate congestion, and internalize the external costs of vehicle emissions and pavement damage.[1] Yet others argue that 'the prospects for widespread adoption of congestion pricing are extremely limited' because only a small political constituency (principally transportation economists and planners) favors this kind of pricing (Wachs 1994, p.15).

While the use of tolls to manage the externalities of congestion and pollution is relatively new in the realm of highways, road pricing to build and maintain infrastructure has a long history. However, most roads are still financed through gas taxes and general revenue. Future trends and policies may again shift the balance.

Implementing congestion pricing on existing toll roads is straightforward, as the adoption of time-of-day variation on roads such as the New Jersey Turnpike and many toll bridges has shown. Many different services already have prices that vary by time-of-day, including telephones (cheaper evening and weekend rates), movie theaters (the matinee show) and restaurants (the 'early bird' special). Giving discounts to travelers during the uncongested off-peak should attract much less opposition than an extra (punitive) toll on peak period travelers. Setting the right tolls, so that time-of-day pricing is as efficient as possible without being too complex, is a challenging but surmountable problem. However, establishing toll roads in the first place is difficult. This problem has two components: constructing new toll roads and converting old 'free' roads.

New or widened roads can be financed either through tolls or from more broadly based revenue sources such as gas taxes. With the completion of the interstate highway system, American localities must bear a greater share of the cost of new highways. But along with the greater financial responsibility comes increased flexibility. While the federal government generally prohibits tolls on newly constructed interstate highways,[2] no such restriction exists on locally funded roads. Besides raising otherwise unavailable funds, toll financing ties use more closely to payment. A number of new toll roads have been started in the past decade, these include two private roads in the United States as well as many in other countries.

America's current toll roads have never had to face the issue of conversion from the 'free' road model (aside from limited experimentation with high-occupancy/toll lanes, which allow toll payers voluntarily to buy into excess capacity on high-occupancy vehicle lanes, as discussed in Chapter 11). Though there is a historical precedent for the conversion of 'free' roads to the toll model, as discussed in Chapter 2, it is nevertheless a politically contentious issue. Its success depends on how government spends the new toll revenue.

A popular saying insists 'There is no free lunch'. Similarly, there is no 'free way'. The real issues are the directness of the charge and who bears it. Directness varies by means of collection. Payments may be collected by time of day, on each road segment, for every trip, at every fill-up of the gas tank, or once a year as a tax. Depending on the mechanism, different individuals may pay more or less than their fair share. Those who pay nothing for the use of the road are *free riders*. Though the ride may be free to them, it costs someone else. Although there is no free way, some may take a free ride.

States in the east of the United States continue to finance many highways with tolls, but this is rare in the west. Clearly one can point to historical and political reasons explaining this fact, but underlying the history is a set of preferences that shape each state's decision. In brief, the preference can be summed up by the folk saying 'Don't tax you, don't tax me, tax the fella behind the tree'. Local governments typically rely on a mix of revenue sources, each of which is borne by a different set of people. For instance, taxes on car rentals, hotels, and entertainment are common in tourist areas. Speed traps on major highways through small towns are another example. While many conventional taxes cannot reach non-residents – who don't have to pay local income, property, or sales taxes – road tolls can. And the proportion of non-residents using the road in the physically smaller eastern states, or tourist areas like Florida, is greater than in the west.

If a state places a toll booth near the state line (referred to as a *boundary toll*), it expects that at least one-half of the tolls will be paid by non-residents. However the proportion of tolls paid by non-residents is higher than the share of total distance they travel.

This book argues that the issue of who gets to use roads without paying the full cost is critical to understanding the choice of highway finance mechanism. In larger localities employing boundary tolls, an increasing number of trips stay inside the boundary and thus do not incur tolls. However, the larger the community under tax financing, the more trip-makers there are who are subject to taxation. A tax-based financing system, particularly in a small jurisdiction, is inequitable to local residents and may not be politically stable. On the other hand, a toll-based system is inequitable to non-residents, which does not create the same political instabilities. A similar argument applies to placing the burden of new infrastructure on existing rather than future residents.

Table 1.1 illustrates this idea: taxes, particularly property or income taxes, but even gas taxes when drivers buy their gas near home, fall disproportionately or entirely on local residents, while non-residents ride for free. Many tolls, particularly boundary tolls, fall hardest on non-residents, while residents get off easy.

Table 1.1 Incidence of revenue mechanisms on user groups

	Residents	Non-residents
Tax	Hard ride: Payment exceeds fair share	Free ride: No payment for use of road
Toll	Easy ride: Payment less than fair share	Hard ride: Payment exceeds fair share

This book explores many of the underlying reasons that localities choose to use taxes or tolls of various kinds. One hypothesis is that smaller political units have more motivation to impose tolls than large ones. First, the smaller the community, the greater the share of toll revenue from non-residents. Second, for larger regions, tolls collected at the state or county line may prove insufficient to recover costs. However, under the right circumstances, boundary tolls enable a jurisdiction to achieve the locally ideal policy of 'taxing foreigners living abroad' as suggested in the opening quote.

While tolls are common for certain expensive facilities such as tunnels and bridges, they are less common on streets and highways, which are more typically funded through user taxes or general revenue. This research identifies critical technological, economic, geographic, and political factors associated with a government jurisdiction's choice of revenue mechanism (for instance, taxes or tolls) for its network. In contrast to the large thread of research which focuses on optimal financing decisions, this book frequently uses game theory to analyse the political and economic implications of alternative revenue mechanisms and organizational structures for the road network.

This book analyses roadway network financing, constructing models that include the basic features of the economic structure of transportation networks. It examines the demand and supply interaction, the choices available to actors (consumers and producers), and the linkage between the two when the residents of a jurisdiction own the local network. The idea of decentralized, local control and multiple jurisdictions (for example, different states) and user groups distinguishes this analysis from one where a central authority (such as the federal government) tries to maximize global welfare. The model's theoretical results should be consistent with what is empirically known about network financing. It should thus explain what network financing choices are made under various circumstances. Policies that alter circumstances to affect the desired choice of revenue mechanism can then be drafted.

Four main rationales for road pricing motivate this research: financing infrastructure and relieving congestion through capacity expansion; changes in the vehicle fleet and tax base for highways; social costs; and allocating existing infrastructure more efficiently.

RATIONALES FOR ROAD PRICING

Financing Infrastructure

Historically, the primary rationale for road pricing was to finance both the capital and operating costs of infrastructure. Construction of new highways can result in cross-subsidies when financed out of general revenue, or even gas taxes. Typically, a new highway only serves a portion of the population, those using the origin–destination pairs that it connects, but is funded by a broader population. The political impact of the cross-subsidies can be reduced if a large 'package deal' is assembled (for instance, with new highways in every political district). This was the case with the interstate highway program of the 1950s to 1980s, and with many recent highway bills. However, the ability to form package deals of new roads becomes more difficult as the conventional highway system reaches maturity. There are strong arguments on both equity and efficiency grounds for users (those who benefit directly) paying for its use. Road pricing, unlike the gas tax, much less property or income taxes, ties revenue for the use of roads to the users of that specific facility.

Measuring the monetary flows into and out of the highway system is a complex task. Table 1.2 shows a simple balance sheet analysis from the 1999 highway statistics. The vast majority of highway revenue comes from

Table 1.2 Highway revenues and expenditures: 1999

Revenues and Expenditures	$ millions
Highway revenues	
Motor-fuel and vehicle taxes	76,937
Tolls	4,978
Bond issue proceeds	11,276
Intergovernmental transfers	1,762
Total revenues	94,953
Highway expenditures	
Capital outlay	59,499
Maintenance and traffic services	29,212
Administration and research	8,714
Highway law enforcement and safety	9,946
Interest on debt	4,584
Bond retirements	5,471
Net funds placed in reserves	12,473
Total expenditures	129,899
Revenues minus expenditures	(34,946)
Ratio of revenues to expenditures	0.73
Non-highway user revenues	
Property taxes and assessments	6,066
General fund appropriations	14,693
Other taxes and fees	5,519
General investment income and other receipts	6,715
Intergovernmental transfers	1,952
Net non-highway revenues	34,945
Non-highway expenditures from additional highway use taxes	
Non-highway purposes	8,873
Mass transportation	8,951
Collection expenses	3,199
Territories	212
Net non-highway expenditures	21,235
Revenues minus expenditures	13,711
Ratio of revenues to expenditures (adjusted)	0.89

Source: Federal Highway Administration (2000), Highway Statistics 1999, Table HF-10.

user fees in the form of gas taxes, licensing fees, and related vehicle taxes. Tolls represent under 5% of total revenue. Furthermore, general (non-highway-user) revenues have been limited since the early 1980s, though growing in recent years. While highway user revenues cover 73% of expenditures, highway users pay additional taxes that go to non-highway purposes, such as mass transit. Counting those payments (adding the amount to highway revenue), highway users cover 89% of their costs. This compares with less than 40% of operating costs that transit users pay, which does not include transit capital costs. Highway finance is principally a pay-as-you-go system, with a relatively small role for bonds, even for capital expenses with a long lifespan. Net bond usage (bond proceeds minus bond retirements minus interest on debt) is just $1.2 billion, compared with nearly $60 billion in capital expenditures. Funds placed in reserve (in a sense, the opposite of bonds in that they are savings for future expenses rather than borrowing for them) exceed net bond payments approximately ten-fold.

Highway infrastructure here can be divided into two basic types, conventional and advanced, though the logic for the two is largely the same. Advanced highway infrastructure can be distinguished from more conventional infrastructure by its use of intelligent transportation systems. Automated highways, while now on the back-burner, have been suggested to address roadway congestion. While it is unclear at this early date what shape advanced highway systems will take, certain forms may require complete separation of traffic into groups equipped with the appropriate technology and groups which are not so equipped. Without the appropriate financing mechanism such as road pricing, constructing this infrastructure would entail cross-subsidies from the existing (non-equipped) fleet users to those with the new technology, a transfer from poor to rich.

Change in Tax Base with Alternative Fuels

In the absence of a property rights framework and a market solution for air pollution, policy makers have focused on regulation. California and the northeastern United States have mandated that a certain fraction of the new car fleet be either low emission or zero emission vehicles (ZEVs). ZEVs are intended to reduce air pollution, or at least relocate it to the place where electricity is generated, hopefully an area where fewer people will be affected. While the precise rules are subject to change and delay (and have been altered several times to date), the trend toward switching to non-gasoline based fuels is at least nascent. To the extent that roads are financed through gasoline-based excise taxes, a shift to alternative fuels would result in a decrease in revenues for roads.

Some (albeit limited) evidence for this trend are incentives provided for ZEVs (California Air Resources Board 1997). The federal government offers a tax credit of $4,000 toward the purchase of a ZEV. Several California air-quality management districts offer 'buy-downs' to a manufacturer for each ZEV sold for a limited number of sales. Some utilities offer discounted electricity rates for off-peak electric vehicle recharging. A memorandum of agreement reached in 1996 between the California Air Resources Board and seven auto manufacturers postponed the previously announced ZEV mandates. In its place there was agreement to produce (in total) 3,750 advanced battery-powered ZEVs in 1998, 1999, and 2000 (California Air Resources Board 1996) and some measures to provide an equivalent emission reduction through production of cleaner light-duty vehicles. While this level of non-gasoline based vehicles is unlikely to cause major financing shortfalls, future targets of 10% ZEVs as in California, or even higher levels if technological breakthroughs in fuel cells manifest themselves, suggest that it may become a more significant issue in the future.

Social Costs

At the center of social cost debate is the question of whether various modes of transportation are implicitly subsidized because they generate unpriced externalities, and to what extent this biases investment and usage decisions. A proposed solution is to price travel based on the amount of externalities generated. To the extent that externalities vary in space, it may be appropriate to charge for them through road tolls rather than more general sources such as gas taxes. The main externalities include congestion, air pollution, carbon emissions, noise pollution, pavement damage, and increased accident damage. Chapter 3 discusses social costs.

Congestion Pricing

The Bureau of Transportation Statistics (1999) reports that between 1980 and 1997, highway lane-miles increased by 4%, registered motor vehicles increased by 31%, and vehicle-kilometers traveled by 67%. This was despite roughly stable journey to work times (Levinson 1998). At some point, rising congestion costs outweigh construction costs (after accounting for other social and private costs), indicating a net social benefit for the construction of new roads. Road pricing has effects which bear on this issue, including reduced demand (and improved short-run efficiency) in the absence of additional infrastructure and increased revenue for constructing new infrastructure.

Congestion reduction and more efficient allocation of resources are often cited as some of the main benefits of road pricing, particularly peak period pricing. Clearly road pricing is a necessary prerequisite to congestion (or time-differentiated) pricing. Qualitatively, the idea behind congestion pricing is that different people have different values of time. Without pricing, everyone travels slowly. But if roads are priced, individuals with a high value of time will be able to pay money and travel faster, while others will not pay the money and not travel at that time (or travel on more congested and slower alternative free roads).

To increase the welfare of travelers (or potential travelers), the money collected needs to be redistributed in some fashion, either through lowering other taxes, through direct payments, or by reinvesting it in transportation. If a driver's value of time saved plus the amount returned is greater than the amount paid, that driver is better off. If the amount of money returned to another commuter is greater than the cost of deferring the trip (or traveling at a slower speed), then the commuter is better off. Road pricing will inevitably create both winners and losers (usually losers) without redistribution of the toll revenue. However, under the right redistribution policy, most people can be made better off. Chapter 10 discusses congestion pricing and Chapter 11 considers compensation policies.

OUTLINE OF THE BOOK

Chapter 2 provides a positive explanation for the historical rise and fall of turnpikes, as well as speculation about some of the necessary conditions for a significant re-emergence of turnpikes. The historical evidence is compared with specific analytical hypotheses about the effects of jurisdiction size and trip length on the choice of financing mechanism. Road tolls, present since ancient times, were deployed widely in the eighteenth century. By the middle of the nineteenth century, most intercity land travel in Britain and the United States used turnpikes. Yet, at the onset of the twentieth century almost all tollgates had been dismantled and the turnpikes converted to publicly owned, operated, and free highways. Disturnpiking occurred simultaneously with the centralization of control over roads – management moved from small local agencies, companies, and authorities to larger regions or states. Longer-distance travel was viewed as a responsibility of a higher level of government, which saw more users as local residents. What is non-local to a county may be local to a state. By the 1940s, the desire for limited-access highways serving long-distance auto trips led to another upsurge in toll road construction by states. The 1956 Federal Aid Highway Act arrested this trend by guaranteeing federal funding for a designated interstate highway system free of tolls. Just as before, what is non-local to a state is local to the nation. Thus, the vast majority of intercity roads in the United States constructed in the interstate era are not tolled because of centralized national policy-making. Recent interest in tolls in the United States has picked up with the completion of the interstate highway program. New road financing has largely become a state and local problem again. Because of the reduction in the transaction costs to government and travelers with electronic toll collection, tolls are more widely viewed as a feasible option. New public and even private toll roads are being constructed with electronic toll collection, while existing toll plazas are being converted.

Chapter 3 reviews the theoretical and empirical literature on the cost structure of highways and specifies and estimates cost functions. It develops a full cost model which identifies the key cost components, and then estimates costs component by component. It estimates a user's costs of owning and operating a vehicle. It builds a model of long-run total infrastructure expenditures on infrastructure by states. Data on Californian bridges are used to estimate a model of manual toll collection costs. The operating costs of electronic toll collection systems throughout the United States are also modeled. Measures of each externality: noise, air pollution, accidents, and congestion are constructed.

Chapter 4 examines the question of why some states impose tolls while others rely more heavily on gas and other taxes. A model to predict the share of street and highway revenue from tolls is estimated as a function of the share of non-resident workers, the policies of neighboring states, historical factors, and population. The more non-resident workers, the greater the likelihood of tolling, after controlling for toll roads planned or constructed before the 1956 Interstate Act. Similarly, if a state exports a number of residents to work out-of-state and those neighboring states toll, it will be more likely to retaliate by imposing its own tolls than if those states do not toll. Decentralization of finance and control of the road network from the federal to the state, metropolitan and city and county levels of government will increase the incentives for the highway-managing jurisdiction to impose tolls.

Chapter 5 considers questions of financing and the hierarchy of roads and investigates the various relationships between governmental and network hierarchies. Both infrastructure networks and government are typically hierarchically organized. The hierarchy of roads separates access from movement. There are both advantages and disadvantages to managing roads with a higher jurisdiction. While larger jurisdictions may be able to exercise scale economies, they also have a larger span of control, which implies increased management costs and slower decision times.

Chapter 6 investigates the problem of financing infrastructure over time when the number of users changes. The problem is confronted in many fast-growing communities desiring to coordinate the timing of infrastructure and development, yet still achieve economies of scale where they exist. The temporal free-rider problem is defined, whereby the group that finances the construction at a given time is not identical with the group that uses it. The continuous recovery method, which effectively establishes a property rights framework for infrastructure, is described. Continuous recovery enables existing residents to be appropriately compensated by new residents, independent of the number of new residents who ultimately arrive. The system is illustrated and compared with practice in a case that uses a non-continuous cost recovery system.

Chapter 7 considers the factors affecting the choice of revenue mechanism on a beltway in a cost recovery framework. The size of jurisdictions and the length of trips on the network dictate the proportion of trips which pass through each jurisdiction and the proportion which remain entirely within that jurisdiction. The spatial free-rider problem depends on the nature of the financing system; either through trips or local trips can be free riders. Free riding distorts equity and efficiency and produces potential political problems. The fixed and variable cost of collecting tolls and taxes may favor one method over the other and influence the spacing of tolls and thus the number of free riders.

In Chapter 8, a similar but more sophisticated model is constructed to examine a long road representing an intercity highway crossing many states, such as the I-95 on the East Coast of the United States. Here, it is assumed that each locale acts to maximize the benefits to its residents from traveling plus the profits accruing to the local road, or local welfare. This measure explicitly excludes any benefits to non-residents. Each community selects a revenue instrument (such as taxes or tolls) and sets a rate of tax or toll to achieve its goal. The interaction between multiple political units and their residents complicates the analysis. Each jurisdiction's residents use both local and non-local streets, while residents and non-residents alike use its roads. The proportion of trips on a community's roads made by residents and by non-residents directly shapes the local welfare resulting from a particular revenue mechanism. This proportion depends on the size of the relevant city, county, or state. The choice between tax and toll must trade off the number of system users who don't pay their full cost because of where they live and travel, and the costs of collection. The sensitivity of travelers to tolls limits the revenue recovered. The decision of whether to impose taxes, tolls, or some combination of the two therefore depends on jurisdiction size.

Chapter 9 considers the tax toll problem in a repeated game context along a state border. Frontiers provide an opportunity for one jurisdiction to remedy inequities (and even exploit them) in highway finance by employing toll booths, and thereby ensure the highest possible share of revenue from non-residents. If one jurisdiction sets policy in a vacuum, it is clearly advantageous to impose as high a toll on non-residents as can be supported. However, the neighboring jurisdiction can set policy in response. This establishes the potential for a classical prisoners' dilemma consideration: in this case to tax (cooperate) or to toll (defect). Even if both jurisdictions would together raise as much revenue from taxes as from tolls (and perhaps more, since taxes may have lower collection costs), the equilibrium solution in game theory, under a one-shot game, is for both parties to toll. However, in the case of a repeated game, cooperation (taxes and possibly revenue sharing), which has lower collection costs, is stable.

In Chapter 10, a new graphical approach to congestion pricing is suggested to disentangle revealed demand at the given level of service (recognizing that level of service and demand are jointly determined) and underlying demand for travel at a given level of service. It is this underlying (or implicit) demand which should be used for welfare calculations, and which can suggest new approaches to differentiate the road network by level of service. This chapter then develops a disaggregate game theory approach to understanding congestion and congestion pricing, examining in depth the simplest case, that of two individuals choosing when to go, when the payoffs are interdependent.

Chapter 11 develops frameworks for evaluating the effects of financing decisions which will be considered in this study. Efficiency, our usual criterion, loosely speaking, says that no one can be made better off without worsening the condition of another. However, there are also equity considerations: while it may theoretically be possible to compensate individuals for losses from changes designed to make the system more efficient, unless that compensation is undertaken, winners and losers emerge. This chapter considers several compensation schemes associated with congestion pricing to try to achieve the efficiency goals while maintaining equity in the system.

Chapter 12 examines the deployment of electronic toll collection (ETC) and develops a model to maximize social welfare associated with the toll plaza. A payment choice model estimates the share of traffic using ETC as a function of delay, price, and a fixed cost of acquiring the in-vehicle transponder. Delay in turn depends on the relative number of ETC and manual collection lanes. Price depends on the discount given to users of the ETC lanes. The fixed cost of acquiring the transponder (not simply a monetary cost, but also the effort involved in signing up for the program) is a key factor in the model. Once a traveler acquires the transponder, the cost of choosing ETC in the future declines significantly. Welfare, which depends on the market share of ETC, includes delay and gasoline consumption incurred by travelers, costs to the toll agency, and social costs such as air pollution accruing to society. Finding the best combination of

ETC lanes and toll discount maximizes welfare. Too many ETC lanes causes excessive delay to non-equipped users. Too high a discount costs the highway agency revenue needed to operate the facility. The model is applied to California's Carquinez Bridge.

The conclusion summarizes the text and considers possible deployment scenarios leading to the widespread adoption of road pricing.

NOTES

1. See for instance: Bernstein and Muller 1993; de Palma and Lindsey 1998; Downs 1994; Dupuit 1849; Gittings 1987; Keeler and Small 1977; Mohring 1970; and Sugimoto 1994; Roth 1996; Small 1983; Small, Winston, and Evans 1989; TRB 1994; Verhoef, Nijkamp, and Rietveld 1996; Vickery 1963, 1969; Viton 1981, 1990.
2. Tolls are allowed on interstate highways in a few circumstances. Toll bridges, grand-fathered toll roads begun before the interstate system and extensions of those roads, and a few value pricing experiments permitted in the recent surface transportation bill (TEA-21) are the main exceptions.

2. History

INTRODUCTION

Transportation financing has been around since the beginning of organized transportation. The ancient Greeks placed a coin, Charon's toll, in the mouth or hand of the dead person to pay Charon for ferrying the spirit across the River Styx to the Elysian fields. And it is still traditional in some places to place pennies on the eyes of a dead person prior to burial, as noted in the Beatles song 'Tax Man'.[1]

Given the long history of paying tolls, the past, both ancient and recent, may have something to teach us about the future of toll road financing. In particular, fundamental factors in the historic rise and decline of turnpikes, such as transaction costs, jurisdiction size and trip length, and the nature of the free-rider problem (in both the original and modern sense of the term), need to be understood before new efforts are likely to succeed. Hybrid solutions which have been tried in the past and remain in limited current use, such as lower rates for local traffic and mixed financing between toll revenue and local tax rates, may enable new efforts, while theoretically efficient solutions such as pure usage charges remain politically infeasible or economically impractical. This chapter provides institutional background both to corroborate the free-rider hypothesis posed in this book and to show the complex issues which suggest that additional factors need to be considered to fully explain revenue choice.

Explanations for the decline of turnpikes in the nineteenth century cite the new modes of transportation, the canal and then the railroad, which diverted a great deal of long-distance traffic, while urbanization and its concomitant use of public transport further changed travel patterns.[2] Yet the railroads brought with them an expansion of the economy and a growth in total traffic, if not an increase in long-distance road traffic. But when the automobile truck highway system emerged in the twentieth century, toll financing did not resume its previous significance. A positive explanation of the rise and fall, and of the conditions for a significant re-emergence, of turnpikes is called for.

This chapter examines the history of turnpikes while developing evidence for an explanatory hypothesis of the choice by jurisdictions to finance roads using tolls. It is posited that jurisdictions generally attempt to maximize net benefits to their own residents. Jurisdictions consider the amount of additional revenue raised by tolls from non-residents against the inconvenience of tolls for their own residents and the costs of toll collection when choosing whether to tax or to toll. Whether toll roads are managed by government, quasi-governmental organizations, regulated franchises, or unregulated private firms is a secondary question. The underlying hypothesis predicts that when jurisdictions responsible for managing sections of the road network are relatively small compared with the length of trips, an attempt will be made to shift the financial burden from local residents (local trip-makers) to those who make through trips.

The hypothesis can partially explain the rise and decline of turnpikes. When trips by road were long distance (made by out-of-towners), they were expedient to toll by the simple placement of a barrier one could not cross without paying a toll. But when long-distance trips were diverted to canals and rail, imposing sufficient tolls on local residents to raise the required revenue was politically difficult and inefficient, and the toll-financing system collapsed. The hypothesis also suggests that in the present era one is more likely to see tolls on highways constructed by a small jurisdiction (such as Delaware or other states in the northeastern part of the United States), than on those constructed by large states (such as California or other western states).[3] This idea is developed in Chapter 4. Furthermore, when roads are financed by a large integrated jurisdiction (like the United States federal government), where all trips are 'local' in that they remain within the large jurisdiction, the motivation to reduce the transaction costs which have traditionally been associated with toll roads is higher than when financing is by a smaller jurisdiction (any state which is a subset of the larger United States).

The burden of the transaction costs of tolls in the smaller jurisdiction falls in part on those who do not vote in that jurisdiction. In the larger jurisdiction, where road use is pervasive (voters and road users are essentially identical groups), there is no apparent immediate gain to residents from using tolls rather than taxes (aside from the efficiency arguments of congestion pricing and focused internal organization), while in the smaller jurisdiction, the benefits of tolls falling on non-residents is clear. Still, if toll financing is the only means available to construct new roads, there may be benefits even in the larger jurisdiction.

This hypothesis does not claim to be a total explanation under all circumstances, as a socio-political system such as infrastructure financing has many influences. For instance, the ability to exclude non-toll payers from toll roads coupled with the presence of 'free' alternatives, reductions in toll collection costs, and private ownership, may all increase the willingness of a jurisdiction to tolerate tolls even on local residents. Further, the influence of key players in business and politics with specific preferences is unpredictable and may greatly shape the decisions made over time. A third factor is the prevailing ideology of government. In the eighteenth and nineteenth centuries, a philosophy of limited, decentralized government, or *laissez faire*, was conducive to private enterprise at all levels, including roads. However, this philosophy declined in America in the twentieth century, at least through the early 1970s. Finally, regional rivalry and the idea of progress certainly have their place, promoting one-upmanship and construction for the sake of construction.

This chapter begins with a review of tolls in the ancient and medieval world and then examines the status of roads before modern turnpikes. The weakness of the pre-toll financing system of statutory road labor led to the creation of turnpikes. The next sections discuss the factors which led to the expansion, and ultimate contraction, of turnpikes. A discussion follows of what has happened since the beginning of the twentieth century, the era of modern roads, which assumed importance first with the bicycle, then more importantly with the automobile. A wave of turnpike construction beginning with the introduction of limited access ended with the construction of the interstate highway system. Finally, current efforts at building toll roads in the post-interstate era and various road pricing schemes are discussed. General conclusions are drawn from an examination of this history.

TOLLS IN THE ANCIENT AND MEDIEVAL WORLD

The idea of charging for transportation was known in the ancient world, as the myth of Charon, the ferryman in Hades, tells us. However, in fact, rather than myth, 'We know very little about commerce carried by land [in Greece] and the probable reason is that there was very little of it' (Pritchett 1980, p. 183). In the Greek city-states, most intercity trade and travel occurred by sea. Roads in Greece were financed in one of two ways: either a levy on the rich was used to build the road, or the roads were maintained by the adjacent property owners as mandated by *Corpus Juris Civilis* (Casson 1974).

References to tolls in Greek literature are ambiguous and thus conclusions are speculative. Tolls and tariffs were conflated in their collection, so conclusions about toll collection must be treated with caution. Fees from non-local traders were levied at ports and markets, though the revenue was not specifically dedicated to transportation. Thus tolls in this era are different from later appearances. The ideas of tolls and tariffs are distinct today, because tolls are for passage from here to there, while tariffs are assessed at the final destination, not necessarily on pass-through, which is generally exempt. Such distinctions were not so clear in the ancient and medieval world. Customs stations at ports, frontiers, and provincial boundaries exempted items for personal use, but items for trade were subject to duties.

In areas with more land transportation, road tolls were employed, Aristotle in *Oeconomicus* (Book 2) notes land tolls in Asia's Satraps (Pritchett 1980). Similarly, Pliny, in *Natural History*, cites tolls in the Arab parts of the Roman Empire (Chevallier 1976). India's text *The Arthasastra* mentions tolls prior to the 4th century BC (Lay 1992). Strabo, in an example from his *Geographies*, written in the time of Augustus, reports tolls on the Little Saint Bernard's Pass maintained by the Salassi tribe. In economic terms, the local mountain peoples were exploiting their monopoly on the passage to raise revenue from travelers. Part of the toll paid for guidance across the mountains and included portage. The practice employed by tribes such as the Arimani from Lombardy involved leading the traveler across the pass before demanding tolls. The tribes were given toll concessions by the Roman Empire. As the empire declined, the central authority necessary to build and maintain a safe and free (to travelers) road system declined with it, so tolls (not necessarily authorized) became more widespread (Chevallier 1976).

Where the literary evidence is sparse, the archeological evidence may be used. Tolls may leave certain telltale signs: an inexplicable bend in a road on an otherwise flat plain, a lack of ruts on an otherwise (intentionally) rutted road. However, despite the occasional possible tollgate location, the absence of tolls in Greece is more notable than their presence. Speculatively, there are hints of tolls on the road between Athens and a quarry at Mt Pentelichus (Casson 1974). Chevallier suggests some tolls in northern Italy are indicated by bends in the road.

In the middle ages tolls were widely used to support bridge construction and were less widely collected on roads in some areas. A major issue during the reign of Wenceslas as Holy Roman Emperor (1378–1400) was the insistence of territorial lords on imposing tolls on city merchandise in transit through their lands. The justification for road tolls on road and river traffic relied on the protection of merchants and their goods. However, the frequent spacing of toll stations hampered trade and provoked disputes, often culminating in the lords seizing both merchants and their merchandise. Later reports from Montaigne in the late 1500s suggest longstanding tolls in the Appenine mountains, across various passes (Chevallier 1976).

ROADS BEFORE MODERN TURNPIKES

The road network of Britain has been heavily studied, and as English common law has become the underlying standard throughout much of the world, it is a reasonable starting point for understanding the status of roads before the imposition of modern tolls. Following the research of the Webbs (1913), it is believed that roads (in Britain and elsewhere) began as trails, running from high ground to fordable points on rivers or seaports. Through a process of cumulative causation – a cleared path attracts more traffic, which helps keep the path clear – these tracks became ensconced as the backbone of the original transportation network. The Roman occupation of Britain resulted in the construction of four main roads, principally for military communication, and numerous minor ones. After the Romans left, road use may have diminished, though it certainly did not vanish.

The road in this period is better conceived of as a right than as an object. A road is a right of passage on another's land, rather than the paved surface owned by some central authority that we imagine today. The highway constituted 'good passage' rather than the beaten track, so if the track were in poor condition, travelers could skirt it. The English word 'road' comes from the same root as the word 'ride' – the Middle English 'rood' and Old English 'rad' – meaning the act of riding (*Webster's II* 1984). Lay (1992) notes that tollgates were cited in the English *Domesday Book of 1095* and that as early as 1286 London Bridge had tolls. Edward III legislated tolling rights on the Great North Road out of London to Philippe Litchfield in 1364 in return for his work in improving the road.

The first English law dealing with roads was the 1285 Statute of Westminster, requiring residents of manors to clear 200 feet on each side of their roadway of 'bushes, woods, or dykes' where a 'man may lurk to do hurt'. The wide right-of-way was to ensure protection from highway robbery rather than enhance movement. However, the roadways began to deteriorate over the late Middle Ages and Renaissance. An important cause was the decline of the religious orders associated with Henry VIII's break with Rome, which reduced pilgrimages and levels of traffic on the roads. Monasteries which had maintained roads were no longer able to do so, while the successors to their property had much less incentive. As cumulative causation works in one direction in creating the roads, it also can work in reverse, leading to their deterioration through neglect.

The next legal milestone, 2 and 3 Philip and Mary, C.8., was passed by the Parliament of 1555. This law set the obligation of maintaining public highways upon several parties: the parish and every resident thereof, the newly created Surveyor of Highways for each parish, and the Justices of the Peace within the parish's division. Any or all of the parties could be brought before a judicial tribunal if they failed to fulfill their obligation. Parishioners with property were required to send plows, carts and horses to help maintain the roads, while others were required to labor for six consecutive days each year (about 2% of the working year) under the authority of the Surveyor of Highways.

As might be expected with growth in the economy and changes in the price level, over time the penalty for not performing the obligatory labor became less onerous than actually doing the work. By 1649, in some British localities, taxes were beginning to be assessed for road improvements to pay the Surveyor of Highways, formalizing the process. However, the system of compulsory labor remained through the 1700s, until finally being eliminated in 1835. With the decline of the feudal manor system, this mechanism of 'financing' road improvements was viewed as more and more inequitable. Furthermore, it became increasingly inefficient as roads of steadily higher quality were demanded. The efficient division of labor called for something other than everyone serving the same six-day period on roads; it made little sense to have those responsible for spreading gravel on the roads working (or not working) over the same six days as those who had to dig the gravel.

Similar laws existed in North America. For instance, in New York in 1800, all free males over the age of 21 were assessed highway labor 'in proportion to the estate and ability of each', with a minimum of one day and a maximum of 30 days as determined by town highway commissioners. Failure to contribute led to fines which steadily increased over time; commutation of labor cost 62.5 cents per day in 1801 (Klein and Majewski 1994). These laws lasted into the twentieth century in some rural areas, including parts of Texas (Goddard 1994).

The American system collapsed for similar reasons to the British: mandatory labor was viewed as a burden and the laborers did not contribute their utmost effort. There was no incentive to work hard in general, particularly so when your co-workers shirked. Unlike money, which is easily exchanged, labor's value depends on the effort put in as well as the amount of time spent. The stream of money for roads was inconsistent, coming from fines rather than any dedicated revenue, making planning difficult. The districts, which were small, could only draw on local laborers for construction, even if the road which it governed served a broad area.

TURNPIKES IN GREAT BRITAIN, 1656–1900

The initial deployment of turnpikes in seventeenth century Britain, their growth through the eighteenth and early nineteenth centuries, and their decline in the late nineteenth century provides insight into current discussions of private toll roads. The English word 'turnpike' derives from the spiked spear (pike) that was stretched across the road so it could be swung open for toll payers (McShane 1994). Turnpikes were comprised of both new and reconstructed roads (Buchanan 1990). In some important cases, the turnpiking of a road was accompanied by its reconstruction; in others, the government subsidized the reconstruction of an existing turnpike.

The first English turnpike is recorded in the Vestry of Radwell, Hertfordshire, which petitioned Parliament for road improvements in 1656. In 1663, Parliament permitted the County Justices in Quarter or Highway Sessions the placement of three tollgates to raise funds for the repair of the Great North Road (Payne 1956). Some other tollgates followed. The upturn in turnpike acts in 1695 reflects a return to domestic stability in England after the Glorious Revolution (Albert 1979).

Turnpike acts were promoted by local residents (town councils, merchants, manufacturers, farmers, landowners) responsible for maintaining at least part of the road in question. The turnpikes covered multiple parishes, though only a large subset of those parishes were required to pass an act (Albert 1972).

After 1706 in Britain, Parliament chartered 'turnpike trusts' to improve selected roadways. A typical turnpike trust might have well over 80 trustees, although only a dozen or so would attend meetings regularly (Payne 1956). The trusts were chaired by the treasurer, while the turnpikes were managed by an appointed surveyor (who generally did not serve as a trustee, to avoid the accusation of jobbery, or corruption). The surveyor supervised maintenance and construction along the road, and was rarely limited to serving on only one turnpike. Ultimately, the collection of tolls was franchised to toll 'farmers' who, after paying a fixed sum to the trust, were permitted to collect tolls at specified gates on the turnpike or turnpike system. Toll farming began as early as 1702, when the first leases were agreed to. Only in 1773 were tolls auctioned using a formal procedure. Initially the toll farmers were local businessmen, but as the system matured they formed increasingly larger groups. By 1825 one partnership collected three-quarters of the tolls in London, amounting to between £400,000 and £500,000 (Albert 1972).

Pawson (1977) provides the most comprehensive history on the deployment of turnpikes. Figure 2.1 shows the number of turnpike trusts in Britain, approximating the classic 'S-curve' through 1850. The theory underlying the S-curve is straightforward. As knowledge of a technology and realization of its benefits spreads, the rate of adoption increases. Each project acts as a demonstration to potential new users. Furthermore, the advantages to adoption may increase with the number of users if there are network or interfirm scale, scope, or sequence economies. As the technology diffuses, those who expect to attain the most benefit adopt it first. After a point, diminishing marginal returns set in. It is expected that, after complete exposure, technology is adopted by those who gain the most, and then by those who gain less and less from it, until it is fully deployed. The life of a technology may be cut short by competing technologies (such as canals and railroads in the case of turnpikes) or because a technological problem is discovered (as in the case of plank roads). Phillips and Turten (1987) describe two basic patterns of British roadways during deployment: radial roads focusing on towns (initially London and later other places), and interregional roads serving intercity traffic.

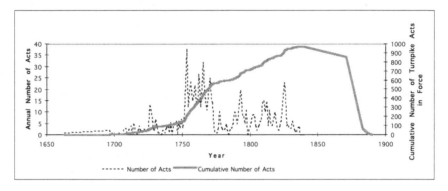

Source: Pawson (1977) and Webb (1913).

Figure 2.1 Turnpikes in Great Britain: 1650–1900

In Britain, not everyone was subject to tolls. The government paid an annual fee in lieu of tolls, while residents of the road's locality typically paid a fixed annual fee rather than a per-use charge (Payne 1956), thereby enabling some degree of free (or subsidized) riding. In economic terms, British turnpikes were viewed as local public goods, with outsiders able to pay for limited use, as with a club good (Cornes and Sandler 1996). It is unlikely the fixed annual fee provided revenue in proportion to the costs of use, though the financial situation in terms of costs and revenues on turnpikes in this era remains to be satisfactorily examined. In other locations, the mails and religious persons were exempt, as were the construction workers improving the roads (Copeland 1963). The tollgates, which generally formed, at minimum, a cordon around the part of the road network operated by a single authority, extracted revenue from trips originating in and/or destined for areas outside the toll authority's coverage. The tolls were used to pay off mortgages incurred by the trusts for road improvements, including extending, resurfacing, straightening, and widening the turnpike, constructing footpaths, arching over sewers, and lighting the road in urban areas.

The deployment of turnpikes was not without some opposition. Prior to the turnpiking of a road, it had been open to free passage under English common law. But because 'free' roads were of poor quality, carriages, belonging mostly to the rich, could not easily pass. The turnpikes, which improved road quality at a price, were thus viewed as a transfer from the poor, who had always been able to pass for free with carts and horses before tolls, to the rich, who gained the most when the roads were improved. This was quite similar to the enclosure movement, which also created similar new property rights. The inequity led to several turnpike riots (Albert 1979). Miners who resented the placement of tolls between the coal mines and market in Kingswood, Bristol, smashed gates and toll houses during riots in 1727, 1731, and 1749. However, unlike laborers in other sectors who also had resentments, the coal miners were far better organized and had been given fewer dispensations than local traffic elsewhere. To combat these riots, the government in 1727 raised penalties on destroying turnpikes or riverworks to three months in prison and imposed a public whipping for the first offense and seven years of transportation (being sent abroad to a penal colony) for a second. Yet the rioters were not deterred. In the 1730s resistance moved to the Gloucester and Hereford regions. The last eighteenth century riot took place in 1758 near Bradford and Leeds, where tolls had been doubled and new gates imposed. In 1843 the Rebecca riots took place in Wales (Duckham 1984), leading to a restructuring of turnpike management.

After the 1843 Rebecca riots, a Welsh commission recommended that turnpikes be consolidated at the county level (Duckham 1984). Further, tolls were to be made uniform throughout the six counties of Wales for each type of good, and toll booths were to be placed only every 12 kilometers (19 miles). Produce was to be exempt and agricultural inputs such as lime tolled at only half the normal rate. In an early recognition of the link between transportation and land use, the road taxes were deducted from the rent paid by tenant farmers. While the counties continued road maintenance, tolls were again farmed out. The tolls were auctioned to the highest bidder, who over time became a representative of a national organization that attained one main economy of scale – the spread of risk over multiple operations. Risk was steadily increasing in the mid-1800s due to the spread of railroads over the countryside; as soon as a railroad arrived, toll revenues dropped. When a railroad came in, or for any other good reason, the toll farmers tried to obtain a reduction in their lease payments from the county boards, who only sometimes acquiesced.

It should be noted that revenue dropped when the road board operated tolls themselves (Duckham 1984). Several reasons have been suggested for this, including higher administrative expenses and less thoroughness in catching toll evaders. A third reason to note is that causation may be in the other direction; when toll revenues dropped, the county road board had to assume toll collection on the turnpike when the toll farmer defaulted. Toll farmers paid only a short period in advance for the right to collect revenue, minimizing capital outlay and providing them with the opportunity for renegotiation with some leverage. While the tolls covered maintenance, the county still subsidized major capital expenses through the road rate (general taxes). In 1889 the county took over the road boards and dissolved the turnpikes.

The arrival and deployment of railroads from the late 1820s eroded the market share for intercity transportation belonging to roads. The railroads, running on steam power, were significantly faster than horse powered transport, a speed which made up for the increased access costs: the railroad depot may not have been the ultimate origin and destination, and trains ran on fixed schedules. Still, since much intercity transport was provided by carriage services, road transport in the mid-1800s more closely resembles a competition between bus and rail than car and rail.

The Times of London in 1816 editorialized on the inconvenience of toll collection every mile (1.6 km), describing the collectors as: 'men placed in a situation unfavourable to civilized manners, and who might be usefully employed in mending the roads which they now obstruct in a most disagreeable manner' (Albert 1972). Certainly tolls were not heralded with universal acclaim, and as the situation made itself amenable, pressure to remove tolls increased. The Webbs (1913) date from the early 1860s the public determination to rid themselves of tolls. Tolls were replaced by local tax revenue for funding roads in Ireland in 1858, and the results were perceived adequate. Member of Parliament George Clive's 1862 retirement was seen as the elimination of a key impediment to removing tolls, more precisely, in not renewing the terms of turnpike trusts as had been done in the past. The main complaints against tolls were that they were a costly and wasteful means of collecting revenue, that they were inconvenient to the public, that they impeded traffic, and that the tax was inequitable. The recommended solution was to vest the roads in a public authority (highway districts or the local highway parish). From 1865, tolls in Scotland were abolished piecemeal. From 1864 onwards, turnpike trusts in Britain were dissolved at a rapid rate, as shown on the right-hand side of Figure 2.1. The final turnpike toll was collected on 1 November 1895 on the Shrewsbury and Holyhead Road.

The loss of turnpike revenue increased the financial burden on local authorities to finance and maintain roads. Grants from the national government were intended to mitigate these factors. Eventually, authority for the roads moved up to the county level outside urban areas, and was paid for by local taxes sent to the county, town, or special district.

TURNPIKES IN AMERICA: 1785–1900

Though the first recorded toll bridge in the United States appeared in Newbury, Massachusetts, in 1656, turnpike deployment began about a century after Great Britain. The causes were similar: the quality of the roads were insufficient to meet the demands placed upon them. In particular, before turnpike deployment, there was a feeling of inequity where rural residents paid to maintain roads used by urban dwellers for intercity travel. Before bringing in private enterprise, states tried solve the problems themselves. Americans unsuccessfully tried to emulate the British Turnpike Trust system, using taxes for construction and tolls for maintenance, but turned to corporations formed by interested merchants and well-to-do landowners after the earliest deployment. Thus the first turnpikes often had the assistance of tax funding in the 1780s, but in later years, outside of Pennsylvania, most turnpike companies received little state aid. The rationale for state assistance was based on the premise of positive externalities or spillovers that roads would increase both land values and commerce (Durrenberger 1931). Without subsidy, it was believed that there would be an underinvestment in roads.

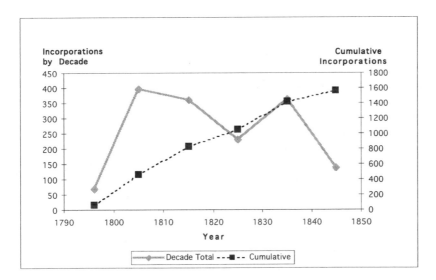

Source: Fielding and Klein (1993).

Figure 2.2 Turnpikes incorporated in the United States: 1790–1845

In 1785, Virginia authorized tolls on public, tax-funded roads, and chartered a short-distance turnpike from Alexandria to Berryville (USDOT

1976); Maryland followed suit in 1787 (Klein and Majewski 1994). The first significant United States turnpike company was chartered in Pennsylvania in 1792, connecting Philadelphia and Lancaster, and completed two years later (USDOT 1976). To look at the rate of deployment, Figure 2.2 shows the number of turnpike companies chartered in eastern states from 1790 to 1845. Like turnpikes, bridges were private toll facilities. From 1786 to 1798, 59 toll bridges were chartered (Klein 1990). Baer et al. (1993) illustrate the basic pattern in New York as a series of roads radiating from that state's main artery, the Hudson River, and later the Erie Canal. In California, most toll roads were deployed in the mining counties of the Sierra Nevada (Klein and Yin 1996).

The Federal Government was not permitted under the Constitution to collect tolls, according to President Monroe, who vetoed attempts to place tolls on the National Road (running from the Potomac River to the Ohio River), which was already beginning to deteriorate less than ten years after its 1813 opening. By the 1830s, Congress turned over the road to the relevant states, which then imposed tolls to maintain the road (USDOT 1976).

Much of the American turnpike construction was due to competition between towns to gain trade. Durrenberger (1931, p.47) argues that 'The rivalries and jealousies that existed among the states seems unbelievable today' and one can extend the observation to rivalries between towns. The subscribers to turnpikes, as with canals, were a mixed group that included citizens, municipalities, and state governments, as well as foreign nationals in later years. Although the federal government had subsidized new turnpikes and roads through land grants in the public lands (western) states prior to 1830, attempts to have the federal government subscribe to turnpike company stock offerings were ended by President Jackson's 1830 veto of the Maysville Road Bill, which had been sponsored by the state of Kentucky to get federal funds for what Jackson deemed a purely local road. It was 20 years before federal subsidies for infrastructure, at the time railroads, returned (USDOT 1976).

Despite the sparse federal involvement, town leaders realized that an early edge in attaining access to other areas, and thus becoming a key crossroads, would have long-term payoffs (Klein and Majewski 1994). Individuals would relocate to the towns with turnpike access, which would attract others individuals, provide revenues to the turnpike, and encourage additional transportation investments. Towns without access would wither.

Klein and Majewski (1994) argue that after the first few had been chartered, turnpike investments were recognized as unprofitable, and were really an example of voluntary private provision of a public good for the good of the public. Towns and their leading citizens were looking for economic spillovers from the roads. Because towns were more autonomous in this era, citizens felt more obligated to contribute. Investors, constituting the social elites of towns, invested in turnpikes to promote the town's interest (and only indirectly their own). The voluntary private provision of public goods can be rational individually if the provider's contribution is outweighed by the benefits received from their own contribution (Olson 1965). Furthermore, social pressures were placed on members of the elite to ensure sufficient subscription to new investment. These pressures enforced good behavior (meeting social obligations) due to the repeated interactions of the local business elite, in multiple spheres, which would socially or economically discipline a member who shirked responsibilities. Gray (1967) finds similar practices in the chartering of the Chesapeake and Delaware Canal.

Although there is some aspect of voluntary private provision of a public good with possible private benefit from spillover in the construction of many turnpikes, other turnpikes were just as surely speculative ventures attempting to be profitable in their own right. Foreign (or even non-local) investment provides evidence of this (USDOT 1976). However, Durrenberger (1931, p.100) states that 'while foreign capital was in abundance after 1815, it played a very minor part in turnpike finance', and that the largest part of foreign impact was associated with dollars lent to the state of Pennsylvania. Durrenberger suggests that capital was mostly local; at no time did state ownership exceed one-third of invested capital, although in a few instances towns and cities did invest. He gives support to the argument that turnpike 'subscribers were usually more interested in the possible benefits the new lines of communication would bring them than in the [profitability] of the investment' because of the wide distribution of stock and the character and interests of subscribers. From the point of view of dividends and capital return, turnpike stocks were poor investments; at best returns were 8% annually, with 3% being more common, and financial problems set in even before the deployment of canals and railroads.

In New York, toll booths were spaced at 10 mile (16 km) intervals, thereby allowing local trip-makers to be free riders. The free-rider problem was significant. For instance, Massachusetts law exempted people going to or from gristmills or church, people on military duty, and those travelling on common and ordinary family business within the tollgated town (Rae 1971). Furthermore, 'shunpikes', illegal tollgate bypasses, frequently arose to allow travelers to avoid the road section with the toll booth. These two factors limited the profitability of turnpikes.

The California turnpike experience differs from that in the eastern states. In addition to beginning about 50 years later, in the wake of the gold rush, the rationales for the road differed. California law borrowed heavily from eastern states, including financial requirements that may have hindered the deployment of the new roads (Klein and Yin 1996). In the eastern states toll roads emerged from community enterprise, without a significant profit motive; in California turnpikes operated more like businesses, interested in the residual revenues from roads. It is unclear to what extent the Californian roads succeeded in being profitable enterprises: some were and some were not, though the exact proportions are not known (Klein and Yin 1996). Many of the owners of California's toll roads were resource extraction companies such as mines and lumber companies. In addition, a number of tourist roads were built, including to Yosemite and on Mount Wilson (Klein and Yin 1996).

Spin-offs of turnpikes included taverns (early rest stops), which were a highly structured market. Three different kinds of taverns were typical, showing up as often as one per mile (1.6 km) on the heavily traveled Philadelphia and Lancaster Turnpike (Durrenberger 1931). They catered to the relatively freer-spending stage passengers, to wagoners, and to livestock drovers. While stage passengers required food and sleep, wagoners needed yards and stables, and drovers needed pasture and feed for their herds.

The argument can be made that some of the toll roads were required as a component in the production process. For instance, roads and mines (particularly in California during the nineteenth century) are complements. A mine without access is useless, but the traffic to the mine does not utilize the full capacity of the road. Because roads exhibit economies of scope – it doesn't matter whether the trip is to the mine (or resort) or not, the road serves both equally – and are lumpy investments (the lanes of a road cannot be made significantly smaller in proportion to the scale of traffic; they represent an indivisibility), California road owners used tolls to capture rents from the external benefits associated with the necessary construction of a road.

In the first turnpike era, turnpikes were believed to increase the value of the land where they were placed and decrease it elsewhere by changing the pattern of relative accessibility. The changes resulted in a reduction in rents in some areas in competition with those newly turnpiked. The consequence was a push to improve transportation accessibility in many localities, either to increase rents or to prevent them from falling. Adam Smith (1776) notes: 'not more than fifty years ago, that some of the counties in the neighborhood of London petitioned against the extension of the turnpikes into the more remoter counties. These remoter counties, they pretended, from the cheapness of labour, would be able to sell their grass and corn cheaper in the London market than themselves, and would thereby reduce their rents, and ruin their cultivation.' The complementarity between transportation and the points they access has also been noticeable in the construction of streetcars and their associated suburbs in the late nineteenth and early twentieth century (Warner 1962) and more recently in developer-financed roads, including some toll roads, opening up new areas such as the Dulles Greenway in Virginia.

As in Britain, opposition to toll roads arose in the United States for many of the expected reasons. On principle, many believed that roads were a public, not a private, function, and that payment of tolls was a payment to usurpers of public roads (Durrenberger 1931, p. 81). More practically, locals were opposed to paying a toll when travel had been free; much of this opposition was mitigated by charters that enabled local residents to be free riders. Further, there was resentment against those who owned the turnpike, who would get rich (or at least were thought to get rich) at the expense of travelers. There was also opposition to the corporate form in general, which was new in the early 1800s (Klein and Majewski 1994). Over the long term, these opponents of corporate governance had little effect, as the corporate form has become the dominant means of organizing business. The opposition to urban highways that emerged after the interstate program was initiated was due to the destruction of local communities as well as the phenomenon now known as NIMBYism (not in my back yard), opposition to having noxious facilities nearby. There is no record that opposition in the first turnpike era had any similar causes. As in Britain, laws protected infrastructure and punished vandalism. The main arguments for abolishing turnpikes derived from those opposing their establishment: that roads were utilities and should be free, that turnpikes derived patronage mostly from local traffic, which meant taxing the farm class, that people would benefit from freer social intercourse, and that tolls were an annoyance to travelers (Durrenberger 1931).

As in Britain, the driving force behind disturnpiking was the development of other modes of transport: canals and railroads. At first these modes, particularly canals, killed the competing trunk roads, while in fact promoting the construction of complementary branches (Baer et al. 1993). The Erie Canal opened in 1825 and soon found its first victims: the First, Second, and Third Great Western Turnpikes, which saw annual revenues decline. As the turnpikes declined, the fortunes of towns on the turnpikes declined, while those on the canal rose. Nevertheless, the turnpikes were not immediately put out of business.

Turnpikes were not helped by the Supreme Court's 1837 decision in the case of *Charles River Bridge* v. *Warren Bridge*.[4] In 1785, Massachusetts legislators authorized the proprietors of the Charles River Bridge to build a connection between Boston and Charlestown. In 1828, the legislature authorized Charlestown merchants to build the new Warren Bridge, and to collect tolls until they were reimbursed, at which time that bridge would be free and revert to the state. The Charles River Bridge proprietors sought an injunction against the new bridge. The question turned on whether the Charles River Bridge proprietors had a vested right to a monopoly between the two locales, or simply permission to operate a bridge and collect tolls. The ambiguity in the original contract permitted multiple interpretations. Taney, a Jackson Democrat and recent judicial appointee, wrote the majority opinion in a four to three vote which justified the destruction of old property 'rights' so that new ventures might prosper. The state was authorized to provide new charters so long as the narrow constitution of the private property right in the original charter was not diminished, that narrow interpretation being simply toll collection. The consequences of this decision were broad and not helpful for turnpikes, which had hoped to use exclusive franchises to delay competing canals and railroads (McShane 1994).

The roads in New York faced a second blow with the advent of major railroad construction beginning in 1848: 'The turnpikes disintegrated in stages, abandoning their road piece by unprofitable piece' (Baer et al. 1993). By the end of the 1850s New York's major trunk turnpikes had been dissolved and become public roads. Partial abandonments were permitted, and this was the most common form of the dissolution of turnpikes (Durrenberger 1931, p. 156). However, as older turnpikes saw long-distance traffic wither and collapse, new feeder roads were being constructed as complements to the railroads. Rose (1953) and Durrenberger (1931, p. 154) argue that the number of new charters did not diminish greatly until 1875. The number of charters from 1830 to 1860 exceeded the number from 1800 to 1830 in the middle Atlantic states: in Pennsylvania the numbers were 630 and 200 respectively, while in New Jersey they were 124 versus 48. Still, it must be remembered that the later roads served as feeders to intercity transportation via canal and railroad, while the earlier roads were themselves more often trunk roads (Durrenberger 1931, p. 139).

A brief exception to the decline of turnpikes occurred with the emergence (and disappearance) of plank roads between 1846 and 1857 (Klein and Majewski 1994). Plank roads overcame many of the competitive disadvantages suffered by gravel roads – they were smooth and thus enabled faster speeds. They were most prevalent in areas where lumber was cheap. Unfortunately, the planks deteriorated after only a few years, much sooner than expected, and plank roads were abandoned shortly after they had been deployed. In New York, the length constructed was over 5800 km between 1846 and 1853, where the plank roads served principally as branch roads in the Erie Canal and Hudson River regions, as well as radial roads to several upstate cities.

Though the first turnpike abandonments were found in 1817 in New York, turnpikes did not go out with a bang; in 1898 in Maryland there were still 828 km of turnpiked road, and in Pennsylvania in 1903 there were still 1835 km (Durrenberger 1931). The Lancaster Pike, the first significant turnpike, was not finally dissolved until 1902 (USDOT 1976).

Durrenberger suggests several main causes of unprofitability: poor organization and management, the high overheads (fixed costs) of toll collection relative to their scale, early undercapitalization and excessive debts so that tolls were diverted to interest payments rather than maintenance, poor location and insufficient traffic due in part to speculative construction in advance of traffic which never materialized, and competition from railroads and canals.

Turnpikes were established under charters which had intended them ultimately to revert to the states, typically after a 99-year run in the private sector or the achievement of some maximum return on capital. The actual method of reversion or disturnpiking was through abandonment, condemnation, or sale; few actually lived out their charters. In the 1870s counties and towns were given authority to purchase and disturnpike roads and bridges at local expense. In New Jersey and other states, by 1897 rules had been drawn up permitting a two-thirds majority of fronting property owners to petition the state public roads commission to disturnpike the road, with a fair and just price being paid to the turnpike's owners by the state (33%), county (57%), and frontage properties (10%) (Durrenberger 1931, p. 164). In the early 1900s, as states established state highway systems, the remaining toll roads were acquired by state and local governments.

TURNPIKES IN AMERICA, 1900–PRESENT

The advent of the bicycle, and then the automobile, created a new set of needs for highways. While originally roads had been designed primarily for pedestrians and animals (pack animals to carry people and goods, and cattle and swine being herded to market), wheeled carts and carriages required an improved surface. The technological change of the wide(r)-spread adoption of wheeled vehicles, coupled with socio-economic factors and regional growth, had led to a change in highway financing in the eighteenth century. Similarly, rubber-wheeled vehicles traveling at higher speeds required a smoother surface. To support the new vehicle stock, roads needed to be improved with smoother surfaces and more gradual curves that could be taken at higher speeds. In the United States, two highway systems were deployed in the twentieth century to support the automobile. The first 'United States Highways' created a national network of paved roads, the second 'Interstates' created a network of grade-separated freeways. Both were largely free of tolls. In 1914, before significant federal involvement but after the beginning of the good roads movement, the United States had some 428,800 km of surfaced roads (Flink 1990).

Prior to federal involvement with 'United States Highways', some modern twentieth century roads had been toll-financed, though this was limited in scope. In 1908, William Vanderbilt started a turnpike company to construct the Long Island Motor Parkway, intended for car enthusiasts in New York (McShane 1994); but the road, only one lane in each direction, never made much money and there were technical problems with its surface. The toll idea was borrowed by Robert Moses, New York's Park Commissioner, to fund 'parkways' throughout metropolitan New York from the 1920s (Caro 1974). Ironically, Moses' Northern States Parkway paralleled the Vanderbilt route, and bankrupted it in 1938 (the Vanderbilt route became a power line right of way). The DuPont family built a similar private roadway in Delaware (McShane 1994). In 1935 Moses created the Henry Hudson Parkway Authority to build a toll road connecting Manhattan with the Bronx, financing it by issuing bonds tied to traffic forecasts.

Financing in the era of United States Highways was principally by gas tax, beginning in Oregon, New Mexico, and Colorado in 1919, and national in scope by 1929. In 1921 property taxes and general funds paid about 75% of the cost of roads; by 1929, 21 states no longer used any general funds or property taxes for funding, and most money came from gas taxes (Flink 1990). The federal aid program paid for no more than 7% of the road length in a state; by 1924, this amounted to $9000 per km. Beginning in Britain in 1909 came the idea of non-divertability of gas taxes, which said that gas revenue would be spent on roads, not on general budget items or even other transport modes. This concept disappeared in Britain in 1926 (Flink 1990), and later in the United States. (In 1973 some gas tax revenue could be diverted to other transport modes and in the 1990s some gas tax revenues were diverted to the general fund at the federal level.)

Before the federal government's involvement in grade-separated roads, a number of states, particularly in the northeast, had already chartered turnpike authorities to construct some intercity roads. Proposals by the Roosevelt administration from 1934 for a transcontinental toll road came to naught (Goddard 1994). In 1939, the Bureau of Public Roads, a long-term opponent of tolls, published *Toll Roads and Free Roads* which argued that tolls would cover less than half the annual cost of a system of interstate roads (Rae 1971). However, their estimates proved to be quite inaccurate, given the experience of actual toll roads opened in the next two decades; for instance, their projection of 715 vehicles per day on the Pennsylvania Turnpike versus actual demand in the tens of thousands (Rae 1971; Gifford 1983). Gifford argues forcefully that the decision of the bureau to oppose federal toll roads would have been reversed had accurate demand forecasts been used and accepted. Even President Eisenhower thought the interstate system should be toll-financed, though Congress, led by Senator Albert Gore, Sr, disagreed (Goddard 1994).

Many tunnels and bridges were constructed as toll facilities, both before and during the interstate era. Those before the interstates include the

Golden Gate and San Francisco Bay Bridges in the Bay Area, and the Holland and Lincoln tunnels and George Washington Bridge in New York.

Just as the first American turnpike was in Pennsylvania, so was the first in the new era of limited access highways. The Pennsylvania Turnpike, constructed in part along the abandoned South Pennsylvania railroad right-of-way and through already partially bored tunnels, opened in 1940. It connected Pittsburgh with Harrisburg along a higher quality and shorter route than the existing United States 30 (Lincoln Highway) and United States 22 (William Penn Highway). The South Pennsylvania had begun construction under the direction of Commodore Vanderbilt and Andrew Carnegie as a competitor to the Pennsylvania Railroad, which had a spatial monopoly on long-distance freight traffic through the state. Vanderbilt, who owned the New York Central, believed the Pennsylvania Railroad was supporting a competitor in New York, and began the South Pennsylvania as a competitive response. J.P. Morgan brokered a deal which led to the abandonment of both competitive projects (Cupper 1990).

Though the road was built without any federal transportation funds, other New Deal financing sources were used, including a $29.25 million grant from the Public Works Administration and a $40.8 million purchase of bonds by the Reconstruction Finance Corporation (Deakin 1989; Cupper 1990). The road was not only the first new-era toll road, it was also the first long-distance limited access highway built in the United States. The original toll was $1.50 end to end but that was not enough to keep the road uncongested. The first traffic jam (27,000 vehicles on a single day) occurred on the sixth day the road was open, as Sunday drivers took advantage of views of fall foliage (Cupper 1990). The toll road was extended several times, ultimately to Ohio and to New Jersey; the road was widened and improved in places; and by 1989 the toll had tripled and traffic flow increased to 97 million vehicles per year.

Owen and Dearing (1951) note that the cost of collecting tolls ranged from 3.5% of total revenue on the Pennsylvania Turnpike to 18% on the Merritt Parkway, while the gas tax in the same era entailed a 4% collection loss. The capital cost of constructing toll booths on the Maine Turnpike was 1.3% of total costs. The advantages of turnpikes recognized at the time included a decentralized institutional structure enabling market evaluation and a limit to the misplaced uniformity (all roads at the same standard, a ubiquity of construction even in areas without demand) of a centralized, publicly funded system. The disadvantages were empire building by a quasi-autonomous government agency that might use cross-subsidies against the public interest, and overextension in cases where forecasts outpaced actual demand.

There was considerable controversy over how to treat toll roads in the context of the toll-free interstate highway system, particularly whether states should be compensated for toll roads already constructed. Ultimately, 4300 km (2700 miles) of the pre-interstate toll roads were included in the interstate system. Over 6400 km (4000 miles) of toll facilities were built in the period from 1940 to 1960 in over 30 states (Shaevitz 1991). These are shown chronologically in Figure 2.3.

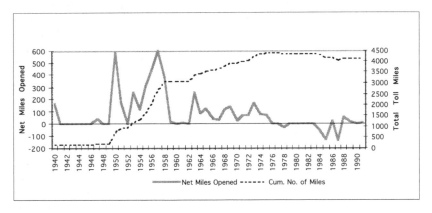

Source: Gomez-Ibañez and Meyer (1993).

Figure 2.3   Toll roads in the United States: 1940–1991

Toll roads were built largely in the physically smaller eastern and midwestern states, while the large western states relied on 'free' roads. At least two factors that help explain this difference are tested empirically in Chapter 4. The first factor relates jurisdiction size with trip length. In general, a larger proportion of traffic in smaller states is made by non-residents than in large states. The welfare of local residents increases when others (for example, residents of other states) pay for a greater share of road construction, operation, and maintenance. Thus it is expected to find toll financing more in smaller states than in larger states. While taxes have lower collection costs than tolls, in small states this is more likely to be offset by the gains from non-local revenue than in large states, where almost all of the traffic is local. This hypothesis assumes that trip length distributions are similar, and are independent of jurisdiction size. This is not strictly true, but the differences in trip lengths are much less significant than differences in size between states in the east and west.

The second factor has to do with federal land ownership, which is significantly higher in western states, and led to higher federal matching shares for construction of 'free roads'. In eastern states, the federal match was only 50% before the advent of the interstate program; in the public lands states, the match was as high as 85% (Gifford 1983).

A few additional toll roads have been built since the completion of the interstate system, several under private ownership (Deakin 1989; Schaevitz 1991; Gomez-Ibañez and Meyer 1993; Reason 1994). Some of these roads are intended to accommodate new development, others to serve existing travel demands. The Dulles Greenway, a private road, was built with major donations of land from adjoining landowners hoping to develop their land. Along California's SR91, in the median of an existing highway, high occupancy/toll lanes were constructed with control of the land transferred from the state to a private company.

RECENT INTERNATIONAL EXPERIENCE

While in the United States the twentieth century toll road experience has been almost completely public, the same is not true in other countries, where private sector toll roads have been constructed with the government's consent. Unlike many toll roads in the United States, these roads apply perfect excludability, so no one can free ride on the roads. A price for this is longer spacing between exits than traditionally found in the United States, where toll roads are more often (though not exclusively) cordons on a state line or across a waterway. A key transportation implication is the increase in backtracking costs, as users must drive beyond their destination to exit and then backtrack, or spend more time in travel on the slower parallel free roads, as illustrated in Figure 2.4.

France granted concessions to private and mixed public–private corporations to finance, build, operate, and receive revenue from intercity toll roads, while the government retained ownership and the right to repurchase at the end of a fixed time period. By the 1990s France had constructed 6000 km of intercity autoroutes, all but 500 of which are tolled (Gomez-Ibañez and Meyer 1993). However, the 1500 km of urban autoroutes remain untolled. The intercity routes compete with a 30,000 km network of untolled national roads, built to less stringent standards and often not grade separated. The eight major concessionaires originally had significant private sector involvement, but only one, Cofiroute, which operates 732 km, remains; the rest were taken over by government when they hit financial difficulties. Those difficulties were not solely the product of a free market; rather, the government in the 1970s took to regulating prices and allowing them to rise at a rate lower than that of inflation, hurting the companies' balance sheets. In the 1980s the socialist government forced consolidation and conversion of the private companies to mixed public–private companies, and implemented cross-subsidies between routes.

Spain began like France, establishing Autopistas in the 1960s, a private concession to operate toll roads. This system was followed by an untolled publicly owned intercity highway system, the Autovias, promoted in the 1980s. In advance of the 1992 Olympics and World's Fair, some new Autopistas routes were established. Gomez-Ibañez and Meyer (1993) concluded that the system as a whole was profitable, though not each route.

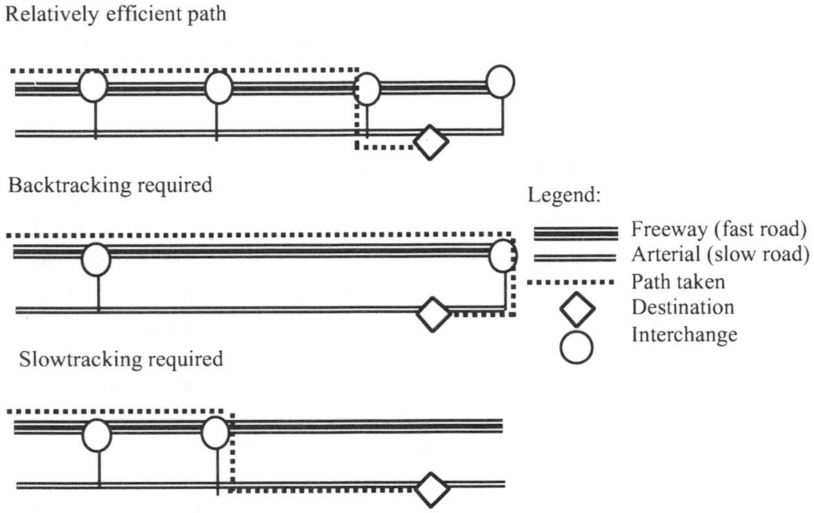

Relatively efficient path

Backtracking required

Legend:

Slowtracking required

— Freeway (fast road)
— Arterial (slow road)
······· Path taken
◇ Destination
○ Interchange

Figure 2.4   Implications of freeway interchange spacing policies

Mexico established publicly owned toll roads in the 1950s and had constructed about 1000 km by 1970 (Gomez-Ibañez and Meyer 1993). During the 1980s two concessions totaling 215 km were granted to the national development bank, with equity split between the bank, contractors, and state governments. In 1989, a program to build 4000 km of toll roads was proposed. The government selected the roads, performed the design and set the initial tolls, which would be permitted to rise with inflation. Twenty-nine new concessions, of an average duration of 11 years, were signed between 1989 and 1991, and roads were opened at the rate of 500 km per year. The toll rates were set high and the roads were underutilized (as of 1994 only five concessions had traffic in excess of forecasts, the remainder being below forecast) (Ruster 1997). Ruster suggests a variety of reasons for the toll road's problems, including the Mexican currency and debt crisis of 1994 and scarcity of financial resources, bad network planning, an inadequate tendering process and poor concession design, poor financial discipline, underdeveloped financial institutions, and mismanagement. The toll road program essentially failed. In 1997 the Mexican government assumed ownership, debt and management of a majority of the country's toll road concessions, reimbursing the original owners in the form of bonds (McCormack and Rauch 1997). McCormack and Rauch believe the bailout was intended as much to bail out the banks as the toll road concessionaires or bond holders.

Malaysia, Indonesia, and Thailand have also experimented with private toll roads (Gomez-Ibañez and Meyer 1993). In Malaysia, a private firm connected with the government received a concession to collect tolls and operate 424 km of road that had already been constructed by the government in exchange for completing the 785 km road from Thailand to Singapore. The Indonesian government had built 318 km of toll roads and four bridges by 1990. As in Malaysia, firms with government connections were given the authority to build private joint-venture toll roads, where the government provided the right-of-way and the firm undertook the construction. Thailand has constructed public toll roads in and around Bangkok, and in 1989 signed a concession with a private firm to complete a beltway around the capital and construct spokes. Tolls are to be shared between the public and private roads.

Economists have long suggested widespread road pricing as a solution to financing and congestion problems. However, comprehensive pricing has only been carried out in a few areas and to a limited extent. These experiments have all operated with the government acting as central planner, dictating road prices to users. The best example may be in Hong Kong, where in the 1980s a full-fledged test of road pricing technology was implemented (Hau 1992). A sample of 2500 vehicles tested electronic road pricing. Each vehicle was fitted with an electronic license plate, and tolls were collected at 18 sites buried in the ground. While the system was technically successful, it failed the political test because of perceptions that it was just another tax (despite government protestations that it would be revenue neutral) and that it enabled 'big brother' to monitor travel, of particular concern with the transfer of Hong Kong to the People's Republic of China in 1997.

Singapore has had an area licensing scheme since 1975 (Hau 1992; McCarthy and Tay 1993), where, in order to enter the downtown cordon, cars must possess a license, which can be read as the cars travel at full speed. The program did significantly reduce vehicle travel into the cordon, though off-peak traffic increased. Hau (1992) concludes that the government is using the area licensing scheme as a traffic management device rather than as a revenue generator. McCarthy and Tay (1993) argue that the toll is too high, and that tolled 'peak' period congestion is now lower than the untolled 'off-peak'.

Bergen, Norway, has established a ring around the central business district and imposed tolls on the traffic crossing that ring. Bergen allows the purchase of a seasonal pass, which has zero marginal effect, as there is no immediate out-of-pocket charge, no delay, and no incentive not to travel after the pass is purchased. Traffic did decline somewhat after the program was put in place. The revenue was used to finance construction and expansion of the toll system. This system has been adopted by Oslo and Trondheim, and considered by many other cities. The tolls use electronic as well as manual collection, and provide volume discounts for frequent users (PRA 1996). The extent to which volume discounts increase automobile travel is not yet known.

CONCLUSIONS

Both push and pull factors created the pressure to charter and build turnpikes. Pull factors included the economics of promoting more longer-distance trade. The push factors were the difficulties in the existing system which utilized statutory labor to maintain roads. Toll roads have come in four eras. The first, which began in the 1700s and peaked in the early to mid-1800s, saw turnpikes under the control of local companies and trusts chartered by states or Parliament.

The differences between the American and British experiences during the first era are instructive. In Britain, turnpikes were quasi-governmental organizations which sold bonds to fund construction. In the United States, turnpikes were owned and built by private companies, which were granted charters by the state to sell stock and raise tolls on given roads. Turnpike authorities were permitted to lay out roads and negotiate with property owners whose land they needed to take; legal procedures were implemented when this was a problem. On both continents, the turnpike authority's obligations were similar, to maintain roads at an acceptable standard. In Britain, turnpikes were viewed as local public goods, with some club aspects, built by the community for the good of the community because no private individuals would build it themselves under the then current economic and legal circumstances. In America, turnpikes were privately provided. However, the motivations in the United States included both the case of voluntary provision of public goods – with profits forgone, and the attempt to undertake a profitable enterprise. Free riders were present in both America and England: first, shunpikes enabled the skirting of tolls; second, many classes of trips which crossed the tollgate were exempt; and third, trips remaining within the toll cordon paid no tolls and raised no revenue, though they imposed costs on the turnpike authority. Local residents in Britain and in some American towns subsidized the roads through annual taxes, or through municipal subscription to an unprofitable road, and even through use of required contribution of local labor on occasion, but whether these subsidies covered the full private cost of travel by local residents is doubtful. As the competition from canals and rail diverted long-distance trips, toll revenue declined, even if local traffic did not, leading to the bankruptcy and abandonment of turnpikes in the United States and the disturnpiking and public takeover of the quasi-autonomous trusts in Britain. Because more trips were local to the larger government level (states in the United States or counties in England), and revenue could be raised from multiple sources, tolls were removed.

A brief second wave came about with the automobile and the first significant deployment of smooth paved roads. However, in the United States most roads were financed by states, and later the federal government, by means of a gas tax. With the relatively slow speed of highway travel, most trips remained within states; through trips were not as significant as they would become later in the twentieth century. However, a number of parkways featuring the property of excludability were toll-financed.

A third and significant wave of toll financing arrived with the deployment of grade-separated highways. As both vehicles and highways improved, trips of longer distances could be made in the same time and trip lengths increased. This in turn implied more trips between states, and the emergence of the free-rider problem when the basis over which roads were financed (taxes or tolls) did not coincide with those who used the system. While financing was at the state level, turnpikes were an effective means of collecting revenue from all users and mitigating the potential free-rider problem. But when national financing became dominant, the definition of 'local' changed to include everyone, and the revenue mechanism with lower collection costs (the gas tax) was preferred to tolls. As a result, new toll roads were no longer built in the United States, though international experience varies. Furthermore, unlike earlier roads, grade-separated roads were easily excludable, that is, the number of entrances was limited and tolls could be assessed cost-effectively at each. The same was not true of roads without grade separations.

Finally, with the completion of the interstate (intercity grade-separated highway) system in the United States, new road financing has largely become a local problem again, and new toll roads are being constructed, including some private roads. Because of the length of trips and the ease with which tolls can be collected on these excludable roads, as well as a reduction in toll collection transaction costs on both the government and traveler side with electronic toll collection, tolls are again a feasible option. New road pricing proposals depend on electronic toll collection.

Cordon tolls are being placed around a number of cities. These will collect revenue from non-local residents for traveling on urban streets. The cordons establish excludability for use of a network from outside, though not for any particular link once the network is entered. In places where cordons can easily be established, such as river crossings and ring roads, this is a feasible option for localities wishing to switch the road-financing burden to suburban residents. Ironically, the attempts of localities subject to obsolete political boundaries to finance infrastructure for the 'wrong' reason – the offloading of costs on to non-residents – creates opportunities to achieve a more efficient infrastructure pricing and financing system.

From the evidence presented here, two key conditions are required to bring about more widespread use of toll financing. First, a decentralization of the road operation authority to the point where a significant number of the trips are non-local to the relevant decision-making body would foster a greater willingness to use tolls, following the traditional saying 'don't tax you, don't tax me, tax the fella behind the tree'. Second, a decline in transaction costs to the point where they are equal to or lower than the costs of other revenue streams is necessary, where transaction costs include both delay to users and collection costs for operators. These two factors should shift beliefs about the utility of imposing tolls, as they are designed to toll someone else (not the individual making the decision to support them) and they raise at least as much revenue at similar levels of or less inconvenience.

NOTES

1. There are several rationales for placing pennies with the dead:
   - Charon's toll: A coin, about equal to a penny, was placed in the mouth or hand of the dead to pay Charon for ferrying the spirit across the river Styx to the Elysian fields. *Brewer's Dictionary of Phrase and Fable*, (1898).
   - It is said that putting pennies on the eyes of someone you kill will prevent his ghost from haunting you.
     <http://fyndo.myip.org/dbd/mirror/septembermove.html>.
   - An old method to keep the eyes closed was to place pennies on the closed eyelids. <http://www.globalideasbank.org/reinv/RIS-240.HTML>.
   - The pennies covering the eyes is an old European burial tradition. The church would put coins over the closed eyes of the paupers who died in the town and couldn't afford to be buried with a cross or some other religious symbol. The pennies were a symbolic way of giving the paupers something to take into the afterlife. The practice stopped in Europe ages ago because grave robbers would dig up the dead bodies to steal the pennies.
     <http://www.stormloader.com/users/newtopian/finaldream/dream2.htm>.

'Tax Man'
(Words and music by George Harrison)
> *Now my advice for those who die*
> *Tax Man!*
> *Declare the pennies on your eyes.*
> *Tax Man!*

The irony of course is that the pennies on the eyes may be viewed as a transportation tax to begin with, so the Tax Man is taxing tax payments.

2. See for instance: Goodrich 1960; Hilton and Due 1960; Warner 1962; Gray 1967; Bobrick 1986; Smerk 1991; Dilts 1992; Martin 1992; Hood 1993.

3. To demonstrate the point that intercity roads in western states carry more local (in-state) traffic than in eastern states, examine trip length distributions between the various areas. While trips are on average slightly longer in western than in eastern states, the difference is not significant compared with their size differences.

Travel Distance in Miles (km), All Trips

Region	Mean	Std. Dev.	N
Northeast	10.8 (18.1)	39.7 (66.2)	24591
Northcentral	10.5 (17.6)	41.2 (68.6)	24175
South	10.9 (18.1)	40.2 (67.0)	28756
West	11.5 (19.2)	50.8 (84.7)	16248

Source: 1990/91 Nationwide Personal Transportation Survey (FHWA 1991).

4. The Charles River Bridge case (11 Pet. (36 United States) 420 (1837)) is discussed by Monroe in Hall (1992).

3. Costs

INTRODUCTION

Highway transportation financing involves the costs of building and operating infrastructure, the private costs of owning and operating a vehicle, and other costs borne by society. While the public costs of infrastructure and the private costs of vehicle operations are generally understood, social or external costs are hidden to the users and operators of the transportation system. As such, they engender controversy as to their magnitude and significance. In particular, the debate over the existence and desirability of cross-subsidies in transportation centers in large part on the extent of environmental externalities – the dark matter of transportation economics. A growing line of research has attempted to unveil these costs, so that they can be used in a full accounting of transportation.[1]

On the one hand, claims of environmental damage as well as environmental standards formulated without consideration of costs and ·benefits often result in the slowing or stopping of investment in new infrastructure. On the other hand, the real social costs of new infrastructure are typically not recovered when financing projects, and are rarely considered when charging for their use.

A distinction between *output* and *outcome* is in order. An output is the desired end of the production process; an outcome is what actually results. Highway segments can be thought of as producing two outputs: traffic flow, which requires capacity in terms of the number of lanes, and standard axle loadings, which require durability in terms of the thickness of the pavement. Some outcomes of the use of highway segments are clearly not intended, including noise and air pollution, wasted time, and risk to life and property.

The cost characteristics for infrastructure providers include scale, scope, and density economies. Scale economies in the provision of highways exist, for instance, if it is cheaper (per lane) to build three lanes than two, or if it is cheaper per kilometer to build five kilometers of road rather than four. When total costs per user (or average costs) decrease over a broad range of outputs as the size of the producer expands in both output and capacity, economies of scale arise. Formally, when average costs exceed marginal costs (the change in total costs with an additional user), then there exist economies of scale; when marginal costs exceed average costs, there are diseconomies of scale.

Typically, a highway is used to produce a large number of conceptually distinct products, differentiated by time, space, and quality. This sharing of costs, called joint and common costs, gives rise to economies of scope, the cost characteristic whereby a single organization producing multiple outputs has lower costs than multiple firms each producing one of those outputs. Whether and the extent to which scope economies exist will depend upon both the number of products and the level of each output.

Understanding scale economies has practical value for the viability of alternative road-pricing strategies. The financial viability of an infrastructure facility, under optimal pricing and investment, will depend largely upon the characteristics of its cost function (Mohring and Harwitz 1962). Marginal cost pricing refers to charging a vehicle for the addition to total costs that results when it uses a roadway, particularly with regards to the delay that it creates. This contrasts with average cost pricing, which simply divides total costs by the total number of users. When highway capacity and durability costs both have constant returns to scale, then marginal cost pricing will fully recover capital and operating costs. However, when there are increasing returns to scale, marginal cost pricing will not cover costs. Similarly, when there are decreasing returns to scale, marginal cost pricing produces excess revenue.

Economics has a long tradition of distinguishing those costs which are fully internalized by economic agents (internal or private costs) and those that are not (external or social costs). Agents (individuals, households, firms, and governments) interact in interrelated markets by buying and selling goods and services, as inputs to and outputs from production. The costs and benefits that voluntarily interacting agents convey or impose on one another are fully reflected in the prices charged. When the actions of one economic agent alter the environment of another economic agent in the absence of a voluntary exchange, there is an externality.[2] The essential distinction is harm committed between strangers, an external cost, and harm committed between parties to an economic transaction, an internal cost.

Central to the definition and valuation of externalities is the definition of the agent in question. One way is to define agents as comprising each vehicle. A vehicle influences other vehicles (agents) by generating effects (such as congestion and increasing the risk of accident) largely contained within the transportation system. A vehicle also influences unrelated agents by generating effects (such as noise and air pollution) not contained within the transportation system. Alternatively, the infrastructure operator may be selected as the agent, thereby internalizing the first set of effects. This analysis uses the first definition, giving a broader scope of externalities to examine.

Second, the appropriate externalities to consider in this context must be determined. This depends on how the transportation problem is defined. Overall, the transportation system is open, dynamic, and constantly changing. Some of the more permanent elements include streets and highways. The system also includes the vehicles using those roads at any given time. The energy to propel vehicles is part of the system, but it is not obvious whether the extraction of resources from the ground (for example, oil wells) should be counted as part of the system.

Any open system influences the world in many ways. Some influences are direct, some are indirect. The transportation system is no exception. Three examples may illustrate the point:

- First order (direct) effect: a road improvement reduces travel time.
- Second order (less direct) effect: reduced travel time increases the amount of land development along a corridor. This is not a direct effect because other factors may intervene to exacerbate or prevent this consequence.
- Indirect effect: The new land development along a corridor results in increased demand for public schools and libraries.

As can be seen almost immediately, there is no end to the number or extent of indirect effects, which may follow in turn from the less direct, second-order effects. While recognizing that the economy is dynamic and connected in an enormous number of ways, it is almost impossible consistently to quantify anything other than the proximate, first-order, direct effects of the transportation system. Rather than building a structural model of the economy tracing the reverberations and interactions of all choices, decisions, and outcomes, correlation between cause and effect is used. Many effects have multiple causes that influence the outcome only probabilistically. If the degree to which 'cause' (transportation) and 'effect' (negative externality) are correlated is sufficiently high, the effect is considered direct; the lower the probability of effect following from the single (transportation) cause, the less direct is the effect. The question of degree of correlation is fundamentally empirical, and the appropriate level of correlation to use is inevitably arbitrary.

Several costs are excluded because they are outside the strictly defined transport sector. In order to evaluate costs, borders must be drawn around the system considered; otherwise one is drawn into a full evaluation of the entire economy. Pecuniary externalities, the effect on other markets due to changes in price associated with changes in demand, are excluded. For a limited project, for instance a single corridor, it is unlikely that prices in most commodity markets will change noticeably. Some researchers ascribe a fraction of US defense costs to the transportation sector, since much of that defense is of the Middle East, an oil-producing region, which would not otherwise be defended. The links are tenuous, and certainly outside the market. It is unclear whether such defense expenditures actually lower energy costs, and they may be undertaken for a variety of geopolitical reasons. Others consider parking to be a cost associated with transportation. Parking is not 'free', it is either charged directly to the consumer or subsidized by the provider (a shopping center, or office building, or the community which builds wider than necessary streets). Sprawl and the increased costs of serving dispersed land uses are sometimes blamed on the automobile. Certainly automobility enables dispersed housing, but so does telephony and any number of other technologies. It is at least a second-order effect.

There are also costs which have long been recognized but are seemingly impossible to quantify accurately, including social severance or the cost of dividing communities with infrastructure, or ecosystem severance, the cost to the environment of driving a highway through local ecologies. Such costs will involve value judgements or further empirical research. Thus the overall levels of external costs here can be taken as a lower bound in this regard.

However, this chapter estimates the amount of economic damage produced by the externality, rather than the cost of preventing that damage in the first place. Rational economic actors would choose the lower of prevention costs or damage costs when costs are internalized. This should bias the results upward (if there were a cheaper prevention measure, it could be used, but if prevention were more expensive, then the actors would accept damages). In short, some externalities are missing, but there are moderately high estimates of the externalities included.

The next sections estimate costs, component by component. First, the total vehicle ownership, operation, and maintenance costs borne by users of the system are measured. These include the cost of vehicle ownership (as measured by depreciation) and the cost of operating and maintaining the vehicle (including gas, tires, repairs and such). Costs borne by users also include taxes and insurance. Although these costs are borne by users, they are transfers to other cost categories (infrastructure, accidents, and safety). The next category is infrastructure costs. Here, state-level expenditures are examined, including federal transfer payments as well as the expenditures of lower levels of government. Highway travel, like other modes, is wrought with common and joint costs between different trip classes and vehicle types. Econometric analysis is used to estimate the long-run costs per vehicle-kilometer traveled accounting for different vehicle types. Toll collection costs are estimated. These vary according to the type of toll road on which they are placed. Time costs are divided into two components, one reflecting free-flow travel time (which is an internal cost), the other reflecting the increase in time due to congestion (the external costs due to and imposed on other users). Other social costs estimated include the full cost of accidents, regardless of incidence; the decline in property values due to noise; and damage to the environment, which is the monetized consideration of pollution and property damage in addition to the estimated costs of global climate change. While noise and environmental damage costs are pure externalities, in that their incidence falls on those outside the system, accident and congestion costs are inflicted by one system user on another.

VEHICLES

The first element in the full cost model are vehicle costs borne by users. The cost of operating a vehicle depends upon numerous factors, many of them (such as the size and quality of the vehicle) decided by the user. The operating costs considered in the analysis include gas, oil, maintenance and tires. Insurance costs (fire/theft, collision, and property damage/liability) and license, registration, and taxes are considered to be transfers (at least in part). They must not be double counted, and so are not considered here, but rather in later sections. For instance, the full cost of accidents can be considered neither solely a social cost nor solely a private cost. Insurance simply transfers part of the financial incidence of accidents from drivers to an insurance pool. Theft just transfers a good from one party, the rightful owner, to another, the thief. Similarly, license, registration, and taxes pay for part of the cost of constructing, maintaining, and operating the highway system. This can be expressed as follows:

$$T_U(D) = (C_g + C_o + C_t)D - \beta_1 A - \beta_2 D$$

where:
   $T_U(D)$ = Total user cost as a function of distance
   C_g = cost of gas ($/km)
   C_o = cost of oil and maintenance ($/km)
   C_t = cost of tires ($/km)
   D = distance traveled per year (km)
   A = age of vehicle (years)
   β_n = coefficient estimated from model.

Depreciation occurs for two main reasons: wear and tear on the vehicle, and changing demand. Demand for an aging (unused) vehicle is replaced by the demand for a newer vehicle equipped with technologically advanced features. Demand is also affected by changing preferences. In order to estimate the various cost components of depreciation, and thus to distinguish between average cost and marginal cost, a database of used car asking prices was developed from an internet site for used car trading. This analysis uses the intermediate sized cars (Honda Accord and Ford Taurus) as an illustration, though the analysis can easily be generalized. The user cost model tests the hypothesis that depreciation increases with age and distance. A used car price model was estimated using ordinary least squares regression. The results are shown in Table 3.1, and illustrated in Figure 3.1.

Table 3.1   Used car price model

Variable	Description	Coefficient	*T*- Statistic
β_0	Constant	$20,053	26.44[c]
β_1	Age ($/year)	-$1,351	-6.69[c]
β_2	Distance depreciation ($/vkt)	-$0.014	-1.53
β_3	Make (1 if Ford, 0 if Honda)	-$2,738	-3.46[c]

Note: : *a* – significant at the 10% level, *b* – significant at the 5% level, *c* - significant at the 1% level; $R^2 = 0.861$.

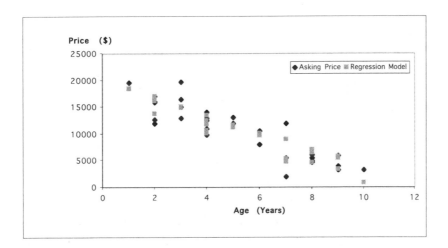

Figure 3.1   Used car age versus price

The analysis implies that a car loses $0.014 per vehicle kilometer traveled (vkt) and $1,351 in value per year. The model also implies that a Ford Taurus sells for $2,738 less than a Honda Accord, all other things being equal. The intercept term suggests that a new Honda Accord (1996) with no kilometers is valued at $20,053. These are not actual transaction prices, but asking prices so an additional markup is included in the price. For a car that is driven 16,000 km per year, the model gives a depreciation of $1,581. Even considering markup, this is less than the depreciated value of $2,883 given by the American Automobile Association (AAA 1993). Used cars suffer the problem of adverse selection, so prices may tend to underestimate their actual value because of the possibility of 'lemons'. The buyer offers a price lower than what he would pay if he were certain of the car's quality.

Estimates for average unit costs ($0.13/vkt) and marginal cost ($0.49/vkt) imply that for a 1000-km trip, the average cost for the automobile user is $130, but the marginal cost is only $49. In all likelihood, the driver perceives the cost of the trip as the marginal cost, if not lower, since he is likely to discount the cost of oil, tires and depreciation from the calculation.

The AAA (1993) estimates a series of unit costs for transportation, including a gas cost of $0.036/vkt, excluding tax. However, the retail price of a gallon of gas (excluding tax) at the end of 1995 was about $0.18/liter, though noticeably higher in 2000. At the corporate average fuel economy standard for new cars (about 11 km/liter), which all manufacturers must achieve as a fleet average, this translates to $0.015/vkt for gas. The cost of gas is close to the cost of oil and maintenance because special excise taxes are removed from the price of gas (as they are considered a transfer to infrastructure), while general taxes on oil are included in the price. AAA (1993) estimates for the price of oil and maintenance ($0.014/vkt) and tires ($0.0054/vkt) are employed.

INFRASTRUCTURE

The second component in the full cost model is infrastructure costs. This section presents a model predicting long-run total expenditures on infrastructure as a function of price inputs (interest rates, wage rates, and material costs) and outputs (distance traveled by passenger vehicle, single unit truck, and combination truck). The hypothesis of the expenditure model is that total expenditures increase with outputs and prices, so all signs should be positive. However, the amount of increase with output depends on the nature of the output.

Total expenditure data are developed from two sets of information: data compiled by the Federal Highway Administration on maintenance, operating, and administrative costs (FHWA 1993); and capital stock data collected by Gillen et al. (1994). The capital stock series was inflated from

1988 to 1993 levels, and then was discounted to reflect an annualized cost. The annual cost was assumed to equal the total cost multiplied by the price of capital or interest rate – a state with a higher interest rate has a higher opportunity cost for investing money in fixed assets. The annualized capital cost (C_k) was added to annual expenditures on maintenance (C_m) and operations and administration (C_l) to create an estimate of long-run total infrastructure expenditures (T_l).

Three classes of output (Y) are defined: passenger cars (Y_a), single unit trucks (Y_s), and combination trucks (Y_c) in millions of vehicle miles traveled per year. Based on relative damage to the roadway, costs associated with passenger cars are expected to be less than those associated with single unit trucks, which is less still than those associated with combination trucks. However, this may not be the case if there are economies of scope associated with roadways. For instance, suppose a network is designed for peak rush-hour flows, and that these flows are dominated by passenger cars. In the off-peak hours, capacity is underutilized. If it is during those hours that trucks use the roadway, then the government expenditure on transportation to serve those trucks may in fact be less than that for passenger vehicles. At a minimum, because these two effects (efficient capacity utilization versus greater damage) are offsetting, the relative additional costs to serve trucks would not be as great as that indicated by an engineering analysis based solely on damage and that does not consider scope economies.

Several price measures are included in the model. The price of capital (P_k), including the entire built stock of the highway network, is measured by taking the interest rate, which reflects the cost of borrowed money. States with lower bond ratings or higher interest rates must pay more to borrow, and have a higher opportunity cost for fixed investment. Moody's ratings for each state (Bureau of Census 1993) and typical interest rates paid for lower-rated bonds garnered from recent offerings are employed to estimate the price of capital. The price of labor (P_l) is measured by taking the average wage rate of state government employees (normalized to the national average) for 1993 (Bureau of Labor Statistics 1995). The third main input is the price of materials (P_m). The principal material used in highway construction is bituminous concrete for pavement. Indices of construction materials prices are computed by taking the price of an input (FHWA 1994), and dividing by the national average of the price of that input. The indices, reflecting relative prices, with a mean at 1, can then be added to create a composite index for construction materials. For instance, the price of bituminous concrete in a state, and divided by the national average of the unit price of bituminous concrete, provides an index representing the relative price of bituminous concrete. The materials for which data were available – bituminous concrete (price per ton), common excavation (price per cubic yard), reinforcing steel (price per pound), structural steel (price per pound), and structural concrete (price per cubic yard) – were included in the database. Boske (1988) discusses the data and the use of indices with these data, though only bituminous concrete was used in the final regressions.

The long-run total expenditure model presented below was estimated with feasible generalized least squares regression.[3] The results below present a Cobb–Douglas functional form, using the log of both dependent and independent variables modeled in the regression. Largely, the hypotheses were borne out. As shown in Table 3.2, the signs were generally in the expected direction, though the price of materials was not significant.

Table 3.2   Long-run total infrastructure expenditure model

	Variable	Coefficient	*T*-Statistic
Capital	$ln(P_k)$	1.831	11.247[c]
Labor	$ln(P_l)$	0.786	3.346[c]
Materials	$ln(P_m)$	0.005	0.222
Autos	$ln(Y_a)$	0.439	9.824[c]
Single Unit Truck	$ln(Y_s)$	0.179	4.885[c]
Combination	$ln(Y_c)$	0.225	5.016[c]
	(Constant)	11.280	20.050[c]

Note: a – significant at the 10% level, b – significant at the 5% level, c - significant at the 1% level; $R^2 = 0.995$.

Table 3.3   Long-run marginal and average infrastructure costs and scale economies

	Auto	Single Truck	Combination Truck
Marginal Costs	0.019	0.043	0.051
Average Costs	0.017	0.063	0.101
Economies of Scale	0.92	1.45	1.96
	Decreasing	Increasing	Increasing

Note: in $/vkt.

The total expenditure model can be used to compute the marginal and average costs for the each class of vehicles. These are solved for average values and are given in Table 3.3.[4] With economies of scale, the cost of producing more transportation output within the same network is lower for larger levels of output. The economic interpretation of economies of scale

(*S*) is the ratio of average costs to marginal costs. Where *S* is greater than one, there are economies of scale; where *S* is less than one there are diseconomies of scale.

Prior to determining economies of scale in this multi-product case, the measure of economies of scale for each output, or the product- specific economies of scale, must be examined. Small, Winston, and Evans (1989) reported the existence of significant economies of scale associated with the durability output of roads, the ability to handle axle loads. This is because the pavement's ability to sustain traffic increases proportionally more than its thickness. They also found evidence that there are slight economies of scale in the provision of road capacity, that is, the capacity to handle traffic volume. However, they reported diseconomies of scope from the joint production of durability and capacity because, as the road is made wider to accommodate more traffic, the cost of any additional thickness rises since all the lanes must be built to the same standard of thickness. They conclude that these three factors together result in highway production having approximately constant returns to scale. In other words, the output-specific scale economies are offset by the diseconomies of scope in producing them jointly.

Our results argue there are economies of scale for trucks, and diseconomies of scale for passenger cars (as shown in Table 3.3). This suggests complementarities in the provision of infrastructure, probably explained by the peaked nature of capacity requirements for cars as compared with trucks, which offsets the requirements for thicker pavement. Cars, which are used relatively more intensively in the already congested peak period, impose a higher marginal cost than average cost on infrastructure. The next infrastructure expansion will cost more than previous expansions; as many roads have already taken advantage of the easy opportunities for expansion, any additional construction costs will require land acquisition in already developed (and therefore more expensive) areas.

TOLL COLLECTION

Collection costs depend on the technology used to collect tolls. The two main turnpike toll collection systems on limited access facilities are dubbed cordon (or open) and perfect (or closed), illustrated in Figure 3.2. Open, or cordon, tolls use a mainline barrier, this allows local, short-distance traffic to use the facility without paying tolls, but all traffic crossing the barrier must pay the toll. Examples of open systems include the Connecticut Turnpike and Bee Line Expressway in Florida. Closed, or perfect, tolls use tickets (or their electronic equivalent). Toll booths are located at each point

Financing Transportation Networks

of entry and exit. Tickets are issued at the entry points and revenue collected at the exit based on the amount of travel in the system. Examples of closed systems include the New Jersey, Pennsylvania, and Ohio turnpikes. There are numerous hybrid combinations between these two idealized types. Some mix use of mainline barriers and entry and exit tolls to increase the probability of getting revenue for each trip without imposing as high a collection cost as a closed system. Others combine mainline tolls with entry tolls to ensure some revenue from every trip without having to track origin and destination. Hybrid systems will generally be more equitable than open systems and less equitable than closed systems, where equity is defined as paying in proportion to use. Examples of hybrid systems include the Illinois Tollway and Garden State Parkway. For a single link (such as a bridge), with one entry and one exit, open and closed systems are identical.

Closed toll system

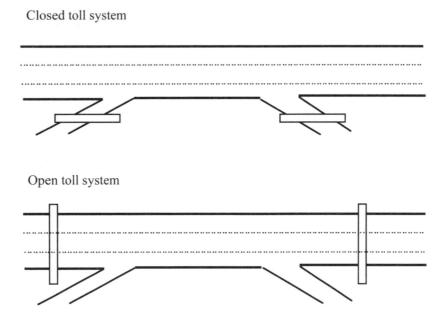

Open toll system

Figure 3.2   Schematic illustration of closed and open toll systems

Existing, non-toll, limited-access highways have a higher density of interchanges and are more accessible than typical closed-system toll roads, as shown in Table 3.4. This is due to the high cost of collecting revenue in a closed system. Thus imposing perfect (closed) tolls implies increasing the backtrack or slowtrack (early exit to a slower speed route) costs of users, as shown in Figure 2.4.

Table 3.4   Interchange spacing on free and closed-toll highways

Type	State	Facility	Length (km)	Interchanges (no.)	Spacing (km)
Free	Ohio	I-70	408	70	5.8
Toll		Turnpike	386	19	20.3
Free	Pennsylvania	I-80	509	62	8.2
Toll		Turnpike	573	28	20.5

Source: Gittings (1987*).*

In general, the cost per barrier on a closed system will be much lower than in an open system, since the closed system's barrier typically guards only one lane (the entry or exit ramp), while the open system must cover an entire toll plaza. However, the lower unit cost is unlikely to entirely offset the costs of the increased number of barriers which must be constructed. Also, although this section does not compute delay directly, it should be noted that a manually operated open system with three or more barriers is likely to cause more user delay due to tolls than a closed system (where a user faces only two barriers).

There are several ways to estimate the collection costs. We use data for California toll bridges to estimate these costs. Table 3.5 gives the result of an OLS regression, shown in Figure 3.3. Allocating the annual fixed cost to the peak hour gives $91.65 per hour for collecting tolls on all lanes per bridge, the empirical value for fixed collection costs. If there are 300 vehicles per toll lane per hour, then the fixed cost of collection amounts to $0.03/vehicle, compared with $0.085/vehicle for variable costs.

Table 3.5   Regression on collection costs from California bridges

	Coefficients	T-Statistic
Constant	334523	2.90[b]
Total Vehicles	0.085	14.33[c]

Note: a – significant at the 10% level, *b* – significant at the 5% level, *c* - significant at the 1% level; $R^2 = 0.96$.

Turnpikes in New York and Pennsylvania lose between 14% and 19% of revenue collected to collection costs using current (labor-intensive) technology (Gittings 1987). This compares with 9–31% found on

California's bridges, with the highest efficiency on the most heavily traveled San Francisco to Oakland Bay Bridge. When tolls doubled on California's bridges in 1998, the cost of collection relative to revenues collected was halved (aside from additional delays due to the need to give change). While looking at percentages is interesting, it does not help solve the problem, because there is no reason to expect these percentages to remain stable as tolls vary.

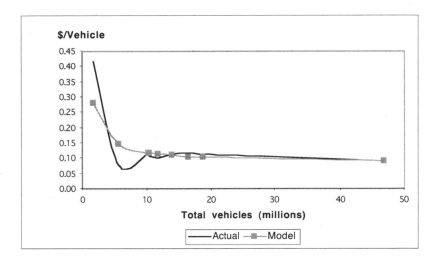

Note: Bridges (by revenue smallest to largest) are Antioch, Vincent Thomas, San Diego-Coronado, Dumbarton, Richmond San Mateo, Benicia-Martinez, Carquinez, San Francisco-Oakland.

Figure 3.3   Manual toll collection costs

Electronic toll collection (ETC) systems are operating or being tested today in locations across the United States and around the world. Automatic vehicle identification (AVI) technology makes these systems possible.[5] ETC increases toll lane capacity, thereby reducing toll processing time and queue lengths at toll plazas. Thus both delays and the number of toll-takers are reduced. For instance, where conventional toll collection takes 14 seconds per car in Japan on average, ETC takes only about 3 seconds per car.[6] Furthermore, ETC can substantially reduce or even eliminate the need for future expansion of toll plaza lanes. It also offers users a payment alternative. Opening pre-payment accounts eliminates the need for patrons to be concerned with having cash ready for each toll plaza passage. Having dedicated special AVI lanes eliminates the need for AVI-equipped vehicles to stop at toll plazas, which can reduce noise pollution, air pollution, and fuel consumption. AVI systems can also significantly reduce reconstruction costs and operating costs. Lennon (1994) reports that a manual toll lane can accommodate 400–450 vehicles per hour while an electronic lane on New York's Tappan Zee Bridge peaks at 1000 vehicles per hour. Clean Air Action (1993) found a significant reduction in tons of pollutants in Oklahoma. The average emissions reduction was 72% for carbon monoxide, 83% for hydrocarbons, and 45% for oxides of nitrogen per mile of impacted operation. Philip and Schramm (1997) have shown that ETC can reduce the cost of staffing toll booths by 43.1%, money handling by 9.6%, and roadway maintenance by 14.4%. Mitretek Systems (1999) for the Oklahoma Turnpike System reports that the annual cost to operate an automated lane in the Oklahoma Turnpike System is only $15,800 while the annual cost to operate an attended lane is $176,000. (Deployment of ETC is discussed in Chapter 12.)

On the other hand, the implementation of ETC will also increase the capital outlay and other costs of toll facilities. In particular, consideration must be given to the costs of lane operation and maintenance expenses, computer hardware and software, and transponders for the different technologies. It is important to note that, when the equipment is purchased in large quantities, the unit cost will likely decline.[7]

An operating cost function, with data from 68 toll facilities (including highways, bridges and tunnels, but excluding ferries) throughout the United States, is estimated. The first task is to specify an operating cost model as a function of demand, capacity, and technology used. Here, annual transactions (in thousands of dollars) measures demand. Total traffic is not used because some toll facilities only charge for one direction while others charge vehicles for both directions. The number of toll lanes serves as the capacity variable. Technology is defined using the market share of the AVI system, a numerical percentage. A log-linear OLS model is estimated.

The cost data, which include maintenance disbursements, operating disbursements, and administration costs, are from *Highway Statistics 1998* published by the Federal Highway Administration. The annual transactions and the market share of each toll facility are from the Electronic Toll Collection and Traffic Management website statistics (ETTM 2001). Because the data were collected by different agencies, some problems arose when they were transformed to fit the above models. The first problem is the collection time difference. The cost data from *Highway Statistics 1998* are the costs of all the toll facilities in 1998. However, in ETTM statistics, the data which include annual transactions and the number of toll lanes range from 1995 to 1999. It is assumed that the number of toll lanes of the observed facilities did not change from 1995 to 1999 and that the annual total transactions were unchanged in these four years. The second problem is that each database contains observations that do not appear in the other, so some data had to be dropped.[8]

Other desirable data are not available. In particular, the location of toll plazas, whether they are on a freeway mainline, or on an on-ramp (or off-ramp) toll plaza, may affect costs. Another factor is the technology used by each ETC system. There are at least three available AVI technologies, the costs of which may be expected to differ. Also, there are some gaps in the data collection process. Because the cost data are from *Highway Statistics 1998*, ETC systems opened after 1998 are not included in the data. However, many highways, bridges and tunnels began to implement various AVI systems after 1998.

The models were estimated using the data with 68 observations. The resulting estimates an OLS regression are shown on Table 3.6. The coefficient of the variable, representing AVI status is -0.125, meaning the operating cost reduction due to implementing an AVI system is 25%, but is not statistically significant.

Table 3.6   Toll operating costs model results [Ln (Total operating cost)]

Independent Variables	Coefficient	T-Statistic
Constant	1.087	2.05 [b]
Ln (lanes)	0.477	2.48 [b]
Ln (annual transactions)	0.490	2.76 [c]
Market share	-0.125	0.637
Number of observations	68	

Note: a – significant at the 10% level, *b –* significant at the 5% level, *c -* significant at the 1% level; $R^2 = 0.70$.

TIME

The time a trip takes can be divided into two components, uncongested and congested time. The uncongested time is a simple function of distance and uncongested (or free-flow) speed, and is clearly an internal cost. Congested time depends on the number of other vehicles on the road, and thus is external to the vehicle but internal to the transportation system.

The exact relationship between volume and delay for a specific location can best be determined by a detailed, site-specific engineering study. For highways, the *Highway Capacity Manual* (TRB 1985) provides some estimates. For a segment with a 112 km/hr design speed, under ideal conditions the capacity (Q_o) is taken to be 2000 passenger cars per hour per lane. The following is an equation for limited access freeways derived from the data given in HCM (1985) and graphed in Figure 3.4:

$$T_T = Q\left(L/V_f + 0.32(Q/Q_0)^{10} \right)$$

where:

T_T = total travel time in vehicle minutes of highway time per km;
L = length (km);
V_f = free-flow speed (km per minute);
Q = highway flow in vehicles per hour per lane; and
Q_o = highway maximum flow (capacity) (2000 veh. per hour per lane).

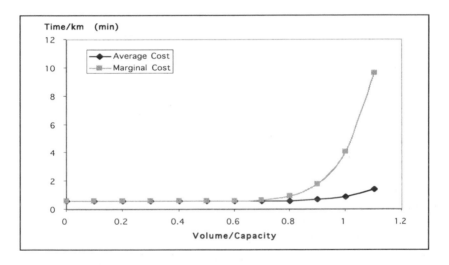

Source: TRB (1985), author's calculations.

Figure 3.4 Highway travel time: average versus marginal costs

The incremental delay caused by an additional vehicle, at capacity (moving from 1999 to 2000 vehicles per hour), can be calculated to be almost four minutes of total delay on a single one-kilometer segment. Of course, any estimates of the amount of delay depend on estimates of volume, and vice versa, so the problems will need to be treated together before a definitive answer can be determined.

The value of time depends on factors such as the mode of travel, time of day, purpose (business, non-business) of the trip, quality or level of service of the trip (including speed), and specific characteristics of the trip-maker, including income (Hensher 1995).   Furthermore, the value of time saved depends on the amount of time saved – 60 people saving 1 minute may not be worth the same as one person saving 60 minutes. Time in motion is valued differently from time spent waiting. Unexpected delays are more costly than the expected, since they are built into decisions. All of these factors need to be considered in a detailed operational analysis of the costs of travel time and congestion. There are a number of approaches to valuing travel time, ranging from utility theory to marginal productivity. Conservatively, a $10/hour value of time for all trips is adopted, although it is easy to see how the monetized costs of time change with changes in this value.

Congestion costs, assuming an average traffic level of 1500 vehicles per hour per lane, at $10/hour value of time and 1.5 persons per car (delay victims) amount to a marginal cost of $0.049/vkt imposed on other travelers and an average cost of $0.0045/vkt suffered by the vehicle driver and passenger. Free-flow costs can be calculated making assumptions about speed and value of time. If a speed of 100 km/hr, and a value of time of $10/hour, and 1.5 persons per vehicle are assumed, this amounts to an average of $0.15/vkt separate from congestion costs. For intercity travel, free-flow costs outweigh congestion costs.

ACCIDENTS

There are a number of sources recording highway accidents. The National Highway Traffic Safety Administration has two databases: NASS, the National Accident Sampling System, and FARS, the Fatal Accident Reporting System. In addition, each state keeps records, as does the insurance industry with its National Council on Compensation Insurance Detailed Claims Information (DCI) database. Injuries are typically classified according to whether they result in fatalities, and by the degree of injury or property damage. Many crashes, particularly minor accidents without loss of life or major injury, are not reported to the police or insurance industry.

Sullivan and Hsu (1988) have estimated the rate of accidents as a function of traffic during the peak periods (5:00 – 9:30 a.m. or 3:00 –7:30 p.m.). It should be noted that while there are more accidents proportionately in urban areas, the share of fatal accidents is much less than in rural areas, as urban accidents tend to occur at a slower speed. While accidents are often assumed to occur at a fixed rate, this 'linearity' conjecture should not be assumed to be true.

The principal means of estimating the cost of accidents is to estimate their damage costs. The method employed here is a comprehensive approach which includes valuing years lost to the accident as well as direct costs. Several steps must be undertaken: converting injuries to years of life, developing a value of life, and estimating other costs. Placing a value on injury requires measuring its severity. Miller (1992) describes a year of functional capacity (365 days/year, 24 hours/day) as consisting of several dimensions – mobility, cognitive, self care, sensory, cosmetic, pain, ability to perform household responsibilities, and ability to perform wage work – and calculates the number of years of functional years lost by degree of injury. Central to the estimation of costs is an estimate of the standard value of life, which Miller summarizes from a number of studies and gives as $2.7 million.

Table 3.7   Estimated value of life by type of study

Type of study	Description	Value of Life (1995$ millions)
Market demand versus price	Extra wages for risky jobs (average of 30 studies)	2.5–4.4
	Safer cars	3.4
	Smoke detectors	1.6
	Houses in less polluted areas	3.4
	Life insurance	3.9
	Wages	2.7
Safety behavior	Pedestrian tunnel use	2.7
	Safety belt use (2 studies)	2.6–4.0
	Speed choice (2 studies)	1.7–2.9
	Smoking	1.3
Surveys	Auto safety (5 studies)	1.6–3.6
	Cancer	3.4
	Safer job	2.9
	Fire safety	4.7
	Average of 49 studies	2.9
	Average of 11 auto safety studies	2.7

Source: Adapted from Miller (1992).

After converting injuries to functional years lost, combining with fatality rates, and value of life (see for example Table 3.7), a substantial portion of accident costs have been captured. But these data must be supplemented by other costs, including hospitalization, rehabilitation, and emergency services. The comprehensive costs can be allocated to the various accident categories by severity. Costs vary by location, crashes on urban interstates cost about $70,000 while those on rural interstates about

$120,000 (Miller 1992). Application of the Sullivan and Hsu (1988) accident model results in typical values on the order of $0.040/vkt for rural travel or $0.023/vkt for urban travel.[9] The values are graphed in Figure 3.5.

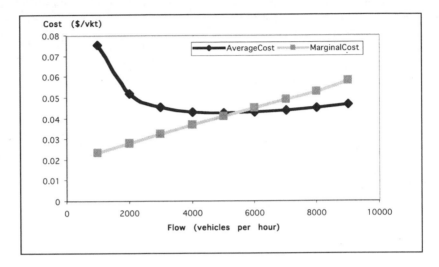

Figure 3.5 Highway accidents: average and marginal costs

NOISE

Noise is usually defined as unwanted sound. The damages caused by noise include loss of sleep, lower productivity, psychological discomfort, and annoyance. These are hard to quantify, but because they are associated with a place, the quantity of damage is often viewed as resulting in lower property values. A number of studies have been performed over the years to measure the decline in residential property values due to noise and its associated vibration. This has not been done for non-residential (commercial and public) buildings, however, where abatement measures are more cost-effective.

Hedonic models of housing collected by Modra and Bennett (1985), Nelson (1982b), and from other studies are summarized in Table 3.8. These studies use a noise depreciation index (NDI) that measures the percentage reduction of house price per decibel (dB(A)) above some base. To determine the amount of noise damage produced by a facility, one must know the noise produced on that facility (as a function of traffic flow) and the location of residences near the facility. Also the house value must be known because the impact of noise is generally found to be a percentage reduction in house price rather than a fixed value. The average NDI for all of the noise surveys since 1967 is 0.62, giving confidence in using that number for the noise depreciation index in this analysis.

Table 3.8   Noise depreciation near highways

Researcher	Site	NDI	Year
Towne	Seattle, WA	negligible	1968
Diffey	London	0	1971
Gamble et al.	All four areas	0.26	1970
	N. Springfield VA	0.21	1970
	Bogata NJ	2.22	1970
	Rosedale, MD	0.42	1970
	Towson, MD	0.26	1970
Anderson and Wise	All four areas	0.25	1970
	N. Springfield, VA	0.14	1970
	Towson, MD	0.43	1970
Hammar	Stockholm	1.4	1972
Vaughn and Huckins	Chicago	0.65	1974
Nelson	Washington, DC	0.87	1975
Langley	N. Springfield, VA	0.32	1977
Bailey	N. Springfield, VA	0.30	1977
Abelson	Sydney, NSW	0.56	1977
Hall et al.	Toronto, ON	1.05	1977
Langley	N. Springfield, VA	0.40	1980
Palmquist	Kingsgate, WA	0.48	1980
	N. King Co. WA	0.30	1980
	Spokane, WA	0.08	1980
Allen	N. Virginia	0.15	1980
	Tidewater	0.14	1980
Taylor et al	Southern Ontario	0.5	1982
Holsman, Bradley	Sydney, NSW	0.72	1982
Pommerehne	Berlin	1.2	1985
Hall and Willard	Toronto/Vic. Park	0.335	1987
	Toronto/Leslie St.	2.10	1987
	Toronto/Etobicoke	0.39	1987
	Pooled	0.70	1987
Soguel	Neuchatel	0.91	1989
Streeting	Canberra	0.90	1989
Swiss	Basle	1.26	
Average		0.62	

Source: Adapted from Nelson (1982).

The damage caused by a new highway is determined by comparing the noise before and after the roadway is deployed. This analysis assumes a baseline of background noise exposure forecast (NEF, an index of noise in dB(A) weighted by number of events over a time period) of 30. The model is solved by dividing the area on each side of the road into 10 meter strips (s) parallel to the road, as illustrated in Figure 3.6. Each 10-meter by 1 kilometer strip has a number of housing units (H_s) depending on the density. To compute the total damage for each strip, the number of homes is multiplied by the value (V_H) of each home, the noise depreciation index (NDI) and the net increase in the NEF compared with a baseline. The total damage is converted to a present cost and is summed over all the 10 meter strips for a 1-kilometer stretch.

To estimate the full cost of noise per passenger kilometer traveled, the total change in the prices of homes as a result of noise damage must be converted into an annual charge. For automobile travel, the integrated highway noise model gives a range of between $0.0001/vkt and $0.0060/vkt average cost, depending on flow, given the other assumptions shown in Table 3.9. This charge can then be divided by the total passenger volume per year to determine the charge per passenger kilometer.

Table 3.9 Assumptions in noise model

Variable	Value
Number of years	30
Discount rate	7.5%
Cost/dB(A)	0.62
Home value	$250,000
Residential density	360 houses/km^2
Highway speed	100 km/hr
Heavy vehicles	10%
Distance sound travels from highway edge	500 m

A regression was performed after fixing, with the independent variable being the natural log of highway flow (Q), and the dependent variable being the average cost in $/vkt. It should be noted that the average cost of noise depends not only on same direction flow, but also on opposite directional flow, complicating this problem.[10] The average cost function was estimated ($R^2 = 0.92$), and from it the total cost and marginal cost expressions were derived, the total cost form is given below. Figure 3.7 graphs average and marginal costs (in $/vkt) versus flow.

$$T_N = Q\left(-0.018 + 0.0028\left(\ln\left(Q\right)\right)\right)$$

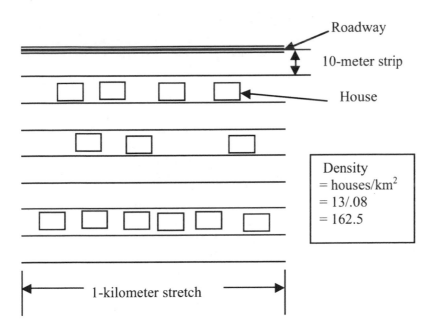

Figure 3.6 Illustration of noise model application

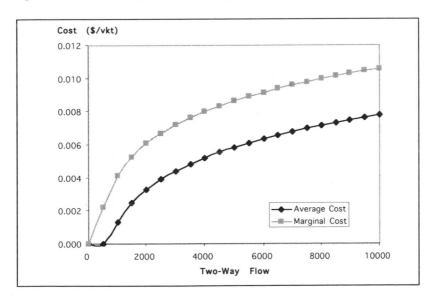

Figure 3.7 Highway noise: average and marginal costs

AIR POLLUTION AND GLOBAL CHANGE

Probably the most difficult external cost to establish is that of air pollution. Determining the quantity of pollutants emitted by an automobile is in principle a relatively straightforward engineering task, though it depends on vehicle type, model year, vehicle deterioration, fuel type, speed, acceleration, and deceleration, and other factors. However, traditionally, emission rates are determined by tests in the laboratory rather than actual conditions, so to some extent these rates underestimate the amount of actual emissions, particularly those of super-emitters, or poorly maintained vehicles (Small and Kazimi 1995). Determining the damage done is more difficult still, depending on the place and time of emission, density and distribution of the population, the climate, and topography. This section synthesizes earlier studies to develop cost estimates.

As used here, the types of air pollution fall into four main categories, photo-chemical smog, acid deposition, ozone depletion, and global warming, though it is only for the first and last that significant research into transportation costs has been undertaken. There is considerable scientific controversy surrounding all of these categories, and there is no direct translation from pollutant emitted to damage inflicted.

- *Photo-chemical smog* occurs low in the atmosphere and at ground level, and results in health, vegetation, and material damages. Seasonal in nature and peaking in the summertime in most areas, smog's principal cause is tailpipe emissions from automobiles. Ozone, formed in the atmosphere by a reaction between volatile organic compounds (VOCs), nitrogen oxides (NOx) and water in the presence of sunlight, is the main cause of smog. Problematic emissions come primarily from the excess byproduct of burning of a fuel, though there are other sources, including evaporation and leakage of feedstocks and finished energy resources, and venting, leaking, and flaring of gas mixtures.
- *Acidic deposition* (acid rain), most prevalent in eastern North America and Europe, is found in the troposphere. Acid rain is formed when sulfur dioxide (SO_2) and nitrogen dioxide (NO_2) react with H_2O to form sulfuric and nitric acid. The principal source of SO_2 is fixed-source burning of fuels, particularly coal, such as in electricity generation.
- *Stratospheric ozone depletion* – Ozone (O_3) is formed when oxygen molecules (O_2) are combined with oxygen atoms photodissociated from other oxygen molecules. The layer of ozone in the atmosphere reflects ultraviolet radiation. Due to man-made pollutants, particularly chloro-fluorocarbons (CFCs), the layer has become thinner over time. The

Montreal Protocol required the phasing out of damaging CFCs, such as those used as refrigerants in air conditioners.

- *Global warming* (the greenhouse effect) is a result of trace gases in the troposphere absorbing heat emitted by the earth and radiating some of it back, thus warming the global atmosphere. The Intergovernmental Panel on Climate Change concluded that man-made pollutants are increasing the amount of heat retained by the earth, with possible long-term consequences. These include a rise in the average planetary temperature, resulting in a slight melting of polar ice-caps and a consequent rise in the sea-level. The impacts on global weather patterns are not well understood; some areas may benefit, but others are sure to lose. There is considerable dispute in the scientific community about the magnitude of changes caused by man-made pollution. In particular, little is understood about feedbacks within the environmental system. For instance, a rise in temperature may increase cloud cover, which will cause more sunlight to be reflected rather than reaching the earth, thereby mitigating the temperature rise. Other feedbacks may make the problem worse. The economic and ecological effects of such changes are not knowable with certainty, although attempts have been made to estimate these costs (Nordhaus 1994).

Despite many simplifications, the science of emissions estimation remains an extremely complicated subject. Models such as the EMFAC series (California Air Resources Board 1991) and the MOBILE series (Environmental Protection Agency 1988) have been developed which characterize emissions generation by a number of factors including fleet mix (size and age of vehicles), fuel usage, the environment (temperature) and travel characteristics. For instance, light-duty trucks pollute about 20% more than autos, while medium-duty trucks (with catalytic converters) pollute about twice as much HC and NOx and the same amount of CO as autos. Heavy-duty trucks emit about two times as much HC and CO as autos, and five times as much NOx. Furthermore, older cars pollute more than newer, a 1972 model is about ten times as noxious as a 1992 car, though most improvements came from standards implemented between 1972 and 1982. It has been noted from studies of pollution in more realistic situations that the rates proposed above may err on the low side.

The EMFAC and MOBILE models provide data only on criteria pollutants, that is, pollutants for which standards have been set for health reasons. Greenhouse gases (principally carbon dioxide and methane) do not have such standards. Carbon estimates are extracted from emission factors developed by the Energy Information Agency (EIA 1994). The use of a macroeconomic/global climate model to estimate a 'carbon tax' which would be the price of damages from pollution has been attempted by

Nordhaus (1994). He used a model to estimate the appropriate tax at a given point of time that would optimize the amount of pollution, trading off economic costs of damages due to greenhouse gases against the damages due to imposing the tax. He estimates the appropriate tax at $5.29 in tons of carbon equivalent for the 1990s. However, environmentalists have proposed significantly higher carbon taxes, ranging from $52.80/tonne to $179.40/tonne (IBI Group 1995). Nordhaus's results already factor in the optimization required to compare the cost of damages with that of prevention, developing an equilibrium solution, while the other estimates consider only the cost of damage (and a high estimate at that), disregarding the economic burden imposed by the new tax or the changes in behavior required to obtain equilibrium. Clearly, this value is subject to a significant amount of controversy, and the consensus of estimated damage, if one is arrived at, is likely to change over time.

     Recent work on the costs of air pollution from cars comes from Small and Kazimi (1995), who analysed the Los Angeles region. They update air pollution emission factors from the EMFAC model to correct for reported underestimation of pollution. They then review evidence on mortality and morbidity and its association with pollutants (VOC, particulate matter 10 microns in size (PM10), SOx, NOx). They combine various exposure models for the Los Angeles region with health costs. Their findings suggest that particulate matter is a primary cause of mortality and morbidity costs, followed by morbidity due to ozone. Of course, costs in densely populated areas, such as the Los Angeles basin, should be higher than in rural areas as the exposure rate is far higher. Whereas Small and Kazimi assume a value of life of $4.87 million in their baseline assumptions, this analysis uses a $2.7 million value of life (V_L) for consistent comparison with accident costs.

Table 3.10: Air pollution and global change costs of highway travel

Pollutant	Health Damage ($/kg)	Auto emissions (gm/vkt)	Cost (cents/vkt)
PM10	12.85	0.0066	0.0085
SOx	13.82	0.0228	0.0315
HC	1.71	2.254	0.3850
CO	0.0063	7.8	0.0049
NOx	1.33	0.756	0.1000
Carbon	$0.0058	46	0.0260
Total			0.56

Source: Emissions: Small and Kazimi (1995), EIA (1994); Damage costs: Small and Kazimi (1995), Nordhaus (1994).
Note: Value of life = $2.7 million.

A review of the literature on material and vegetation damages suggests that those cost components are small compared with the costs of health damages.

Combining emission rates and damages per unit of emission with the data reported in Table 3.10, the cost estimate for local air pollution cost is $0.0053/vkt, while the global environmental impact cost is $0.0003/vkt.

CONCLUSION

Finally, the cost in each category is assembled, being careful not to double count, to produce the estimates of the costs of intercity auto travel shown in Figure 3.8. The total long-run average cost is $0.34 per vehicle kilometer traveled, including user fixed and variable costs, the cost of time to both the driver and passenger in traveling and in congestion, the cost of accidents, the cost of pollution, and the cost of noise. The importance of this chapter is not simply in having a base of solid cost estimates, but to provide a framework for deciding which cost components to isolate – which are more important and which have the greatest uncertainties.

While the marginal cost of infrastructure is higher than the average cost, indicating that new construction is becoming increasingly expensive, the marginal cost of driving (user fixed and variable costs) is less than the average cost, indicating that by increasing travel the user can spread the fixed cost of a vehicle over more trips without penalty while paying a fairly low marginal cost of $0.049/vkt. The conclusion that one can draw is that when infrastructure is priced at its average cost (as it is), users drive more than if infrastructure utilization were priced at marginal costs; when vehicle use is priced at the marginal cost (as it is), users drive more than if it were priced at its average cost. Efforts to change travel behavior through more efficient price signals should consider these facts.

The single largest cost category is free-flow travel time, and as the economy grows (and the value of time becomes higher), time can be expected to remain the most costly input to highway travel barring major increases in travel speed. Congestion is not as important in intercity travel, though for urban travel it may very well be. Accidents are the largest external cost on an average cost basis, though to what extent they are external is the subject of debate.

The uncertainties surrounding the cost of air pollution and global warming are clearly large, but even a ten-fold increase in estimate of these costs would lead to only a 13% increase in the total cost of auto travel (and a somewhat higher percentage of the internal costs of auto travel). Internalizing pollution costs should not be expected to have a great effect on auto demand given the low price elasticity that has been found historically.

Use of the point estimates of marginal or average cost should be treated cautiously. The more important contribution is the development of cost functions which can be applied to specific circumstances and provide information about the economic structure of specific cost items of highway transportation. The value of an externality varies with use, and despite all of the research, the true economic costs of externalities are still unknown. The challenge is not simply to measure the externality but also to value it; requiring a bridging of the fields of engineering and economics.

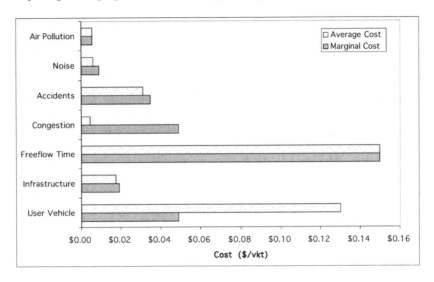

Figure 3.8 Average and marginal costs by category for an intercity trip

NOTES

1. See, for instance: Keeler et al. 1975; Fuller et al. 1983; Quinet 1990; Mackenzie et al. 1992; INRETS 1993, Miller and Moffet 1993; Works Consultancy Services 1993; INFRAS/IWW 1995; IBI Groups 1995; Levinson et al. 1996; Delucchi 1996.
2. Formally, 'an externality refers to a commodity bundle that is supplied by an economic agent to another economic agent in the absence of any related economic transaction between the agents' (Spulber, 1989). An action by which one consumer's purchase changes the prices paid by another is dubbed a 'pecuniary externality' and is not analysed here further. There are many alternative classification schemes for external costs, see: Verhoef 1994, Button 1994, Rothengatter 1994, Rietveld 1994, and Maggi 1994.

Coase (1992) argues that the problem is that of actions of economic agents have harmful effects on others. His theorem is restated from Stigler (1966) as 'under perfect competition, private and social costs will be equal.' This analysis extends and controverts the argument of Pigou (1920), who argued that the creator of the externality should pay a tax or be liable. Coase suggests the problem is lack of property rights, and notes that the externality is caused by both parties, the polluter and the receiver of pollution. In this reciprocal relationship, there would be no noise pollution externality if no-one was around to hear. This theory echoes the Zen question: 'If a tree falls in the woods and no-one is around to hear, does it make a sound?' Moreover, the allocation of property rights to either the polluter or pollutee results in a socially optimal level of production, because in theory the individuals or firms could merge and the external cost would become internal. However, this analysis assumes zero transaction costs. If the transaction costs exceed the gains from a rearrangement of activities to maximize production value, then the switch in behavior won't be made.

There are several means for internalizing these external costs. Pigou identifies the imposition of taxes and transfers, Coase calls for assigning property rights, while government most frequently uses regulation. To some extent all have been tried in various places and times. In dealing with air pollution, transferable pollution rights have been created for some pollutants. Fuel taxes are used in some countries to deter the amount of travel, with an added rationale being compensation for the air pollution created by cars. The US government establishes pollution and noise standards for vehicles, and requires noise walls be installed along highways in some areas.

3. Feasible generalized least square regression is related to the more widely used ordinary least squares regression. However, the reciprocal of variance is used as a weight to correct for the heteroscedasticity in the data, wherein the size of the residual is correlated with the size of the dependent variables

4. This chapter compares marginal and average costs. Simply put, marginal cost is the derivative of total costs T with respect to output Y, while average costs is total costs divided by total output.

$$M = dT(Y)/dY$$
$$A = T/Y$$

The average cost function is well defined for the single output cost function, but with multiple outputs the measure of average costs does not uniquely exist, unless the outputs in the vector Y are assumed to be equivalent or systematically related. Some type of index must be used in place of the vector Y in the calculation of an 'average' cost. In this way, the calculation of average cost requires a weighting of the outputs. The incremental cost of introducing the additional output (vector of flows) Y_n is equal to :

$$A_n = T(Y) - T(Y_{m-n})$$

where:
$Y = \{Y_1,....,Y_m\}$
$Y_n = \{Y_1,...,Y_n\}$
$Y_{m-n} = \{Y_{n+1}, ... , Y_m\}$

The total expenditure function is evaluated at two values to estimate the average cost. For example, to estimate the long-run average incremental cost per unit of automobile travel, the model is solved at the means for all parameters except Y_a, which is evaluated both at the mean and at 1.

5. AVI works by using wireless communications between a tag (or transponder) mounted on a vehicle and a sensor located at the roadside. The vehicle can be a car, truck, or rail car. Sensors can read the information while the vehicle is stopped or while it is moving at high speeds. The communication between the tag and sensor can be one-way (read-only) or two-way (read/write). Most areas use a distributed overhead antenna with tag-based in-vehicle equipment. It provides automatic vehicle identification that allows for toll collection.

6. These results are from a test operation of ETC at the Odawara Tollgate on March 31, 1997 in Japan.

7. The table below represents the computer hardware and software costs for host computer equipment. The unit price of a one-way, read-only radio frequency transponder ranges from $5 to $50 depending on the technology, the vendor, and the quantity of transponders purchased. (So-called 'smart cards' and transponders with read/write capability will cost from $35 to $65.) Alternatively, the unit price for a bar code decal ranges from $1.00 each for large quantities (100,000) to $2.00 each for smaller quantities (2,000 to 3,000).

Table: AVI host and plaza computer equipment cost

Quantity	Equipment	Average cost
2	Host computer	127,200
6	Disk drives	63,100
2	4mm DAT tape drives	7,000
2	Network interfaces	6,600
2	Network routers	10,200
2	Terminal server	7,000
2	Network workstation	7,300
8	Terminals (14 inch monitors)	19,000
4	High speed printers	27,800
12	Modems	10,400
2	Communication cabinet	2,700
1	Power supply system	8,500
1	Host software	10,600
	Host total	307,400
2	Plaza computers	38,500
4	Disk drives	33,400
2	4mm DAT tape drives	8,000
1	Network interfaces	3,800
1	Network routers	4,500
1	Terminal server	4,000
1	Supervisor workstation	4,200
3	Terminals (14 inch monitors)	8,100
3	Printers	3,000
2	Modems	2,000
	Communication cabinet	1,600
1	Power supply system	13,300
1	Plaza software	3,900
	Plaza total	128,300

Source: Dallas North Tollway, Oklahoma Pikepass, and industry cost proposals.

8. For instance, in Florida, the cost data given by *Highway Statistics 1998* are only give by authorities, not facility. For example, the Miami-Dade Expressway Authority comprises four tollways: Dolphin East/West Tollway (SR836), Gratigny Parkway (SR924), Miami Airport Expressway (SR112) and Don Shula Expressway (SR874), but it is unclear how those tollways were accounted for in the *Highway Statistics 1998*. The same thing happened to the Orlando/Orange County Expressway Authority.

9. Application of the Sullivan and Hsu model (reproduced below) gives an average annual total accident rate per hour of 2.214 using the assumptions in the rightmost columns, giving the probability of an accident per hour per vehicle is 0.00000034. Multiply this by the cost of an accident ($120,000 for an rural crash and $70,000 as the cost of an urban crash).

Table: Square root of total annual accidents during peak periods

Variable Description	Coefficient	*T*-Statistic	Assumed Value
L*N The section length (L) in miles times the number of travel lanes (N) (excluding auxiliary lanes)	0.19	3.90	4
IRAMP The average number on-ramps per mile	1.92	6.63	.12
ARAMP = IRAMP if there are auxiliary lanes = 0 if there are no auxiliary lanes in the section,	-0.098	-4.10	1
Qh The average hourly traffic volume in all lanes during the peak period	0.000143	3.90	6000
NONE The average%age of time during the peak period when no queue exists in the freeway section.	-0.017	-3.38	100

Source: Sullivan and Hsu 1988

Note: $R^2=0.95$, N=62.

11. Some of the variables can be re-incorporated into the Noise model through the use of adjustment factors for density (default=1 for all three factors) (f_D = density/360), House value (f_H = house value/$250,000), and the cost per decibel deflator (f_C = Cost per dB(A)/0.0062).

$$T_N = f_D f_H f_C \, Q\big(-0.018 + 0.0028\ln(Q)\big)$$

4. Revenues

INTRODUCTION

States have the opportunity to impose toll financing on many of their bridges and highways and to determine the rate of toll, recognizing the legal and fiscal constraints imposed by accepting federal transportation funds. Yet not all states levy tolls, and those that do vary in their rate of toll. This chapter examines empirical evidence to explain the dependence of state highway finance on tolls.

The term 'beggar thy neighbor' describes strategic trade behavior, essentially mercantilist in nature, designed to give one country a foreign trade advantage at the expense of others.[1] Inevitably, such behavior leads to retaliation and only makes everyone worse off. Countries perceive what game theorists term a 'prisoners' dilemma,' whereby 'cooperating' to reduce barriers only pays off in the long term and only if others do so as well. Highway tolls are in some ways analogous to tariffs. States (or the turnpike authorities they establish) can charge travelers for crossing a boundary. Often, no similar charge is levied on traffic remaining within the boundary. In this way, a toll may be viewed as a tariff on the transportation portion of a good or on labor. Overall, states and users may be better off if other financing mechanisms, with significantly lower transaction costs such as gas taxes, are chosen. However, the inability of states to cooperate and compensate each other for their residents' travel on other states' roads leads to a more direct and costly toll system. When most users are in-state residents, a legislature can develop a reasonably practical cost-sharing solution for highway finance. That is not nearly so simple when states need to cooperate. While the extent to which the behavior of tolling roads is to achieve efficiencies and the extent to which it is price discrimination cannot be established a priori, it can be surmised that one state's perception of efficient financing may be perceived by another as discriminatory exploitation.

Tariffs and tolls do differ in several important respects. First, tolls may be seen as efficient user charges, as states provide a service in exchange for payment of a toll. Second, because of the nature of surface transportation, the toll may affect 'through trips', travel conducted between two other states. Third, the presence of externalities, particularly congestion, may make it socially beneficial to use tolls rather than other sources of revenue (Walters 1961; Vickery 1963). To date this use of tolls has been much more promise than practice.

While road tolls differ from tariffs, this chapter argues that beggar thy neighbor policies help explain their extent. For states that import a significant number of workers during the workday, tolls may seem an ideal way to raise revenue with few political implications. Because out-of-state residents can't vote in the state's elections, toll policies will be more prevalent in states that import labor, as it enables them to raise revenue from non-voters. While complicated, the economics suggest that there will be some effects (both positive and negative) on local residents of tolls assessed against non-residents, principally through the mechanism of real estate. Furthermore, a toll policy may provoke a retaliatory response from the labor exporting states, but the response will be less than full force. In labor exporting states, the burden of tolls (collection costs and all) falls disproportionately on residents. States with large shares of resident workers (and thus fewer imported or exported laborers) are most likely to rely on taxes.

This chapter begins with an examination of the data used in the statistical analyses. Then the specific hypotheses for the essential variables are presented, accompanied by the results of a regression analysis. A sensitivity analysis is conducted using Californian data to examine the possible effect on share of toll revenue when states devolve the power to toll and responsibility for roads to counties and to metropolitan areas. The main difference is that the number of interstate trips is much smaller than the number of inter-county trips, so the incentive structure shifts. Finally, the research is summarized and some policy conclusions are drawn.

DATA

Several sources of data are used in this analysis. Highway finance data comes from the Federal Highway Administration's *Highway Statistics* tables, which provide information on total revenue by state (FHWA 1995, tables SF-1 and HM-20), and revenue by source, including tolls and other sources. Alaska is excluded, because that state's data identify the 'Alaska Marine Highway' as a highway toll even though the service is a ferry. The District of Columbia does not have independent authority over its own roads, but faces a veto from Congress, and so it too is excluded. The remaining 49 states are included in the analysis.

The journey-to-work survey (United States Census Bureau 1998) is used to develop state-to-state traffic flows. The author developed a state-level trip table from the journey-to-work data. This table provides the number of work trips from each state-by-state of destination (in-state or out-of-state). It also provides the number of work trips to each state by state of origin, not available from published data. The trip table can be used to determine the level of interaction between states, so that the effects of neighboring states' policies can be estimated.

To apply the model to geographic units smaller than states, and thus test the implications of a policy for decentralizing highway finance, Census Public Use Microdata Areas (PUMAs) were used. PUMAs are the smallest geographic unit of analysis in the Public Use Microdata Sample (PUMS) data set. The Census constructs PUMAs such that they contain approximately 100,000 people within them. They can be as small as a few city blocks or as large as several counties. An exact description of PUMAs is available from the University of Virginia Library Geospatial and Statistical Data Center (1998).

In preliminary analysis, the American Travel Survey (1995) was also used to construct a trip table of long trips (those greater than 100 miles). While the journey-to-work survey focuses on short trips (though not the very short non-work trips), it does not consider long trips, which may have some effect on policy. State-level summaries from this trip table were also tested in the regression models, but turned up insignificant upon the inclusion of the journey-to-work data and so were excluded from the final analysis. Several special cases are thus missed, such as that of Florida, a major tourist destination that may have a special incentive to export road costs to visitors.

Data on land area and population by state (and thus density) were also obtained from the Census Bureau. Historical data representing the miles of toll road in operation in 1963 by state were obtained from Rae (1971). A summary of state-level data is provided in the notes.[2]

HYPOTHESES

This research hypothesizes that states impose tolls to ensure a significant revenue flow from non-local travelers. Individuals pay income and property taxes to the state in which they live, not necessarily where they work or travel. Furthermore, because drivers can control where they purchase gasoline, particularly for shorter trips, the gas tax does not guarantee revenue from non-resident travelers. Unfortunately, there is no single systematic source of data on interstate trips. The American Travel Survey captures long trips and the Census journey-to-work survey captures work trips, but data on short trips for non-work activities are not collected in sufficient detail to measure interstate travel. Because most non-work trips are shorter than most work trips, it seems reasonable to suppose that interstate non-work trips are relatively small in number compared with work trips. It might also be supposed that the number of non-work trips between states is proportional to the number of work trips between those states, although this cannot be corroborated using the available data. A positive and significant relationship between the share of non-resident workers (*O*) and the share of toll revenue (*S*) is expected.

A state which exports labor may find some of its residents paying tolls to other states. It may respond by tolling in return to try to recapture some of that revenue. However, a situation where both states taxed instead of tolled could be better overall, especially for the labor-exporting state. Therefore, the labor exporter may be less likely to toll initially – where initial tolls will bring about retaliatory tolls. If its labor-importing neighbor taxes, the labor-exporting state may retain taxes as well. In game theory terms, it will cooperate initially, and only be non-cooperative if its neighbor is as well. The outcomes of alternatives are illustrated in Table 4.1.

Table 4.1   Outcomes from tax and toll policies

		Importing neighbor	
		Tax	Toll
Exporting state	Tax	Cooperative	Exploited
	Toll	Exploiter	Non-cooperative

It is unlikely that the effect of a neighbor's tolls will be as strong as the effect of non-local trips, because tolls in a labor-exporting state will disproportionately affect its own residents. (A labor-importing state is in a politically much better position to exploit its neighbors than a labor exporting state.) Furthermore, only a fraction of its own residents will travel out of state and pay tolls to their neighbors. So this can be thought of as a second-order effect. It is hypothesized that the toll share will be positively and significantly affected by the tolls of neighboring states. The neighbor tolls (*N*) are measured as the share of revenue from tolls in each neighboring state weighted by the share of that state's residents commuting to those neighbors.[3]

Before the interstate highway act, states were responsible for funding their own limited-access highways. As noted in Chapter 1, many of these highways were toll-financed. Tolls capture out of state traffic as well as securing a source of funds against which an independent public authority can borrow. Many of those roads are extant and still operated as toll roads. Because of historical inertia, the present share of toll revenue certainly depends on the presence of toll roads built 40 years ago. Since the dependent variable is a ratio, the independent variable is constructed similarly. The ratio of toll miles in 1963 to miles of limited-access highways in 1995 measures the effect of historical toll miles (*M*). Toll miles in 1963 reflect linear miles of toll roads built or under construction before the interstate program took full force. Limited-access highways in 1995 are measured as the linear miles of toll roads, interstate highways, and other freeways and expressways. Revenue and miles are not directly related; revenue depends also on the rate of toll and the usage of the facility, both of which are affected by the other variables described here. Certainly the theory applies before 1956 as well, but data on interstate trips from that era are unavailable for testing.

The size of a jurisdiction may affect the share of revenue from tolls. Jurisdictions that are more populous may have higher costs for building and maintaining highways and greater congestion. Furthermore, states that are home to large cities may be more likely to import workers than rural states. Finally, states in the Northeast and Midwest tend to be more populous than the national average (recognizing some obvious, very populous, exceptions in the south and west), and have a smaller land area than the average. They also have many more miles of toll roads, due to their early start building limited-access highways. The 1990 population (*P*) is expected to be positively and significantly associated with share of toll revenue, but this is tested in combination with population density and land area.

If states have higher costs, then they should have higher expenditures, and may require more revenue from tolls (to avoid the losses caused by gas-tax border effects). If population is important because of costs, then expenditures may also be a significant variable.

In the interstate act, interstate highways were financed with a 90% federal share and a 10% state share except in the 'public lands' states. In those states up to 95% federal financing was provided. Under the interstate act, federally funded roads had to be free of tolls. This additional incentive to use federal dollars may be apparent in today's tolls share. A variable indicating the percentage of land in a state that is federally owned was tested to capture this effect.

RESULTS

To test the hypotheses, a series of regressions were run, with the dependent variable being the share of state revenue from tolls.[4] The results are shown in Table 4.2. After preliminary analysis, several hypotheses were rejected. The variable for the percentage of federal lands variable turned out statistically insignificant, and so was dropped from the final analysis presented here. Similarly, variables for capital and non-capital expenditures were tested as possible explanatory variables and rejected as statistically insignificant. While land is an important variable if the share of workers residing out-of-state is excluded, it is clearly the number of workers, rather than the less direct estimate based on land area, which is significant. Population and density were tested, but density was dropped because population was a much more important and significant variable whereas density was statistically insignificant.

Table 4.2   Share of transportation revenue from tolls

	Model 1		Model 2	
	Coefficient	*T*-Statistic	Coefficient	*T*-Statistic
Intercept	-0.0343	-1.91[a]	-0.0362	-2.18[b]
Population (*P*) (x10^6)	0.00383	1.83[a]	0.00385	1.94[a]
Mile ratio (*M*)	0.300	2.34[b]	0.352	3.14[c]
Imported workers (*O*)	0.843	2.04[b]	0.839	2.14[b]
Neighbor effect (*N*)	89320	1.70[a]		
Adjusted R^2	0.62		0.60	
Observations	49		49	

Note: a, b, and c denote significance at 10%, 5%, and 1% on a two-tailed *T*-test respectively.

The regression corroborates the hypotheses concerning the effect of population (*P*), out-of-state workers (*O*), the neighbor effect (*N*), and the historical toll miles (*M*), which are all positive and significant. As expected the neighbor effect was less significant than the share of non-resident workers. Overall the model explains 62.4% (adjusted R^2) of the variance in states' share of highway revenue from tolls. In order of importance, the ratio of toll miles explains 49.4%, population explains 7.1%, out-of-state workers explains 6.7% and the neighbor effect explains 2.3% of that variance. All four variables are statistically significant at the 10% threshold (two-tailed *T* test).

Each 1% increase in the share of non-resident workers increases the share of toll revenue (*S*) by 0.85% on average. Each 1% increase in the toll mile ratio increases the *S* by 0.30%. Each additional million people increases *S* by 0.38%. The effect of a neighbor's tolling policy on a state's residents is more complicated because of the non-linearity involved. To illustrate, if *N* = 0.01 (for example, in Rhode Island *N* = 0.011), a 1% increase in neighbor's tolls causes S to increase by 0.0036%. If *N* = 0.02 (in New Hampshire *N* = 0.017), a 1% increase leads S to increase by 0.058%, while if *N* = 0.03 (in New Jersey *N* = 0.031), a 1% increase induces a 0.30% increase in *S*.

Table 4.3   Predicted share of toll revenue by geographical area (%)

CMSA	Share	APUMA (Counties)	Share
Bakersfield	0.027	Kern	0.027
Chico	0.014	Butte	0.014
Fresno	0.025	Fresno	0.025
Los Angeles	0.027	Orange	0.125
		Los Angeles	0.087
		Ventura	0.048
		Riverside	0.094
		San Bernardino	0.117
Merced	0.049	Merced	0.049
Modesto	0.057	Stanislaus	0.057
Redding	0.075	Shasta	0.075
Sacramento	0.010	Yolo	0.274
		Placer	0.272
		El Dorado	0.074
		Sacramento	0.094
Salinas	0.017	Monterey	0.017
San Diego	0	San Diego	0
San Francisco	0.011	Alameda	0.213
		Contra Costa	0.208
		Marin	0.222
		San Francisco (city)	0.345
		San Mateo	0.265
		Santa Clara	0.115
		Santa Cruz	0.076
		Sonoma	0.024
		Napa	0.115
		Solano	0.135
Santa Barbara	0.028	Santa Barbara	0.028
Stockton	0.141	San Joaquin	0.141
Visalia	0.012	Tulare	0.012
Yuba	0.057	Sutter, Yuba	0.057
Non-Metropolitan	0.069	Del Norte, Lassen, Modoc, Siskiyou	0.107
		Humboldt	0.061
		Lake, Mendocino	0.066
		Colusa, Glenn, Tehama, Trinity	0.198
		Nevada, Plumas, Sierra	0.074
		Alpine, Amador, Calaveras, Inyo, Mariposa, Mono, Tuolumne	0.035
		Madera, San Benito	0.134
		Kings	0.127
		Imperial	0.000
		San Luis Obispo	0.042

Model 2 in Table 4.2 shows the regression results when the effect of neighbors is dropped. The results are quite similar. However, the implications of the model differ significantly, as seen in the next section, which applies the model to metropolitan and county level data.

SENSITIVITY ANALYSIS

Our model, estimated at the state level, suggests that more localized control over highways will lead to a greater likelihood of toll financing, all else equal. The magnitude of this can be tested by applying the model of state behavior to smaller levels of government (for instance, metropolitan areas or counties). The analysis suggests what might happen if financing responsibility and control over streets and roads were devolved from states to counties or metropolitan areas. Counties that have a great deal of cross-jurisdictional flows are more likely to toll than metropolitan areas, or than the states which contain them. This section hopes to establish the magnitude.

Journey-to-work trip tables using the PUMA definition available from the PUMS database were constructed for the state of California. PUMAs, of about 100,000 residents apiece, either coincide with counties, or aggregations of counties, or can be aggregated to the level of a county. A new definition was created, aggregated PUMA, or APUMA, which was the larger of a PUMA or a county. The APUMA is at a minimum one county, but may be comprised of several small counties. The trip table, created under the PUMA definition, was further aggregated into the larger of the census metropolitan statistical areas (MSA) or consolidated metropolitan statistical areas (CMSA) for each place.

The previous section's model 2 was applied to each of the new geographical units (APUMA and MSA/CMSA). Bridges are not counted as part of the 1963 miles of toll road, so the effect of historical miles is zero for each county and the state of California as a whole.

Table 4.3 shows the resulting share by area. Compared with California's toll share of 2.1%, MSA/CMSAs had an average predicted share of 2.3% and APUMAs of 10%. However, metropolitan APUMAs, part of larger CMSAs, had much higher shares. By definition, very few work trips are between MSAs or CMSAs. However, many do travel between APUMAs within a larger metropolitan area. Consequently, the share of trips originating outside of an area increases as the area gets smaller.

For instance, the Los Angeles metropolitan area, if treated as a whole and given pricing authority over all its roads, was predicted to have a share of toll revenue of 2.7%. However, if the same analysis is done for counties having that authority, the results differ markedly. The shares ranged from 4.8% in Ventura County to 12.5% in Orange County. Interestingly, it is in Orange County that most of the new toll road construction in California is taking place, on SR91 and the Eastern Transportation Corridor.

Similarly in San Francisco, the metropolitan area as a whole would have a fairly low share of toll revenue (1.1%), as most work trips remain within the large area. But the toll share for individual counties would range from 2.4% in Santa Rosa to 34.5% in the City of San Francisco. The counties within the Bay Area have California's highest percentages of inter-county flows. It should be noted that with seven toll bridges and several bottleneck passes, the Bay Area is probably most easily adapted to increasing the share of toll revenue.[4]

SUMMARY AND CONCLUSIONS

This chapter has evaluated the empirical evidence surrounding the hypothesis that jurisdictions' highway finance behavior is determined in part by the share of non-local traffic and by the behavior of neighboring jurisdictions. It found that that the greater the burden of finance which could be placed on non-resident workers, the greater the burden which is placed on those individuals. Similarly, it found corroborating evidence for a weak second-order effect, when a jurisdiction responds to its neighbors' policies. The greater the toll share imposed by neighbors on a jurisdiction's residents, the greater the tolls that the jurisdiction will levy in response.

Whether this is a globally detrimental 'beggar thy neighbor' policy or simply a rational non-cooperative outcome from states behaving efficiently depends on your point of view. This outcome has the potential for internalizing the congestion externality that a more 'cooperative' outcome may lack. Only with the presence of tolls can marginal cost pricing (or its variants of time-of-day or value pricing) be implemented and a more efficient utilization of congested highways achieved. The smaller the jurisdiction, the greater the share of non-local traffic, and thus the higher incentive for tolls. This is especially true when looking at county-sized jurisdictions, such as those within California. Therefore, a way to increase the likelihood of tolling is to decentralize the financial responsibility and governance of highways to more local agencies (for instance, by eliminating federal funding and moving authority from states to sub-metropolitan areas and counties).

This potential could quickly turn sour in cases without congestion (for example, rural interstates), where the tolls may significantly exceed the marginal cost price. Decentralization may also lead to misinvestment, as jurisdictions have monopoly power and may set tolls and build infrastructure with local profits rather than global welfare in mind.

NOTES

1. Beggar-thy-neighbor Policy - 'A course of action through which a country tries to reduce unemployment and increase domestic output by raising tariffs and instituting non-tariff barriers that impede imports ... which, by reducing export markets, tended to worsen the economic difficulties that precipitated the initial protectionist action' (Smith and Blakeslee 1998).

2. Table *Summary data*

	Percentage				Miles	
State	Revenue from tolls (S)	Workers who live out of state (O)	Residents who work out of state	Fed.. land	Toll roads in 1963	Freewayse xpwy, 1995
Alabama	0.0	2.4	3.6	3.3	0	925
Arizona	0.0	1.1	1.6	41.5	0	1250
Arkansas	0.0	4.0	3.2	8.3	0	646
California	2.1	0.5	0.4	44.6	0	3750
Colorado	0.3	0.8	1.0	36.0	17	1170
Connecticut	0.0	4.6	4.7	0.2	194	542
Delaware	25.3	13.8	9.5	2.2	11	51
Florida	7.8	0.8	1.0	7.6	207	1861
Georgia	0.4	2.8	2.4	3.9	11	1413
Hawaii	0.0	1.0	0.5	8.5	0	77
Idaho	0.0	2.6	4.0	60.6	0	613
Illinois	9.3	2.8	2.9	1.3	185	2245
Indiana	4.3	3.3	4.8	1.7	157	1303
Iowa	0.1	3.7	4.3	0.2	0	781
Kansas	6.5	7.1	7.6	0.5	241	1008
Kentucky	0.8	6.3	6.7	4.2	205	855
Louisiana	2.9	2.1	1.9	2.8	0	929
Maine	10.5	2.1	3.1	0.9	112	383
Maryland	7.0	7.0	17.3	3.1	42	711
Massachusetts	10.4	5.0	3.1	1.2	124	762
Michigan	0.7	0.8	1.5	10.1	0	1458
Minnesota	0.0	2.3	1.8	3.1	0	1042
Mississippi	0.0	3.1	5.9	4.3	0	726
Missouri	0.1	7.2	4.8	3.8	0	1460
Montana	0.0	0.8	1.2	27.5	0	1190
Nebraska	0.2	4.3	2.3	1.2	0	497
Nevada	0.0	4.3	1.2	77.1	0	586
New Hampshire	11.8	8.5	16.8	12.8	77	266

New Jersey	27.3	7.0	11.7	3.3	309	728
New Mexico	0.0	1.9	2.5	33.9	0	1003
New York	33.2	5.1	2.4	0.7	629	2328
North Carolina	0.1	2.2	1.8	6.9	0	1237
North Dakota	0.0	5.9	3.7	4.0	0	570
Ohio	3.3	2.8	2.2	1.1	241	1937
Oklahoma	7.6	1.1	2.9	1.5	174	1064
Oregon	0.5	3.7	2.1	51.8	0	780
Pennsylvania	11.7	3.4	4.3	2.2	469	2087
Rhode Island	3.7	7.6	11.9	0.7	0	137
South Carolina	0.0	2.1	1.8	3.8	0	894
South Dakota	0.0	3.0	4.0	5.5	0	681
Tennessee	0.0	4.6	3.3	5.7	0	1176
Texas	2.5	0.9	0.8	1.4	30	4474
Utah	0.1	1.0	1.3	63.1	0	948
Vermont	0.0	4.9	5.8	6.4	0	1329
Virginia	4.7	6.5	9.3	9.4	35	339
Washington	4.1	1.5	2.7	24.1	0	1079
West Virginia	6.6	8.3	9.7	7.0	86	560
Wisconsin	0.0	1.4	3.2	5.3	0	830
Wyoming	0.0	2.6	2.0	48.5	0	916

Note: Toll miles = Toll miles in use in 1963, from Rae (1971) after Bureau of Public Road data.

3.

$$N_i = \left(\frac{\sum_j T_{ij} S_j}{W_i} \right)^{\beta} \quad \text{for } j \neq i$$

Where:
N_i = Neighbor state effect for state i
T_{ij} = Trips from state i to state j
$W_i = \Sigma_j T_{ij}$ for all j.
S_j = Share of revenue from tolls in state j
β = model coefficient.

Raising the term to a power greater than 1 magnifies larger, and reduces noise in the data. The value of β ($\beta = 4$) was arrived at after some statistical experimentation.
4. Other model structures, including binomial logit and probit models were tested (the choice of toll/not toll) as was an aggregate logistic form, where the dependent variable was $S/(1 - S)$. Subsamples of the tolling states were used in some estimates, excluding from the share estimates states that don't toll. Different functional forms (Cobb-Douglas) as well as non-linear transformations of the variables were tested. The linear specification was preferred because it was plausible and simple and the fit was good. The Cook-Weisberg test on an uncorrected ordinary least squares

regression reports heteroscedasticity, so corrected robust estimates using the Huber-White estimator of variance are presented in Table 4.2.

5. Application of Model 1 from the previous section, which included a neighbor effect (N), is somewhat more complicated, especially since a power term is used. The model would need to be applied iteratively or simultaneously, since it is solving for the toll share of each geographical unit (APUMA, MSA/CMSA) depending on the toll share of all other areas. If the estimated power term is used, the model 'blows up' at the APUMA level, most jurisdictions go to 100% toll share very quickly. Toll shares were constrained to fall between 0% and 100%.

5. Hierarchy

INTRODUCTION

Should the federal, state, or local government be accountable for infrastructure's financing, construction, and management? Both infrastructure networks and government are typically hierarchically organized. However, the slope of the hierarchy (the number of layers it possesses) varies. Management by a government layer that is geographically too small or too large brings about costs which can be avoided by associating the infrastructure with the most appropriate layer of government.

In North America, the hierarchy of roads emerged early in the eighteenth century with the division of roads into Great (or Kings) Highways and Common Highways. Great Highways were under the authority of a colony's Governor and Council, while Common Highways were managed more locally by appointed commissioners or the county court upon presentment of a grand jury or petition (Durrenberger 1931, p. 18). This corroborates the general observation of present conditions that roads serving longer-distance trips are generally controlled by a higher jurisdiction than those serving more local traffic.

Conventional traffic engineering suggests that streets and highways have two distinct functions: through movement and land access (McShane and Roess 1990, p. 37). Highway facilities are classified by the relative amount of movement and access they provide, though the share of each falls on a continuum. Figure 5.1 illustrates the issue. The shaded area reflects the share of the network devoted to land access functions as opposed to network movement. Engineers design roads to fall along the diagonal line of Figure 5.1, although not all do. Local streets are slow and low flow, serving primarily the access function. Collectors are medium speed and medium flow, serving both movement and land access. Arterials are often limited-access facilities that serve only movement.

The hierarchy of roads separates the function of access from that of through movement. The reasons for the hierarchy are several. First, it permits the aggregation of traffic to achieve economies of scale in construction and operation, a particular advantage for expensive, limited-access facilities. Aggregation makes the construction of grade separations feasible, for instance. Second, by separating the access and movement function, it reduces the number of conflicts. Third, it helps maintain the desired quiet character of residential neighborhoods by keeping through traffic away from homes. Fourth, a hierarchical network contains less redundancy, and so may be less costly to build. An additional facet of the hierarchy is that the excludability associated with higher levels and the separability associated with each layer create opportunities for efficient network financing. In economic terms, the top level is potentially a competitive market good, while the bottom level is a public or club good.

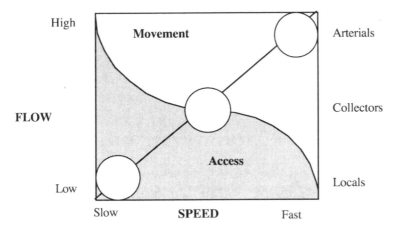

Figure 5.1 Functional highway classification and type of service provided

There are of course disadvantages associated with a hierarchy of roads. First, it trades a minimal trip distance for a minimal travel time. Therefore, a hierarchy may entail increased backtrack costs. Second, it makes a few points critical and thus the system is more vulnerable to catastrophe, that is, the network is less robust. Third, traveler navigation may be more difficult compared with a simple undifferentiated grid.

Just as the network is organized hierarchically, so are political jurisdictions. In the United States, it is typical to find homeowner associations at the lowest level, through towns and counties, to states and then the federal government at the highest level. Different layers of government typically have different functions. A homeowners' association may regulate the aesthetics of the neighborhood and manage common property and driveways; a local government may provide police, schools, and some roads; a state may provide another layer of law enforcement, universities, and larger roads. The federal government provides for the national defense and social insurance, and shares revenue among states – providing funding for major transportation projects.

Two questions arise from these observations, and must be addressed simultaneously. First, what mechanism is appropriate to finance each distinct layer of the hierarchy? Second, which level of government should manage or regulate which level of the network?

This chapter considers the issues around hierarchy in transport and governance to develop the trade-offs inherent in a decision about which layer of government might best regulate or manage a particular layer of the hierarchy using a particular financing mechanism. First examined are the existing network topologies reflected in the hierarchy. Second, the economic properties links possess further help explain hierarchy. The issue of logrolling is then tackled. The definition of link service areas is introduced, and applied to suggest appropriate governmental levels for management of parts of the transportation network. Conclusions from this analysis are drawn in the final section.

TRANSPORTATION HIERARCHY AND NETWORK TOPOLOGY

Two types of transportation hierarchy can be defined: (1) hierarchy between elements, and (2) hierarchy within elements. The first type, hierarchy between elements, manifests itself in both transportation networks and travel decision processes. For instance, the network is comprised of numerous elements, and modelers often speak of nodes (intersections), links,[1] turns (attached segments), and paths (routes composed of multiple segments). Similarly, the travel behavior decision elements – the purpose, frequency, sequence, destination, mode, route, and time of day of trips – may be hierarchically organized. The decision as to whether to make a trip may precede that on what route to take, although feedback loops between decisions exist. However, it is the second type, hierarchy within elements, in particular the link (road segment) layer, which is of concern here. Government hierarchies are inclusive – one tract can fall under many different government jurisdictions. Yet, engineers design road hierarchies to be exclusive; the assignment of a link to a layer of the hierarchy should prevent it from being assigned to a different layer.

There are two basic physical, topological classifications for networks: trees and webs, as illustrated in Figure 5.2. In a tree, some link is common to all paths to a non-tree location; that link is the trunk. A web is a network with multiple paths between all origins and destinations, at least two of which share no links.[2] If classification is based on use patterns as opposed to simple connectedness, a distinction between access and movement functions is useful. The topologies will be discussed in turn.[3] The network topologies and economic properties are necessary to posit the appropriate financing mechanisms for each.

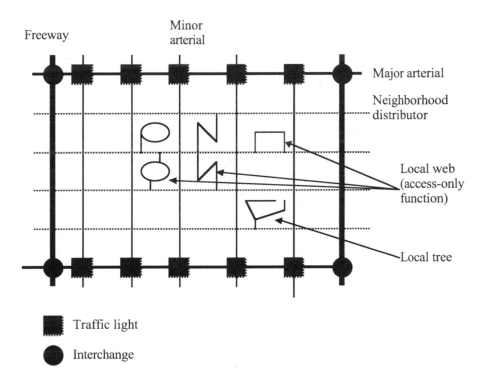

Figure 5.2   Network with topological classifications

The topology has direct implications for the competitiveness of the road. The competitive status of the road can be measured by how easy it is to use alternatives. On a tree link, there are no alternatives; on a web link there are always at least two unique paths. For a tree, each link has a path monopoly for specific origins and destinations. For an origin (destination) on a web link, each traveler has two choices on how to exit (enter), but any division of that link creates a path monopoly. However, for web links that are not serving as origin or destination, that link is competitive (at least nominally) with alternatives.

Link competitiveness neither requires nor prohibits any type of excludability. If private sector management is to be used, some form of excludability is probably necessary.

A property related to competitiveness is contestability – how easy it is to enter a market. In the case of physical networks, it is not very easy to build a new link. High immediate fixed costs of entry, even with eminent domain, are the cause of this lack of contestability. If links are owned by the government and managed by the private sector, the management contract may be auctioned off in some fashion. The market for the right to manage the road may be contestable.

A tree link is a monopoly. The property abutting the pure tree must use the links that form the tree between the property and the tree's roots in order to access the rest of the network, as shown on Figure 5.3.

The link, if it serves an access function, has two excludability properties. First, it potentially has a 'physical-excludability' property, wherein the tree can readily be made excludable at any of its branches or the root; the classic example is the gated community. Second, it has a 'functional excludability' property, that is, it won't be used by anyone except those with an origin and/or destination on the tree. Tree links do not serve through trips, trips with neither an origin nor a destination on the tree.

Links close to the root are complementary to those in the branches, while those in the branches may be competitive with each other if activities can relocate.

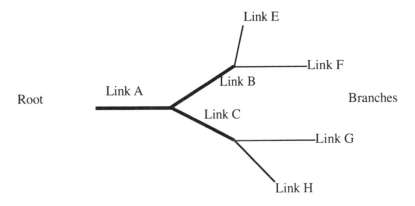

Figure 5.3   Tree topology

All trips using link H that need to exit the tree will use link C and link A. Only a fraction of trips (although the same absolute number) using link C also use link H. Moreover, only a small fraction of trips using link A also use link H. Therefore, the complementarities are asymmetric.

Tree links, particularly those at the lower levels of the hierarchy, are often non-congesting and non-rivalrous. Whether they should be classified as a local public good or a club good is an interesting question. The Tiebout (1956) position that individuals select a bundle of goods and services when they move to a particular jurisdiction, suggests they are essentially joining a club.

Whether tree links belong in the public or the private sector depends on how each is defined. Trees owned by abutting property owners such as a condominium or a 'private' street are little different from those property owners forming a local layer of government that owns the links. The property owners/government may franchise the road to be privately managed (or even owned) subject to a specific contract or under regulation by a firm separate from the property owners. Unregulated private ownership allows the monopoly tree links to exploit their customers. This would result in lowered property values.

A web link is competitive; the degree of its competitiveness is a function of the density of the network. Upon accessing a web, travelers have multiple (at a minimum, two) non-redundant paths between an origin and a destination. However, for individuals accessing a particular web link, that link holds monopoly powers in the absence of residents relocating. While two physical paths may exist, one may be shorter (in terms of time or distance) than another.

At the highest level(s) of the road hierarchy, web links may be excludable, with limited and controlled access. Access may not be given by default to abutting properties or intersecting links.

Web links are always competitive when strictly in parallel. Web links may be complementary or competitive when in series. Routes (serial bundles of links between an origin and destination) may be formed where one route uses a link in competition with another route which uses a second link, while a third route bundles the two links.

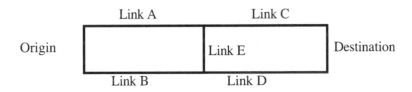

Figure 5.4   Web topology

In Figure 5.4 there are multiple route pairs between origin and destination (AC, AED, BEC, BD). Links A and B are strictly in parallel, as are C and D. In routes AC and BD, links A and D are competitors, as are links B and C. However, links A and D are complements in route AED, as are B and C in route BEC.

Web links are often congesting, but whether they are rivalrous depends on the definition adopted for the term.

Web links may fall in the public or the private sector, but are clearly more ready for market competition than are tree links. The highest-level roads, which are excludable and congesting, and may also have competitors, could easily be considered private goods. How the economic structure of web links is dealt with, such as the size and scope of individual firms managing those links, is a secondary question. Web links which have access functions (and thus are not excludable to abutters), such as non-limited access arterials, are less easily considered for unfettered private management. Private sector management when there are multiple providers allows us to entertain the idea of product differentiation – different links operating with different levels of service.

ECONOMIC PROPERTIES

Economic properties associated with links are important for the classification of roads and the selection of both the appropriate financing mechanism and the appropriate level of governance.

Conventional economics often uses the term *'public good'* to identify products that are logically provided by the public sector, as opposed to *'private goods'*. Two criteria help classify a good as public or private: excludability and rivalry. Excludability implies that the good's provider can prevent a user from obtaining it without charge. Rivalry implies that one person's consumption of a particular good prevents another individual from consuming it. Table 5.1 summarizes the goods by type.

Table 5.1   Public, private, club, and 'congesting' goods

		Excludability Yes	No
Rivalry	Yes	Private	'Congesting'
	No	Club	Public

The classic example of a pure public good is national defense, although many goods exhibit these properties to a greater or lesser degree. The extent to which roads are public goods depends on what degree of the excludability and rivalry that they contain.

Rivalry implies that the consumption of a good by person A prevents its consumption by person B. If transportation is defined as a time-dependent good, in terms either of the time it takes to make a trip, or at what time the trip is made, then user A's consumption may prevent user B from consuming it. However, if travel occurs on uncongested links, with no interference between vehicles, then roads are non-rivalrous.

Properties related to congestion include capacity, free-flow time, and demand. Link capacity is defined as the maximum throughput in a given amount of time. A link's free-flow travel time is the time it takes a single vehicle to traverse the link safely if there is no vehicle-to-vehicle interference. Demand is defined as approach flow (rather than throughput), the number of vehicles that are attempting to use the link during a window of time, given a link travel time. Typically, the hierarchy of roads is constructed such that links with high free-flow speeds and high flows are at the top of the hierarchy, while slow and low-flow links are at the bottom. Roads that experience congestion are inherently rivalrous in the economic sense.

Various scale economies may exist. These properties bear directly on the appropriate jurisdiction to manage the road. The economies may be located at various stages in the lifecycle of the road (construction, operation); they may be advantageous to the producer or the consumer; they may relate to the length, width, or thickness of the road; and they may be confined to a single link or emerge when multiple links are connected.

Economies of scale are present when the cost of constructing, operating, managing, or regulating two things (say A and B) independently is greater than the cost of treating them jointly. In transportation, *length economies* exist when it is cheaper to build two segments together rather than separately. *Width economies* exist when it is cheaper to construct two adjacent lanes than two separated lanes. *Thickness economies* can be found where each inch of the roadbed costs more constructed separately than together. *Scope economies* inhere if it is cheaper to serve multiple classes of users (cars and trucks or peak and off-peak users) with the same facility than with different ones.

Economies of scale in roads can emerge from multiple sources and may result from a joint fixed cost that is spread over these things, or joint variable costs. For instance, in terms of the construction, repair, and maintenance of roads, it may be more efficient to perform such tasks on multiple roads at once when equipment and crews are present. Similarly, snow clearance is more efficient when done on multiple roads with one plow compared with the absurd notion of sending a plow out for a single road segment, and then having it return to base. In terms of traffic regulation, there may be advantages to having a larger system under the control of a single agent. Information and knowledge express increasing returns to scale and carry-over, including confidence in police enforcement, knowledge of traffic laws, and familiarity with the political process.

Network economies involve the use of multiple links. The denser the network (over space or time), the more valuable the average link on the network is, and the higher the demand for that link.

Excludability is the capability to prevent some class of users from using a facility in a certain way. There are three relevant classes of excludability:

- immediate excludability to abutters (for example, a limited-access facility),
- excludability to non-local traffic (for example, a tree network, gated community, or cul-de-sac), and
- perfectly non-excludable – so that anyone can use it, (for example, a collector street with abutting access).

The top level of the road hierarchy is excludable -- all traffic using that level can be metered and restricted, and other alternatives paths exist. But, the bottom level(s) must allow all abutters access, and is often the only access to the network for a land parcel.

LOGROLLING AND DECENTRALIZATION ECONOMIES

Buchanan and Tullock (1962) provide an argument in favor of local and decentralized decision-making. They suggest that larger governments are more subject to logrolling. Logrolling is the situation where, in order to achieve a majority in a parliamentary body, votes must be traded. However, the traded votes are for projects of purely local interest, that is, 'pork barrel' projects. Overspending results from allowing these local projects to be funded more globally. The costs are diffuse over the entire population, while the benefits are concentrated. So the incentive for getting the larger community to pay for a local project is high, particularly so when other local areas are playing the same game. Interestingly, the Buchanan and Tullock example uses a local road and the question of maintenance. The local road can be thought of as a cul-de-sac serving only a few adjacent residents (farmers in the example), but the road is required to access the major highway serving the entire community. The entire community consists of many local roads. Several voting systems are given to compare.

In the first, each road improvement is voted up or down by a referendum of the entire community, and because each improvement benefits only a small percentage of the entire community (and would cost all members), self-interested voters reject it.   This results in an underinvestment of resources in roads.

In the second, logrolling is permitted, so instead of each road being voted on separately, they are voted on as a package (in fact or through an agreement on votes). In order to secure a stable majority in favor of the package, some overinvestment is required. Buchanan and Tullock (1962) write: 'This apparent paradox may be explained as follows: Each voter pays enough in support for the repair of other roads to attain a position of equivalence between estimated individual marginal costs and individual marginal benefits, but the payments included in his private calculus make up only a part of the costs of total road repair that he must, as a taxpayer in the community, support. There are other roads which will be repaired because of successful bargains to which he is not a party.' So individual rational behavior leads to overinvestment because of overlapping coalitions, and because the entire population pays for projects that benefit the few.

This problem is common in a democracy, and it can be reduced by making government more local so that for instance, only the beneficiaries of a project pay for it. This can be achieved through private sector control or very decentralized (localized) public sector control. There are costs to decentralized decision-making as well. If there are economies of scale, then 20 governments performing a single task (road maintenance for a single road) will cost more per road than one government maintaining 20 roads. If there are economies of information, individuals assigned to a proliferation of single-issue government agencies serving different areas may be unable effectively to undertake their oversight function. The extent of logrolling externality depends on specific circumstances, but clearly it needs to be accounted for in any analysis of the appropriate level of government for a particular project, as does any potential diseconomy associated with local control.

SERVICE AREAS

A useful spatial attribute to apply on top of network properties is that of 'service area'. A service area can be defined as the area from which all trips on a link either originate or for which they are destined, whichever trip end is closer. The service area concept is illustrated Figure 5.5, in which the darkly shaded area (denoted 'L') is the service area for the small tree it surrounds. The lightly shaded area (denoted 'H') is the service area for the larger web (circular road with the thicker line) it contains, including the service areas for the trees. The service area for the local streets might be associated with a lower-level or more local jurisdiction, hence the 'L', while the service area for more regional roads might be associated with a higher level jurisdiction, hence the 'H'.

While all traffic originating in or destined for its service area is local, that area may be large for facilities at the top of the hierarchy, links that serve long-distance trips. The proportion of traffic originating in or destined for the service area is an increasing function of jurisdiction size and depends on trip length. The share of local (nearby originating/destined) traffic is highest on streets lower in the hierarchy. The share of traffic originating in a jurisdiction is greatest for the highest (or largest) jurisdiction level and smallest for the lowest (most local) jurisdiction level on otherwise identical web links.

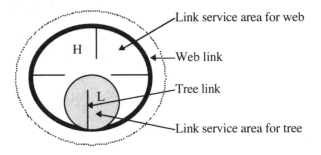

Figure 5.5   Service areas

The reason for defining a service area is to determine the appropriate geography for transportation management (and consequently financing) for a given facility. This is especially important when users cannot be charged directly. It seems clear that if there is a geography to which a link should be assigned, it should be based on the origin and destination of trips using that link. Further, it seems clear that a 'host pays' rule, where the nearest trip-end plays 'the host', is practical compared with its alternatives, 'guest pays' or 'split the bill'. 'Guest pays' involves billing the individual (or, more specifically, the jurisdiction in which he lives) from the farther zone, which would mean collecting revenue and involving decision-makers from many zones rather than a few. A 'split the bill' rule involves more calculations still, as the management must be divided among all zones that use the link, regardless of how small. While the nearest zone is spatially concentrated with many users, the farther zones each have only a few users, but there are many such zones. Because there is a general symmetry in trip-making (each trip has two ends, most trips are round trips, and both parties at a trip-end receive benefits (employer/employee, vendor/customer), adopting a 'host pays' rules should work out to be approximately fair. One can think of problems (unwanted traveling salesmen, for example), but this is seemingly a small issue.

Consider the concept somewhat more formally. An origin zone i is in the service area for link k if

$$\sum_j S_{ik} Z_{ikj} > 0$$

and a destination zone (j) is in the service area for link k if

$$\sum_j S_{kj} \left(1 - Z_{ikj}\right) > 0$$

Note that:

$$\sum_i S_{ik} = 1, \sum_j S_{kj} = 1$$

where:
  S_{ik} = share of users on link k from zone i;
  S_{kj} = share of users on link k going to zone j;
  Z_{ikj} = 1 if $D_{ik} < D_{kj}$, and 0 otherwise;
  D_{ik} = distance from origin i to link k; and
  D_{kj} = distance from link k to destination j.

CONCLUSIONS

As noted in the introduction, roads are often classified according to function, the degree to which they serve the functions of traffic movement and land access. Broadly, three classifications emerge: local roads, which serve neighborhood collection and distribution of traffic; collector roads, which connect neighborhood roads with other collectors; and arterials. There are a number of criteria for dividing the network hierarchically, relating to network function, flow, speed, excludability, competitiveness and alternatives, and locality of traffic. These criteria influence the decision to associate network layers with government layers. These economic properties are summarized in Table 5.2 for each class of road.

There are both advantages and disadvantages to managing roads under a higher jurisdiction. Beginning with the benefits, first, there is no interjurisdictional welfare loss in decision-making, and gouging of neighbors with excessive tolls is eliminated. Second, a larger jurisdiction is more able to achieve the various kinds of scale economies. Finally, the chain of governance is clearer the fewer governmental layers there are. However, there are also costs associated with managing roads under a higher jurisdiction. Higher jurisdictions are more likely to use tax financing rather than tolls, which makes congestion pricing more difficult to implement. Second, larger jurisdictions have a larger span of control, which implies increased management costs and slower decision times. Third, decisions are made remotely with less information about site-specific circumstances, the principal–agent problem is worsened in this circumstance as government is farther from the people. Fourth, as noted before, there are logrolling costs, leading to overinvestment (or perhaps underpricing).   Fifth, there is likely to be innovation loss, as fewer experiments can be run when there are fewer independent governments operating.   Table 5.3 summarizes the basic hypotheses that are suggested when a lower or higher level of government manages roads that serve short- or long-distance trips.

Table 5.2   Roadway classification and economic properties

Property	Locals	Collectors	Arterials
Topology	Tree, Local web	Web	Web
Excludable to abutters	No	No	Yes
Excludable to non-local traffic	Yes	No	No
Congesting	No	Yes	Yes
Competitive	No	Yes	Maybe
Contestable	No	Maybe	Maybe
Locality of Traffic	High	Medium	Low
Capacity	Low	Medium	High
Free-flow Speed	Low	Medium	High
Flow	Low	Medium	High
Scale economies	Small	Medium	Large
Service Area	Small	Medium	Large

Table 5.3   Hypothesized effects of government and road hierarchy

	Short-distance road	Long-distance road
Local government	Fair and efficient	Underinvest or overprice
State government	Overinvest or underprice	Fair and efficient

Following the logrolling argument, a link should be assigned to the smallest governmental jurisdiction that contains its service area.   The problems of logrolling may still arise, however, if there are not appropriately sized small jurisdictions (for example, homeowner associations or small clubs) to manage the very local roads. There are dangers associated with assigning a link to a jurisdiction smaller than its service area. These dangers, discussed more fully in the following chapters, suggest that price gouging might arise if tolling is permitted, or will necessarily result in a cross-subsidy from local to non-local residents where tax financing is used.

If there are a variety of appropriately sized jurisdictions that correlate well with relatively small link service areas, transportation financing should work efficiently. All neighborhood links on a 'tree' are then financed locally, that is, by those on that tree. Since users are all local and local use is pervasive/ubiquitous and approximately equal, then any financing system used can be reasonably fair. For instance, of toll or tax, the preferred method would be the one with the lowest transaction costs, which would depend on technology. On the other hand, 'web' links have relatively large link service areas, which suggests management by a larger jurisdiction. The use of general tax financing is likely to be significantly less fair than user charges in this case.

Another objection to the rule associating a link with the jurisdiction that corresponds with its service area arises from the presence of scale economies. However, scale economies do not necessarily require integration within a single jurisdiction. Contracts for joint construction or maintenance can be used to achieve such economies where they exist.

Such clear differences in the classification and properties of roads suggest that different types of financing and different levels of jurisdictional control may be appropriate. Some solutions for this problem include hybrid and decentralized organizations and the use of oversight rather than direct management by higher levels of the hierarchy. This analysis leads directly to the conclusion that local and intercity roads should be analysed separately. The following chapters consider each in turn.

NOTES

1. A link refers to a road segment between two intersections (the meeting of three or more road segments), or an intersection and a terminus. Driveways are not considered links, and the location where a driveway meets a road is not considered an intersection.
2. Excepting the links on which the origin and destination lie.
3. One can imagine other topologies, for instance webs separated from other webs by a single bridge (a bridge connecting islands). These will not be examined in detail here.

6. Intertemporal Equity

INTRODUCTION

Local jurisdictions must balance present and future needs against costs when financing infrastructure. When a fixed piece of infrastructure is funded and built by one group, and then a new group comes in and uses it without paying, there is a free-rider problem. When one group comes in and borrows money to build infrastructure, and another group is held liable, there is also a free-rider problem. The extent of the problem depends on site-specific circumstances, the nature of financing, and the placement of the tax burden. This chapter will consider these factors and evaluate suggested solutions.

In the past two decades, many localities have levied impact fees to finance new and expanded infrastructure. The fees are designed to be associated with the 'impact' of the development on public services. The impacts include the full gamut of publicly provided services, including roads, sewers, schools, and parks. While development has generally been held responsible for constructing on-site public services, off-site facilities are often addressed by impact payments. Some communities have adopted value capture districts, to tax adjacent development for the benefits associated with new transportation infrastructure (Stopher 1993). Others have implemented stringent growth management regulations tied only weakly to financing (Levinson 1998; Pollakowski and Wachter 1990).

The underlying need for taxes on development arises due to the financing mechanisms used to pay for infrastructure. Suppose a community has adopted 'pay-as-you-go' financing and pays outright for a road. When a residential or commercial development comes along, it does not pay the one-time fixed cost of the road, which has already been absorbed by the earlier taxpayers. Failure to recover funds from the development creates a free-rider problem. Foreknowledge of future failure to recover those funds may discourage the investment in the first place, leading to underinvestment. Cost recovery techniques include user charges and impact fees as well as specially designed policies. Alternatively, a different initial financing system, such as bonds (sometimes called 'pay as you use'), can help alleviate the problem.

Often a piece of infrastructure can be described by a 'U-shaped' cost function.   Average fixed costs decline with additional users, but average variable costs rise. At low demand levels, average fixed costs dominate; at higher demand levels, variable costs are more significant. The appropriate financing mechanism depends on whether costs are falling or rising, while the same system may exhibit different behaviors at different times. When average costs are rising, marginal cost pricing can pay the costs of infrastructure.   Unfortunately, in practical terms, it is unlikely that road pricing will be implemented widely in the near term due to technological difficulties in exclusion and monitoring, as well as political problems in implementation. Further, with rising average costs, and with little incentive to encourage new users of the infrastructure, existing residents may insist on significant compensation.   When average costs are falling, each additional user has little impact on existing users. Yet those existing users who paid for the one-time fixed costs would certainly prefer to be compensated by new residents, who constitute additional users of the infrastructure.

Financing is further complicated because infrastructure is often indivisible; roads, for instance, are built in discrete units. Finally, whether the jurisdiction is open (developers have alternatives locations) or closed (developers can either locate in the jurisdiction or not develop) greatly influences the outcome of negotiations about what charges are paid.

The analysis in this chapter will be similar in some respects to that put forward in the following chapters to analyse tolling along a road connecting adjacent jurisdictions. The foremost difference is that while two groups in time (new and old development) are like two groups in space, the earliest group always moves first, without knowing exactly what the later group will do. Although the first mover acts with uncertainty, the later group knows exactly what the early movers did.

Although this chapter focuses on urban and suburban arterial streets to provide concrete examples, financing in time affects many types of facilities.   Arterials serve the function of enabling both access and movement, are not easily excludable, and are often maintained by city or county governments. Thus, they are unlike neighborhood collector and distributor streets built by the developer of a subdivision – which only local traffic would use.   They also differ from major intercity highways, which are operated by state governments (in the American context) and are often designed as limited-access facilities. Often arterial streets are financed through taxes or developer exactions.

In an ideal world, it would be possible to scale roadways so that they can be added as appropriate by development. There are several practical difficulties with this approach. The first problem is the indivisibility of roads. At best, streets can be built a lane at a time, but a half-lane seldom makes sense. While, at large scales, the indivisibility problem becomes relatively minor, in smaller jurisdictions it remains considerable. A second difficulty is the timing of infrastructure deployment; the cost of congestion rises suddenly compared with the decline in the average fixed costs of infrastructure. To be 'optimal' a community must have a great deal of foresight about when a particular level of congestion will occur and have a road ready to be opened at that point. A third issue is the cross-group use of roads; new residents may drive on existing roads, while existing residents may use the new roads. However, these uses may not be equal.

An alternative to impact fees while still recovering costs is to, in effect, 'rent' the network. This can be accomplished, for instance, by paying for a facility with borrowed funds. Because the community pays annual installments, as the size of the community grows with development, the average cost of the infrastructure for both new and existing residents drops. This encourages the right amount of investment. The downside to renting is that the excess cost of renting may exceed the revenue that can be gained by investing the initial capital elsewhere.

Another alternative is to have an explicit recovery policy in place. At least two kinds of recovery policy come to mind. The first allocates in advance the amount development must pay to the community to recover expenditures on fixed costs. The main difficulty with this approach is its reliance on forecasts, which may or may not materialize. The second, *continuous recovery*, policy dynamically adjusts the charge development must pay, but directs that revenue to compensating existing residents for earlier payment. Existing residents can be thought of as owning the facility.

This chapter proceeds first by outlining a scenario commonly found where infrastructure, with a high fixed cost but low variable cost, must be built to support existing and new residents. Pay as you go, bond financing, and impact fees are compared, and then a continuous recovery approach is developed. While economic theory is geared to using marginal cost pricing, this chapter describes the intelligent use of an average cost approach for cases where marginal cost pricing does not recover sufficient revenue. The issue of relative bargaining power between an existing community and a developer is discussed as a limiting factor to this approach. An example is presented comparing the continuous recovery approach with the cost recovery approach found in some communities for financing water and other infrastructure systems.

OLD VERSUS NEW

Consider this situation: A large community has built a section of roadway, paid for by property taxes. A residential development nestled within or adjacent to the previously existing community is constructed. The landowners of the development site paid a negligible share of the cost of the roadway, since their land was undeveloped at the time of construction. No new roadways are needed to support the development. How much should the development pay to use the existing infrastructure? To whom should the check be written?

Conventional economic theory says that it is efficient that development pay its marginal cost, even if marginal cost pricing does not recover the fixed cost of building the infrastructure in the first place. If the development pays only its marginal cost and average costs are falling, it is free riding on the fixed assets constructed by the previously existing community. Existing residents may not find this outcome fair or desirable. Anticipating this outcome, the older community may attempt to do something to prevent it from happening in the first place, by adopting some regulatory mechanism.

This brings out the first issue: what are the expectations involved? Does the existing community have an expectation (such as a law on the books) of being reimbursed when it decides to expand a capital facility, or does it lack that expectation until after the facility is constructed? That expectation depends on whether a policy has been adopted, and, just as importantly, when that policy was adopted. If the policy was adopted prior to the construction of the existing infrastructure, there is an expectation of recovery (point A on the first row of Figure 6.1). However, if the policy was introduced after the existing infrastructure was built, but before any new development, then recovery is an added bonus to the existing landowners, who still may be able to exact it from new development (point B). If the policy arrives after the development, it has no effect (point C).

However, if development leads to a decision to build infrastructure, then it is likely that both the pre-existing community and the development will be assessed at point D or point E, as shown on the second row of Figure 6.1. This is because separating out the groups after a development has been approved and constructed is difficult (the constitution prohibits ex post facto laws). This case, like point C above, places a greater burden on the community than would have been required prior to the approval of the development.

Infrastructure leads development
Community → [A] → Infrastructure → [B] → Development → [C]

Development leads infrastructure
Community → [A] → Development → [D] → Infrastructure → [E]

Figure 6.1 Timeline of recovery policies

PAY-GO, BONDS, AND IMPACT FEES

Three basic financing schemes can be considered, with numerous variations. The first is pay-as-you-go (Pay-Go), which requires that a facility be paid for when constructed. In the absence of a recovery procedure, the payment falls on the residents at the time of construction. The second is some sort of bond financing, wherein the payments are spread over time, and fall on those in residence at the time of the payment. Bond financing adds an interest charge for the cost of capital. The total costs of bond financing may exceed the total costs of pay-as-you-go financing, depending on a comparison of market interest rates and the return to opportunities available for spending capital. A third financing mechanism is an impact fee, which would be a lump sum charge for new infrastructure imposed on new development

These financing schemes for the two classes of infrastructure affect the two classes of users, as shown in Table 6.1. In the pay-go system, all new infrastructure will have to be paid for by everyone, not just the development. A growing community where new residents are expected to be numerous compared with earlier residents will prefer re-financing old infrastructure with bonds, but for new infrastructure the computation is more complicated. An assessment must be made about future development as well. If the development is the last one a community will see, pay-as-you-go might be preferred to bonds (to reduce future interest costs). However, if the development is simply one in a long string of oncoming development, bonds have advantages over pay-go. With bonds, the base over which payments are made will continue to be expanded (and the per capita payments will decline over time).

This situation can be formulated as a game, with the objective for players (community, developer) being to minimize their own costs given a certain infrastructure deployment. This is a one-time game: while the decisions may recur, they do so with different players. If existing residents choose the financing means for old infrastructure and the developer chooses it for new infrastructure, then (re-)financing both old and new infrastructure with bonds is generally a stable equilibrium. A different solution may result if there is little future growth or if the costs of bonds are large relative to pay-go. However, if the residents set the rules under which infrastructure is financed, then old infrastructure would be paid for with bonds and new infrastructure would be paid for by an impact fee on development. (And if developers set the rules, then old infrastructure would be pay-go and new infrastructure would be pay-go or bond).

Table 6.1: Cost incidence

		New infrastructure		
		Pay-go	Bond	Impact fee
Old infra-structure	Pay-go	$[F/Q+f/(Q+q),$ $f/(Q+q)]$	$[F/Q + r/(Q+q),$ $r/(Q+q)]$	$[F/Q,$ $f/q]$
	Bond	$[(R+f)/(Q+q),$ $(R+f)/(Q+q)]$	$[(R+r)/(Q+q),$ $(R+r)/(Q+q)]$	$[R/(Q+q),$ $R/(Q+q)+$ $f/q]$

Note: For simplicity, assume that new development follows immediately after infrastructure (re-)financing, so that bond payments for old infrastructure are borne proportionally by old residents and new development. Where: R, r = net present value of future bond payment for old (R) and new (r) infrastructure; F, f = fixed cost for old (F) and new (f) infrastructure, and Q, q = existing population (Q), new population (q).

So, *intertemporal equity* in terms of allocating costs to those who cause them, efficiency in terms of internalizing costs of infrastructure to those who benefit from it, and stability all argue for bond financing over pay-as-you-go for financing capital facilities. The primary downside is the additional costs associated with interest payments.

CONTINUOUS RECOVERY

It should be possible to develop a mechanism for achieving the benefits of intertemporal equity and efficiency without the costs associated with borrowing on the open market. This is continuous recovery, which effectively makes the existing residents the owners of a 'capital facility club' that new residents can join by paying their share of the cost to the earlier members.[2]

As shown in Figure 6.2, development (q) pays the average cost of infrastructure (c) to existing residents (Q), this compensates existing residents (Q) for their 'excess' payment. In this case, development pays what it should in terms of 'second best' pricing, it just pays it to the existing residents. If this does not happen, existing residents are paying more than they should (their excess payment), since the recovery of costs was anticipated, and thus internalized in property values. The relationships are expressed below:

$$\left(Q+q\right)c = QC \tag{1}$$

$$C = T/Q \tag{2}$$

$$c = T/\left(Q+q\right) \tag{3}$$

where:

T = total fixed cost,

C, c = average fixed cost of infrastructure before (C), and after development (c); and

Q, q = existing population (Q), new population (q).

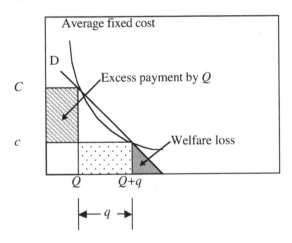

Figure 6.2   Illustration of welfare loss

However, the actual (out-of-pocket) cost of allowing a development of new residents given existing residents is zero if average costs are falling, so anything the development contributes bails out existing residents. This situation applies to the case where the recovery policy is imposed after the existing residents pay for the capital facility, but before the development is constructed (as opposed to before both old and new development). The property right to recover the money invested in the capital facility is not as strong in this case as when recovery was assumed before the initial decision to construct the infrastructure. One might suggest that there is a welfare loss with recovery.

In this case, the welfare loss (demand not realized because it is priced) is denoted by the shaded triangle in Figure 6.2. In this case, no individual would be harmed in the short run by permitting extra development (as there are only fixed costs). This welfare may not change the motivation of the original residents, as the loss accrues not to them, but to some other set of individuals (potential new residents). If the capital facility was already paid for with no expectation of recovery and has no marginal costs to use, why shouldn't additional users be able to free ride? How does free riding harm anyone? Charging for use without an expectation of recovery is 'unfair', just as is being unable to recover costs when there was an expectation that one could. However, 'unfairness' may lead to inefficiencies. These inefficiencies include underinvestment or lagging investment over the long term. Residents may choose not to build in advance if unfairness is perceived. Furthermore, this kind of 'cheating', exploiting a resource without compensation, will eventually lead to a loss of confidence in the system.

BARGAINING

While the right to permit development may always reside with existing residents, the actual ability of residents to impose costs on development depends on the respective bargaining strengths of the community and developers. Perhaps the most important indicator of bargaining strength is the degree of monopoly power the residents of the existing jurisdiction have. That depends on the choices available to a developer and the potential new residents the developer represents.

In a 'closed city' the entire area of analysis is contained within one governmental unit, so the existing residents have very strong bargaining power. New residents (developers) can either pay what existing residents ask or not locate there. A closed city may be an isolated community, or a strong regional government (with growth controls) giving a spatial monopoly to existing residents at the expense of potential residents.

In an 'open city', new residents or developers can play jurisdictions off against each other; if one jurisdiction charges too much, another may undercut it. In an open city, relative bargaining strength resides with developers, who can drive down development exactions. Since something is better than nothing in terms of recovering fixed costs (when there are declining average costs), the existing community may accept less than its full fair-share cost recovery from a new development.

In addition to the open city/closed city distinction, other factors may play into bargaining about recovery. These include other positive and negative externalities of development, in particular tax base changes,

demands on public services, accessibility benefits and congestion costs. If
the existing residents receive a positive net benefit from the development,
the amount they constrict the development should be less than if there is a
negative net benefit (X). Similarly, if the development achieves economic
profits ($\prod$), then the existing community may try to exact some share of
those profits in exchange for permission to develop. The resulting charge
will range between a subsidy to development of up to the amount of a
positive net externality, to a charge on development of up to the economic
profits of the development. More precise values than this depend on market
conditions and the number of competing jurisdictions and developers.

Table 6.2 is the payoff matrix to user classes (community, developer)
under two conditions of recovery from the community and two responses
from a developer. The actual amount of the payment ranges does not
exceed $\prod$, but must exceed X. If the externality is positive, then the
payment may be negative. The precise amount is indeterminate from this
analysis.

Table 6.2   Bargaining

		Developer Do not pay	Pay if required
Community requires	No payment	$[0 - X, \prod]$	$[0 - X, \prod]$
	Payment	$[0 , 0]$	$[\text{Payment} - X, \prod - \text{payment}]$

Notes: X = net negative externality. $\prod$ = economic profit to new development. If X
< Payment < $\prod$ then development will occur with payment.

EXAMPLES

There are a number of cities with capital recovery (or recoupment) fees for
water and sewerage, among them (discovered by the author through an
internet search) Austin TX, Chelmsford MA, Chesterfield County VA,
Concord NC, Conway SC, Dunedin FL, Gurnee IL, Houston TX, Loveland
CO, Montecito CA, Pooler GA, Round Rock TX, San Jose CA, Santa Clara,
CA, and Calgary Canada. There is also a software package that automates
the process of calculating the rates (Ratemod 2000). Capital recovery is
also becoming a significant issue in electricity deregulation; particularly
concerning who will pay for existing expensive generation plants, called
'stranded' costs. However, the use of capital recovery charges does not
seem prevalent in other infrastructure categories.

Loveland Colorado is perhaps the most widely recognized example of a
capital cost recovery impact fee (Heath et al. 1989; Nicholas, Nelson, and
Juergensmeyer 1991). Impact fees comprise 5.8% of the city budget, while

user fees are 9.1% and utilities are 46.3% (Loveland Colorado 2000).
Unlike conventional impact fees, which are used to expand facilities, the
recovery fee allows development to buy into existing excess capacity
provided by the community. A sample calculation for a library facility in
Loveland using this approach and a comparison with the proposed
continuous recovery approach are given in Tables 6.3 and 6.4.

Table 6.3 Loveland capital expansion fee

Category	Loveland
A. Total capital cost ($)	3,354,000
B. Replacement and betterment cost = A $Q/(Q+q)$ ($)	1,571,300
C. Future capacity (units)	14,700
D. CEF Fee = (A – B)/C ($)	121

Source: Adapted from Nicholas et al. (1991) Table 13-2.

Table 6.4 Continuous recovery

Category	Continuous recovery
A. Total capital cost	3,354,000
B. Initial cost per household = A $/Q$	260.00
C. Fee for first new household = $A/(Q+1)$	259.98
D. Fee for 5,000th new household = $A/(Q+5000)$	187.37
E. Fee for last new household = A $/(Q+q)$	121.52
F. Total amount paid (before Returns)	2,550,944
G. Total amount returned to q	$764,575
H. Total amount returned to Q = Net total amount paid by q	1,786,370
I. Amount recovered by Q per household = H/Q	138.47
J. Net payment by Q = B – I	121.52

Notes: Q, q = existing population, new population (32,700, 37,100) in persons (at
2.53 people per household, approximately equal to 12,900, 14,700 households
respectively).
Source: Author's calculations.

Table 6.3 illustrates the Loveland policy as applied to a library,
ignoring corrections for excess capacity, external funding, or splits between
residential and commercial development. The total capital cost of the
facility is allocated proportionately to existing and future households. The

capital expansion fee is simply the share allocated to future households
divided by the number of those households. The continuous recovery
policy (Table 6.4), on the other hand, does not have a single fee. Rather,
the fee depends on the number of units that have actually been developed.
So, for instance, if only 5,000 additional housing units are constructed
(rather than the 14,700 forecast), the cost per unit for those 5,000 will be
higher ($187 versus $121). As additional units are constructed, the earlier
units are given rebates. Small differences in numbers between the values in
the tables are due to rounding errors in the original Loveland example.

There are several differences between the Loveland and other real-
world examples and the proposed continuous recovery system. The first
difference concerns whether individuals or the community is repaid by the
system. Existing capital cost recovery approaches fail to return the funds
directly to the residents who paid in. That is, they are, or are analogous to,
a debt financing system for bonds rather than a community owned capital
facility club. Second, the choice of basis over which to estimate the fees is
critical. Either a historical basis (the cost to actually build the facility for
which excess capacity is being sold) or the cost to replace the facility
(minus depreciation) in current dollars could be used. Loveland assesses
based on replacement cost. However, the use of a replacement basis, while
certainly appropriate for new or future construction, may result in a profit to
existing residents or the community as a whole when the capacity has
already been built. Third, the Loveland program keeps the fee fixed,
whereas a true continuous recovery program as outlined in the chapter
would vary the fee over time based on the number of actual users.
Loveland's program requires forecasting the ultimate number of users, and
then allocating costs accordingly. Should the forecast be optimistic and not
all the new residents materialize, then the original residents of Loveland
will have overpaid (if Loveland does not use bond financing).

SUMMARY AND CONCLUSIONS

When infrastructure needs to be financed through taxes rather than user
fees, the issue of which class of citizens pays for the infrastructure is still
not resolved. A properly designed financing system is still required in order
to have an equitable distribution of the burden while producing efficient
infrastructure. The financing system must operate within the confines of an
institutional structure that attributes the ownership of the infrastructure to
those who paid for it, and does not allow use without buy-in.

The continuous cost recovery system suggested here is an improvement
on top-down financing allocation systems that rely on the realization of
forecasts to achieve an equitable burden. If the forecast levels of

development are not reached, the existing residents are stuck holding a larger payment than are those who moved after the charge was imposed. If property rights to road use are placed in the hands of existing residents, then a mechanism for recovering fixed costs is a necessary feature of a politically viable infrastructure-financing system. The argument was made that an intertemporal equity policy is necessary to encourage an efficient level of infrastructure investment. There are several mechanisms to achieve intertemporal equity, including bond financing or an explicit policy of recovery with pay-as-you-go financing. These procedures do not supplant impact fees to pay for congestion or facility expansion. Rather, they supplement the marginal cost approach to recover fixed costs when marginal costs are zero or falling.

This chapter has dealt with residential development. However, the attribution of transportation infrastructure costs to residential or commercial development is very much like the argument about taxing income or sales. A trip has two ends, and which end pays what share of the infrastructure cost of the trip is in many ways arbitrary. It would be a simple extension of this process to allocate a share of infrastructure costs to different sectors (office, retail, industrial, other, residential), much as is done in the Loveland system. The extent of pass-through of costs from development to consumers depends on the relative competitiveness of markets. Nicholas et al. (1991) discuss the issue of housing costs, but other costs should be similar.

The actual outcomes in terms of the selected financing mechanism and the amount paid rests critically on the institutional assumptions of a 'right' of access to infrastructure for a new development or a 'right' to prevent access by the existing community. It further rests on the relative bargaining power, determined by the alternatives available to a developer or potential new residents in terms of sites to build or locate in neighboring communities. Many of the actual results are indeterminate within a core range of values. In a city where developers have bargaining power, charging more than the market will bear will eliminate the possibility of any recovery.

The application of this approach in a community surrounded by non-adopting jurisdictions is limited by its bargaining power. In the short-run, it may not be possible to recover 100% of fixed costs if neighboring jurisdictions are providing irrational development subsidies. In the long-run, however, a sound financing system and strong public services should be an attractive amenity to new residents and commercial development. Soundly financed services should shift the demand curve, which will increase the community's relative bargaining power, offsetting partially or entirely the short-term problem of neighboring communities' subsidizing development.

NOTES

1. See, for instance: Altshuler and Gomez-Ibañez (1993); Bauman and Ethier (1987); Downs (1992); Lee (1989); Nelson (1989); and Popper (1988).

2. As a practical implementation of this idea, consider forming an infrastructure club. To begin, assume that infrastructure is collectively indivisible, so that no weighting of the cost-share infrastructure by use would be made. All existing households would be grandfathered into the club, but all new households would be required to pay a membership fee to the existing members. The fee would be proportionate to

$$I_n = \frac{T}{Q+q}$$

where:

I_n = fee new households must pay to buy into infrastructure club
Q = population of existing households (excluding new households)
q = total number of new households
T = total fixed cost of existing infrastructure attributed to households

The fee (I_q) would be rebated to existing households periodically (as a tax refund for instance). A similar model could be applied to commercial development.

Thus at the end of a time period, each existing household would be paid J_Q:

$$J_Q = \frac{\sum_{q=1}^{q} I_q}{Q} = \frac{\sum_{q=1}^{q} \frac{T}{Q+q}}{Q}$$

However, new development might also bring with it additional infrastructure. This 'payment in kind' would need to be credited. Calculate a fee that each existing household would have to pay to each new household to compensate it for bringing new infrastructure to the table.

$$I_Q = \frac{t}{Q+q}$$

where:

I_Q = fee existing households must pay to compensate new development for providing infrastructure to add to the infrastructure club
t = total fixed cost of new infrastructure attributed to residential development

Thus at the end of a time period, each new household would be paid J_q:

$$J_q = \frac{\sum_{Q=1}^{Q} I_Q}{q} = \frac{\sum_{q=1}^{Q} \frac{t}{Q+q}}{q}$$

Thus the net payment (K_q) for each new household would be:

$$K_q = I_q - J_q = \frac{T}{Q+q} - \frac{\sum_{Q=1}^{Q} \frac{t}{Q+q}}{q}$$

And the net compensation (K_Q) for each existing household would be:

$$K_Q = J_Q - I_Q = \frac{\sum_{q=1}^{q} \frac{T}{Q+q}}{Q} - \frac{t}{Q+q}$$

While this fee is paid all at once to existing households, new households might see it added to their mortgage. Clearly this is a simplified model; extensions would include spatial differentiation to account for different usage of different facilities by different areas. In each period, the existing population (Q) would grow by the number of new households (q).

7.   Finance Choice on a Beltway

INTRODUCTION

Cordon tolls are becoming a popular method of restricting traffic and financing new infrastructure in cities such as Singapore, Oslo, Trondheim, and Bergen. Imperfect cordons, such as tollgates on a major highway without entrance or exit ramp tolls, have traditionally been used both in the early days of turnpikes and in more recent times on limited-access highway systems. In both cases, local trips do not pay tolls, while through trips (trips crossing the cordon) do. On the other hand, tax financing has been common both historically (where initially the tax was in terms of labor), and more recently for local roads, which are typically not funded through usage taxes such as gas taxes.[1] Taxes also rely on a cordon, the boundary of the relevant jurisdiction within which they are assessed. The preference for either of these two revenue sources as financing mechanism can be modeled as a function of trip length, jurisdiction size, and collection costs.

Earlier chapters argued that since jurisdictions try to do well by their residents, who are both voters and travelers, local effects are central to the choice of a financing mechanism. This chapter approaches the argument analytically in a specific context, that of a beltway. The choice of tax or toll, while being historically contingent, is a function of the length of trips, the size of the jurisdiction, and the costs of collecting revenue and providing infrastructure. These properties indicate the nature of the free-rider problem under the two different financing mechanisms (tax, toll), where a free rider is someone who uses the system without paying his full cost. In the case of tax financing, travelers from outside the taxing jurisdiction do not pay taxes to support the construction, operation, and maintenance of the road. In the case of toll cordon financing, travelers entering and exiting the network within the toll cordon pay nothing. A perfectly excludable toll cordon, that tracks everyone entering and exiting each link, is not without cost and cannot necessarily be implemented everywhere. The free-rider problem will occur whenever there is an incomplete or uneven financing mechanism, that is, when financing does not capture every user. In realistic situations of highway transportation, there are costs involved in collecting revenue which dictate that a complete and perfect financing mechanism is not available on every link.

The gains to a jurisdiction from imposing tolls exceed the gains from taxes under certain circumstances. The gains come from residents of other jurisdictions. Finance externalities are well known in certain cases. For instance, local governments rely on some mix of sales, income, and property taxes, each of which are borne by a different set of people, not all of whom are local.

The use of the terms 'tax' and 'toll' should be defined precisely. Here, a tax is a fee levied by a jurisdiction on its residents in the form of a poll tax. A toll is a fee levied by the jurisdiction as travelers cross a cordon. A jurisdiction is defined as the organization responsible for maintaining the road. For simplicity, residents and network users will be considered identical; but when they are not identical, a cross-subsidy from the taxed population to the traveling population occurs.

For the analysis in this chapter, it is assumed that the revenue collected must cover costs and the network is non-congesting. Costs borne by the system operator are comprised of two main categories: infrastructure costs and collection costs. Each cost category has two components, fixed costs, which are independent of use, and variable costs, which depend on use.

The objective of a jurisdiction managing a roadway, in addition to its obligation to cover costs, is similar to its objective in other domains. Borrowing from Downs (1957), the objective of a jurisdiction is to maximize the welfare of its residents (those who vote for the party governing the jurisdiction, in the case of a democracy). That is, *ceteris paribus*, the jurisdiction tries to minimize the costs borne by its residents in terms of money, travel time, and the time it takes to collect taxes or tolls. Furthermore, the utility of residents is composed not only of costs borne within their jurisdiction of residence, but also of their costs outside that jurisdiction. Interjurisdictional interactions need to be considered.

The stylized model presented in this chapter introduces the assessment of alternative financing mechanisms. Game theory is employed to model the conflict between jurisdictions. Each jurisdiction has the choice to tax or to toll. The payoffs from the decisions are interdependent. This chapter presents an analytic model for examining the free-rider problem in relation to collection costs. This model explicitly compares the number of free riders associated with taxes and those associated with tolls on a simplified network with various jurisdiction sizes. A game between two jurisdictions setting pricing policies (tax, toll) demonstrates that in the absence of cooperation, toll financing is a stable equilibrium under certain circumstances. Those conditions require revenue collection costs to be less than the revenue exacted from out-of-jurisdiction residents to cover the costs of the road, and demand to be relatively inelastic. This result also requires that the burden for financing the road can be placed solely on boundary-crossing trips. By looking at how the number of free riders depends on the number of toll booths, a comparison of collection costs against efficient pricing can be made. General conclusions are drawn from an examination of the model.

THE SPATIAL FREE-RIDER PROBLEM

The first issue is the geographic or spatial free-rider problem. The size of the jurisdiction relative to the length of trips will determine the proportion of trips that are local at least one trip-end and the proportion that are through trips. Who acts as 'free rider' and who provides the subsidy, 'us' or 'them', is central to the choice of financing mechanism. The discussion of free riders returns to the original sense of the word, riding on roads without paying. Trips can be divided into several classes (illustrated in Figure 7.1):

1. trips originating in the jurisdiction and destined for the jurisdiction;
2. trips originating in the jurisdiction and destined for outside the jurisdiction;
3. trips originating outside the jurisdiction and destined for inside the jurisdiction;
4. trips originating outside the jurisdiction and destined for outside the jurisdiction.

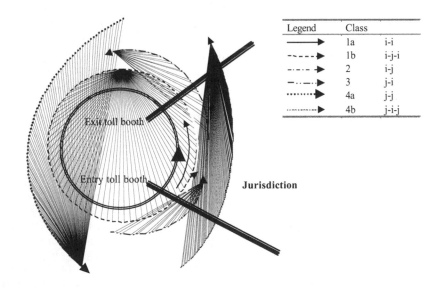

Legend	Class	
⟶	1a	i-i
---▸	1b	i-j-i
-··-·▸	2	i-j
-··—·▸	3	j-i
········▸	4a	j-j
·······-▸	4b	j-i-j

Figure 7.1 Illustration of trip classes

Classes (1) and (4) in Figure 7.1 can be further differentiated by whether or not they stay within a single jurisdiction. Class (1a) trips remain entirely within the jurisdiction; class (1b) trips originate in and are destined for the jurisdiction, but leave the jurisdiction for part of the trip. Similarly, class (4a) trips remain entirely outside the jurisdiction (and are irrelevant for immediate taxing and tolling purposes, though they influence the tolls that residents will pay when entering the other jurisdiction). Class (4b) trips originate and are destined for locations outside the jurisdiction, but travel through the jurisdiction to get there.

Clearly, in the case of local control, there is a preference to attain revenue from through trips (class 4b) and exempt locals (classes 1a, 1b), thereby allowing locals to be the free rider. At the extreme case, that of a single short road segment (a near-perfect cordon), this approaches the efficient financing mechanism of tolling nearly all travelers in proportion to use, as there are very few, if any, 'locals'. However, if those who make through trips control the political process, or through trips are really 'local' because the jurisdiction has a broad geographical scope, then taxes may be preferred because of their lower collection costs.

Collection costs include both the cost to the administrator and the cost to users (and potentially non-users) and depend on the technology used. Historically tolls, requiring human toll collectors, have had the highest collection costs and high variable costs. Advanced toll collection technologies such as automated vehicle identification or the use of radio tags and receivers significantly lower costs over the long term. In the case of toll booths, the costs were borne both by the agency collecting tolls and staffing toll booths as well as by travelers who were repeatedly delayed by those gates.

The size of the jurisdiction administering the roads is not independent of the financing mechanism. Authority can be vested in national, regional, or local jurisdictions. At the most local level, a jurisdiction can be responsible for a single facility, which is common for toll bridges and tunnels. In an untolled situation, generally authority for roads used by local traffic resides with a more local jurisdiction while authority for roads with less local traffic is with a less local (larger) jurisdiction. This internalizes, to some extent, the through trip externality, and so long as road use is pervasive and fairly equal throughout the population, does not create too great an inequity – there is not much cross-subsidy from non-users to users. This issue will be analysed in more detail in subsequent chapters.

The interrelationship between the geographic free-rider problem, associated with cordon tolls or poll taxes, and collection costs can be illustrated with a simple beltway model. The use of a circular road enables simple accounting of flows.

Consider a one-way, circular road divided into sections $(s = 1,S)$ and jurisdictions $(j = 1,J)$. The jurisdictions completely cover the circular road. The size of jurisdiction j, measured in discrete, integer sections, is denoted S_j:

$$\sum S_j = S$$

For convenience there are only two jurisdictions $(J = 2)$. The first jurisdiction's size (S_1) covers a given number of adjacent sections; the second jurisdiction (S_2) covers $S - S_1$ sections. Figure 7.2 illustrates $S = 6$, where Jurisdiction 1 covers one section (section 1), and Jurisdiction 2 covers five sections (sections 2–6).

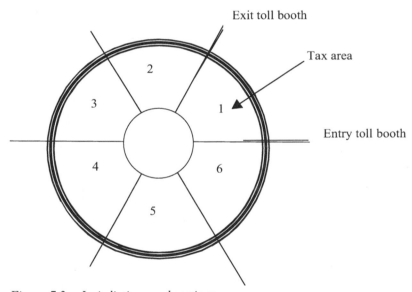

Figure 7.2   Jurisdictions and sections

In the case of cordon tolls, tolls are established before and after the sections in question. It is not important if tolls are collected only on entry, only on exit, or on both entry and exit, as trips are generally round trips, However, collection on both is assumed here. In Figure 7.2, the tolls are collected before and after a one section jurisdiction $(S_1 = 1, S_2 = 5)$. Taxes are only assessed on individuals making trips originating in the jurisdiction. The flow on each segment (the part of the circular road in any section) is assumed to be identical.

Trips have only one route between their origin and destination because the road is circular and one-way (cycling is prohibited). When the origin and destination sections are identical, trips do not need to pass through a tollgate.

FREE RIDERS AND JURISDICTION SIZE

For each size jurisdiction, two traversal matrices are constructed. A traversal matrix gives a 1 (one) if the trip between origin and destination crosses the designated cordon, in this case a toll booth or jurisdiction boundary, and 0 (zero) otherwise. The $S \times S$ matrix is completed for each section-to-section origin–destination pair. For $S = 6$, this requires construction of six 36-cell traversal matrices.

To analyse free riders in the case of tolls, for each size jurisdiction, the number who cross the entry traversal (but not the exit) (class 2), the exit traversal (but not the entry traversal) (class 3), both the entry and exit traversals as through trips (class 4b) or local trips (class 1b), and neither traversal are computed. For those who cross neither traversal, their origin (within the cordon (local, class 1a), or outside (irrelevant, class 4a)) is determined.

To demonstrate the approach, assume that demand between sections is constant and uniform, and perfectly inelastic. The use of a constant and uniform number of trips between sections does not affect the conclusions greatly and simplifies the analysis. A more realistic analysis would consider a distance (time) decay function and sensitivity to price, and would not require the number of trips from each section to be identical. In addition, travelers may not be homogeneous with respect to their value of time. However, this chapter examines cost allocation rather than market conditions. Subsequent chapters consider demand elasticity.

The number of perfect free riders rises as the size of the jurisdiction gets proportionately larger relative to the size of the road, and the number of local trips overtakes the number of through trips. In contrast, consider the case of only using tax financing. Only trips originating in a jurisdiction are subject to taxes. In this case, as the size of the jurisdiction rises, the number of free riders falls. How many trips ride free in a jurisdiction depends on a jurisdiction's size and whether it taxes or tolls. Figure 7.3 compares the number of free riders for the two financing mechanisms. At four or more segments (a jurisdiction represents two-thirds of the network), the number of free riders from tolls overtakes the number of free riders from taxes.

The possibility of using both taxes and tolls to eliminate the problem becomes obvious after examining the results of using one or the other. The problem is politically associated with the ownership of roads by a spatially delimited jurisdiction. This suggests analysis using game theory.

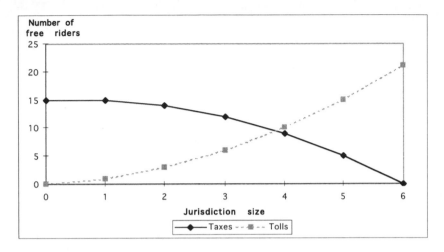

Figure 7.3   Perfect free riders: tax versus cordon tolls

TAX – TOLL GAME

In the previous section one jurisdiction was examined in isolation. Jurisdiction 1 was setting policies assuming no response from jurisdiction 2, which implicitly was paying for its road from taxes on its own residents. Suppose jurisdiction 2 were free to set a policy as well, what would it do? Here, there are two players (jurisdictions) and two policies (tax, toll).

Begin by assuming the net 'profit' to a jurisdiction must be zero. Total revenues for jurisdiction i – those generated by local residents (living in jurisdiction i) (R_{ii}) and non-local residents (living in jurisdiction j) (R_{ji})) must sum to total costs. Total costs are defined as fixed costs of infrastructure (F_I) and toll collection (F_C) plus variable costs associated with the level of traffic (V_{Iii}, V_{Iji}) and toll collection (V_{Cii}, V_{Cji}). The fixed component of infrastructure (F_I) consists primarily of land and construction. The variable component of infrastructure costs, including operating and maintenance costs (V_I), depends on the quantity and quality of use of the system, and is the cost of maintaining and periodically rebuilding the pavement and road structure. The fixed component of collection costs (F_C) includes, for instance, the installation of toll booths or electronic toll collection infrastructure. The variable component (V_C) may vary with the number of users, including the cost of debiting accounts, the labor to collect revenue, and so on. This relationship is summarized as:

$$0 = \left(R_{ii} + R_{ji}\right) - \left(F_I + V_{Iii} + V_{Iji} + F_C + V_{Cii} + V_{Cji}\right)$$

However, revenue from local residents to the local jurisdiction is neither a gain nor a loss, but simply a local transfer. Similarly, paying for the cost imposed by local travel is also neither a gain nor a loss. The fixed cost of infrastructure (F_I) would have to be paid independent of whether any non-local traffic used that infrastructure. However, local residents who pay for travel in another jurisdiction are non-local there, and generate revenue for the other jurisdiction to the amount of R_{ij}, while imposing cost V_{Iij}.

Note that both the fixed and variable parts of the collection costs are included; in the absence of jurisdictional boundaries (and the desire to collect revenue from out-of-jurisdiction users), the collection costs for tolls would not be necessary. By assumption, the additional costs for collecting transportation taxes are small (zero), since taxes are already collected for other purposes, while tolls are not.

The amount of revenue and cost of collection depends on the method of revenue collection. In the case of taxes collected in jurisdiction i, $R_{ji} = 0$ and $V_{Cii} + V_{Cji} + F_{Ci} = 0$; in the case of taxes collected in the jurisdiction j, $R_{ij} = 0$ and $V_{Cij} + V_{Cjj} + F_{Cj} = 0$. Recall, section to section demand is fixed and independent of cost and therefore proportional to the size of the jurisdiction.

Generically, for two jurisdictions, the payoff (net exchange) matrix can be constructed as shown in Table 7.1. The payoff matrices are shown in Table 7.2 for the three different jurisdiction size pairs: (5,1),(4,2),(3,3).

Table 7.1   Tax/toll game between jurisdictions

		J_j	
		Tax	Toll
J_i	Tax	$[- V_{Iji} + V_{Iij}, - V_{Iij} + V_{Iji}]$	$[- V_{Iji} - R_{ij} + V_{Iij}, R_{ij} - V_{Iij} + V_{Iji}$ $- (V_{Cij} + V_{Cjj} + F_{Cj})]$
	Toll	$[R_{ji} - V_{Iji} + V_{Iij} - (V_{Cii} +$ $V_{Cji} + F_{Ci}), - V_{Iij} - R_{ji} + V_{Iji}]$	$[R_{ji} - V_{Iji} - R_{ij} + V_{Iij} - (V_{Cii} +$ $V_{Cji} + F_{Ci}), R_{ij} - V_{Iij} - R_{ji} + V_{Iji} -$ $(V_{Cij} + V_{Cjj} + F_{Cj})]$

Table 7.2   Example of tax/toll game between jurisdictions

(a) $S_1=1, S_2=5$		J_2	
		Tax	Toll
J_1	Tax	[0,0]	[-5,4]
	Toll	[4,-5]	[-1,-1]*
(b) $S_1=2, S_2=4$		J_2	
		Tax	Toll
J_1	Tax	[0,0]	[-8,7]
	Toll	[7,-8]	[-1,-1]*
(c) $S_1=3, S_2=3$		J_2	
		Tax	Toll
J_1	Tax	[0,0]	[-9,8]
	Toll	[8,-9]	[-1,-1]*

Notes: * indicates equilibrium. [n, n] = [total payoff to jurisdiction 1, total payoff to jurisdiction 2]. Variable infrastructure cost = 6 units per segment (that is, cost proportional to number of travelers). Toll collection costs = 1 unit per tolling jurisdiction (fixed + variable).

This situation is quite analogous to the prisoners' dilemma game (Von Neumann and Morgenstern 1944). Using the above assumptions, it is in the interest of each to 'defect', that is, to use toll financing on a one-time game. If jurisdiction 1 levies a tax, it is in the interest of jurisdiction 2 to levy a toll (and vice versa). If jurisdiction 2 levies a toll, it always is in the interest of jurisdiction 1 to levy a toll. If jurisdiction 1 levies a toll, it is always in the interest of jurisdiction 2 to levy a toll. Tolling is a dominant strategy for each jurisdiction, regardless of what the other does, so long as $R_{ji} > V_{Cii} + V_{Cji} + F_{Ci}$. In other words, a jurisdiction will toll so long as the out-of-jurisdiction revenue exceeds the collection costs. Thus [toll, toll] is the stable equilibrium policy in a one-time game.

In general, the [toll, toll] payoff overall is worse than [tax, tax] since tolls have higher collection costs than taxes. In the case of a one-time game, 'defect' may be the equilibrium solution, but in the case of a repeated game, that is not necessarily the case (Axelrod 1984). The case of a repeated game will be discussed in more depth in a later chapter.

OPTIMAL SPACING OF TOLLS

Certainly toll agencies are not limited to placing toll booths at jurisdiction boundaries, they can be at section boundaries. In this section, the number of jurisdictions is not relevant.

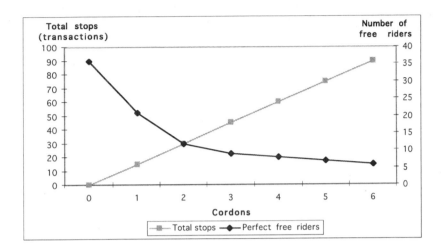

Figure 7.4   Number of cordons, transaction costs, and free riders

Revenue recovery varies with the number of cordons placed on the beltway. Figure 7.4 shows the number of cordons (toll booths), and the number of trips stopped by the cordons. The number not paying is reduced to the minimum (six trips that remain within their section), when the number of cordons is at a maximum (also six). However, there are clearly diminishing returns setting in, with each cordon producing successively fewer new payers. Depending on the cost of a cordon compared with the cost of free-rider losses (and the importance of eliminating intrasectoral cross-subsidies), the optimal number of cordons may be less than the maximum. Figure 7.4 graphs the trade-off, but where the two curves intersect depends on the cost of collection per stop and the cost of having free riders. In any case, as technology reduces the cost of a cordon, the optimal number of cordons increases.

CONCLUSIONS

The analytical model compares taxes and tolls and demonstrates the trade-off between collection costs of toll collection and the number of free riders. In small jurisdictions, tolls have a very high payoff, but as jurisdiction size rises, the payoff declines, perhaps to a point where taxes make economic sense, particularly if the collection costs of tolls are high. The number of free riders declines as jurisdiction size rises when taxes are used. This comports with the empirical evidence that larger jurisdictions are more likely to use tax financing.

This chapter has introduced the analysis of toll versus tax financing, but has made a number of simplifying assumptions. For instance, because demand is considered inelastic, a strict measure of benefit to travelers is not possible. In its stead, the costs of travel consumed in other jurisdictions is used. The next chapter, considering a long road and multiple identical jurisdictions, relaxes this assumption.

NOTE

1. The analysis of financing through a gas tax relies on a large number of behavioral assumptions about where and when gas is purchased, and is not dealt with here.

8. Finance Choice on an Interstate

INTRODUCTION

The previous chapter examined financing on a beltway. The model was simple in that demand was insensitive to price or travel time, jurisdictions were of specific size, jurisdictions could only cover costs, and it was solved with discrete rather than continuous mathematics (algebra rather than calculus). This chapter extends that introductory model by considering an interstate highway that covers multiple jurisdictions, each serving a local objective. As in the previous chapter, the main complication is the joint production and consumption of the key good (network services) by the jurisdiction and its residents. The network operator (jurisdiction) makes the network available while residents consume the network for traveling. Spatial complexity in this problem ensues because jurisdiction residents use both local and non-local networks, and each jurisdiction's network is used by both local and non-local residents. The network is not perfectly competitive and thus retains some monopoly power. The degree of locality in the use of the network directly shapes the local welfare resulting from a particular revenue mechanism, and itself is a function of jurisdiction size. The choice of financing instrument must trade off the number of spatial free riders – system users who do not pay their cost because of the location – and the costs of collection. However, in this chapter, the price charged for a given instrument is limited by the elasticity of demand on those who are charged.

In this chapter a model of network financing is developed which incorporates the basic features of the economic structure of transportation networks. It includes the demand and supply interaction, the choices available to actors (consumers and producers), and the linkage between the two when local residents own the network within their jurisdiction. The idea of decentralized, local control and multiple jurisdictions distinguishes this analysis from one where a central authority maximizes global welfare. The model's theoretical results should be consistent with what is empirically known about network financing. It should thus describe what network financing choices are made under various circumstances.

The central thesis of this book argues that, since jurisdictions try to do well by their residents, who are both voters and travelers, the effects of a revenue instrument on local residents is a key consideration in the choice of that revenue instrument. It is assumed that jurisdictions responsible for network financing behave as if they have the objective of local welfare maximization. Local welfare here reflects the consumers' surplus of residents of the jurisdiction and the profits accruing to the locally controlled network authority that the jurisdiction owns and manages.

Jurisdictions would rather place the burden of financing on non-local travelers in order to maximize local welfare. Therefore, in the case of local control there is a preference to tax through trips and exempt trips which both originate in and are destined for the jurisdiction (locals), thereby allowing locals to be the free riders. The model presented in this chapter provides a strategic framework for assessing the outcome of alternative revenue instruments. This chapter examines the free-rider problem in relation to transaction (toll collection) costs. This model explicitly compares the welfare associated with taxes and those associated with tolls on a simplified network with various jurisdiction sizes. The actions available to network operators and the posited objectives of the two main sets of actors, the network operator (owned by residents) and travelers, are presented. Then, the network geometry of this model is illustrated. The model of flow as a function of trip length and tolls is explained, as is the resultant consumers' surplus. Profit calculations and their component cost and revenue equations are presented. The model is then evaluated using assumed parameters to better understand its implications. Finally, key points, some policy conclusions, and directions for future research are summarized.

ACTIONS AND OBJECTIVES

A jurisdiction is defined as the owner of the road authority responsible for maintaining the road. These jurisdictions, or network operators, have several classes of actions. This research focuses on the selections of a revenue instrument (taxes or tolls) and price or rate (collectively called revenue mechanism). Broadly, the two available revenue instruments are taxes and tolls. As used here, a *toll* (denoted by the tau symbol (τ)) is a fixed sum of money charged for a specific service or privilege (for instance, the right to travel on a link or sub-network). A toll is a fee levied by the road authority as travelers cross a cordon. In contrast, the term *tax* (denoted by the chi symbol (χ)) is defined as a fixed sum of money charged for a general service or privilege, such as the support of government for roads in general, independent of use. A tax is a periodic (for example, annual) fee levied by a jurisdiction on its residents in the form of a poll tax. The distinction between a tax and a toll is in how specific or general the service is which is being provided and how closely it aligns with the revenue mechanism. Thus, a gas tax is more like a toll than is a property, poll, or income tax. Gas taxes are not analysed in this model, as they require the additional complication of determining where, in relation to the home, a driver purchases gasoline.

In general, it is assumed that jurisdictions have the objective of local welfare maximization (max W_L), where welfare is defined narrowly as the sum of profit (loss) from administering the road and consumers' surplus for its residents excluding external costs.

$$\max_{P_I} W_L = \Pi_i + U_i \qquad (1)$$

where:

Π_i = producer's surplus (profit) on network owned by jurisdiction i;

U_i = consumers' surplus (transportation and non-transportation) of residents of jurisdiction i;

P_I = a vector describing price of infrastructure, a function of location of trip origin, destination, location of toll booths, revenue mechanism (including rate of odometer tax, cordon toll, or perfect toll and the basis of that toll), detailed later in the text.

The residents own the network through the jurisdiction. So the jurisdiction which owns the network is comprised of residents who (collectively through their government) can set the policies for the network (revenue mechanism) to achieve a maximization of their own welfare. Because profits are (or can be) redistributed to local residents, revenue in excess of costs from local residents is returned to them. Therefore, treating a jurisdiction and its residents as a single block is not unreasonable.

This model differs from one that treats the network and its users as independent. In that case, the network operator will maximize profit while users will maximize their own utility. Inevitably, the monopolist network operator would raise prices relative to the welfare-maximizing toll and thus result in lower welfare overall. A comparison between various objectives is conducted in the next chapter.

NETWORK GEOMETRY

The network geometry analysed here consists of an infinitely long road, as illustrated in Figure 8.1. There are two types of cordons along the road: *jurisdiction boundaries* and *toll booths*. A *jurisdiction* covers an area that contains, owns, and operates a portion of the road and is located between jurisdiction boundaries. In this model, all jurisdictions are identical in their fundamental features (including size), so one is selected for analysis, called the *jurisdiction of interest* (J_0). The jurisdiction of interest covers the portion of the road between boundary points a and b, so its size is represented by the distance $|b - a|$. All other jurisdictions (to the east and west of J_0) are collectively called the *environment* (E). Jurisdictions to the west of J_0 are denoted by J_{-n}, where n denotes the number of jurisdictions J_{-n} is away from J_0. Similarly jurisdictions to the east of J_0 are denoted by J_{+n}. In the analysis of cordon tolls, it is assumed that all toll booths are located on jurisdiction boundaries, but not that all jurisdiction boundaries necessarily have toll booths. Each jurisdiction that has cordon toll booths has them both at the entrance and at the exit of the jurisdiction.

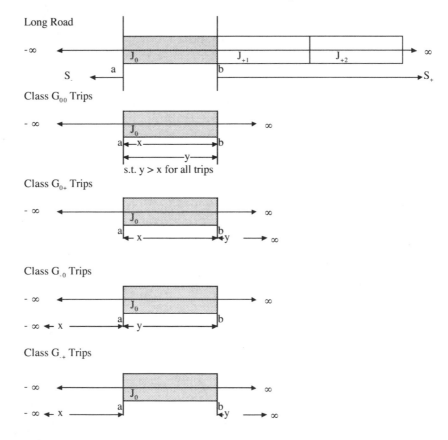

Figure 8.1   One-way, long road and classes of trips

In an intercity context, the geometry represents one jurisdiction (among many) that has authority over its portion of the long road, such as along an interstate highway under the authority of multiple states. In a more general problem, different densities of trip origins and destinations along the road could represent the center and periphery of an urban region.

In order to make the analysis more convenient, *sections* (*S*) will be defined, in this chapter, as aggregations of jurisdictions. For simplicity, three sections are defined: the area comprised of all jurisdictions west of the jurisdiction of interest J_0 $\{J_{-1}, J_{-2} ... \in S_-\}$; the jurisdiction of interest $\{J_0\}$; and the area comprised of all jurisdictions east of J_0 $\{J_{+1}, J_{+2} ... \in S_+\}$.

User *classes* (*G*) are defined as section-to-section (rather than jurisdiction-to-jurisdiction) interactions. In principle the number of section-to-section interactions (classes) is S^2, where S is the number of sections. This chapter analyses a one-way road, but assumes underlying symmetric demand functions, and round trips. On a one-way road, the number of relevant section-to-section interactions is reduced from the number S^2, as trips cannot exit upstream of where they enter. Furthermore, trips that do not travel through J_0 can be eliminated from consideration. Therefore, on a one-way road the three sections define only four section-to-section interactions, the *classes of interest*. The user classes are shown in Table 8.1. For convenience, all jurisdictions are identically sized.

Table 8.1   General trip classification

		Section of	destination	(*y*)
		S_-	J_0	S_+
	S_-	G_{--}	G_{-0}	G_{-+}
Section of origin (*x*)	J_0	G_{0-}	G_{00}	G_{0+}
	S_+	G_{+-}	G_{+0}	G_{++}

Notes: Bold type indicates trip classes of interest on a one-way road.
0 indicates jurisdiction J_0 ; -,+ indicates jurisdiction in S_-,S_+ respectively.

DEMAND

Flow ($f(z)$) across any point (z) on a road can be described by the function below, following and extending Newell (1980):

$$f(z) = \int\limits_{x<z} \int\limits_{y>z} \rho\big(P_T(r, x, y)\big) dx dy \qquad (2)$$

where:

$f(z)$ = flow past point z;

$\rho(\Pi_T(r,x,y))dxdy$ = demand function representing the number of trips that enter the facility between x and $x + dx$ and leave between y and $y + dy$;

$P_T(r,x,y)$ = feneralized cost of travel to users (defined below);

x, y = where trip enters, exits road, $x<y$ (to account for the fact that it is a one-way road);

z = point on the road; and

r = collective toll paid by traveler.

A key assumption is that markets are non-substitutable. This means that there is no cross-elasticity of demand. For instance, trips remaining entirely within J_0 (class G_{00}) are unaffected by price changes by J_{+1}. There remain supply-side effects, so that a change in price by J_+ affects the demand for trips using roads in both J_0 and J_{+1} (such as G_{0+} trips). In turn, this may affect prices faced by travelers in J_0 (say, G_{-0} trips), even if they do not travel in J_{+1}. The following chain of logic can explain this price-demand interdependence. First the optimal tolls in any jurisdiction, including J_0, depend on the demand function for the link. Second, the demand on the link in J_0 depends on the demand of all trip classes using that link. And third, those trip classes that use links in more than one jurisdiction - depend on prices on the links in each jurisdiction.

The argument of the demand function is a weighted sum of the time and money costs of travel. A negative exponential form is used. Therefore, the density function may be rewritten as dependent on the total price users pay (P_T), a decay coefficient (α), as well as a multiplier (δ) representing the number of trips generated per unit length.

$$\rho(P_T(r, x, y)) = \delta e^{\alpha P_T(r,x,y)} \qquad (3)$$

The total price users pay for travel (P_T) is the sum of several components. Direct infrastructure charges (P_I) transferred to the network operators depend on the revenue policy selected by each jurisdiction (cordon tolls or general taxes). In general, the price of infrastructure is a function of the rate of cordon toll (r_τ) and the quantity over which each unit rate is applied (number of tolls crossed). The price of infrastructure can be decomposed into the price inside J_0 and the price outside J_0, which are summed to attain the price paid by users. This decomposition enables a clear analysis of situations where a jurisdiction employs one policy while the environment imposes another. Under a general tax policy, user payment for infrastructure is independent of the amount or location of travel. The rate of toll paid to a jurisdiction that imposes taxes is 0 for all user groups. A toll policy is more complicated than a general tax policy, as tolls affect demand while taxes do not. In the case of cordon tolls, direct infrastructure charges transferred to the network operators depend on the location of the origin and destination, that is, an incidence matrix ($I(x,y,n)$) which represents whether toll booth n is crossed for trips between x and y. Infrastructure charges also depend on the toll per crossing ($r_{\tau v}$), which is a policy variable available to the various jurisdictions. This is illustrated in Figure 8.2.

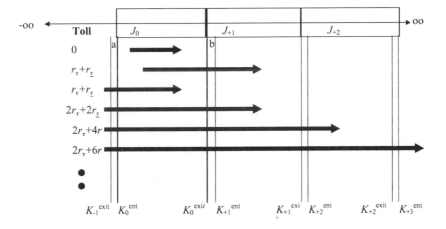

Figure 8.2   Tolls by location of origin and destination

Private vehicle costs (P_V), depend on the distance traveled ($|y - x|$), the cost per unit distance (v) as well as a number of fixed components (ζ) depending on the age and type of vehicle used.

Freeflow travel time costs (P_F) depend on trip length ($|y - x|$) and freeflow speed (S_F), as well as the value of time (V_T). Congested travel time is not dealt with here. Implicit in this model is that jurisdictions have the obligation of maintaining a level of service with a resulting freeflow speed consistent with congested speeds. Thus 'congestion effects' are ascribed to infrastructure costs which are proportional to traffic flow (described in the cost section).

To simplify the analysis, there are no economies or diseconomies of scale and infrastructure costs increase smoothly and continuously. External costs are also excluded, since by definition they do not figure into the calculations of the network operator.

$$P_T = P_I + P_V + P_F = \sum_{n=1}^{\infty} r_{\tau n}\left[I(x,y,n)\right] + \left(\zeta + \upsilon|y - x|\right) + V_T\left(\frac{|y - x|}{S_F}\right) \tag{4}$$

where:

$I(x,y,n)$ = toll incidence matrix, where: $I(x,y,n) = 1$ if $x < L(n) < y$, and
   $I(x,y,n) = 0$ otherwise, and $L(n)$ = location of toll booth n;
n = index of toll booths along road;
$r_{\tau n}$ = rate of toll at toll crossing n;
S_F = freeflow speed;
V_T = value of time;
x, y = where trip enters, exits road;
υ = private variable cost (per unit length); and
ζ = private fixed vehicle cost.

CONSUMERS' SURPLUS

The sum of transportation consumers' surplus for all trips originating in jurisdiction J_0 (U_0) for the two relevant user classes ($U_{00} + U_{0+}$) is given by the following equation:

$$U_0 = U_{00} + U_{0+} \tag{5}$$

$$= \int_a^b\int_x^b\int_r^{\infty}\rho\big(P_T(p,x,y)\big)dpdydx + \sum_{n=1}^{\infty}\int_a^b\int_{n(b-a)}^{(n+1)(b-a)}\int_r^{\infty}\rho\big(P_T(p,x,y)\big)dpdydx$$

where:

U_0 = consumer's surplus of trips originating in J_0;
U_{00}, U_{0+} = consumer's surplus for trips of G_{00} and G_{0+};
$\rho(\Pi_T(p,x,y))dxdy$ = demand function;
$P_T(p,x,y)$ = generalized cost of travel to users at price p;
n = index for number of toll booths on road;
a,b = jurisdiction J_0 cordon locations; and
p = user monetary cost (integrated from r to infinity).

The rate of cordon toll that is assessed by jurisdictions on trips of the appropriate group is multiplied by the basis over which the rate is assessed to compute the price paid (P_l). Local trips (G_{00}) do not pay cordon tolls (because they do not cross the toll cordon). Cordon tolls on locally originating, non-locally destined trips (G_{0+}) are assessed both by the home jurisdiction (J_0 assesses a toll rate r_τ) and by other jurisdictions (which assess a toll rate $r_{\underline{\tau}}$). Because jurisdictions are identical, the effective price under identical policies (and toll-setting behavior) is identical across jurisdictions.

Technically speaking, each x–y pair is a distinct market (rather than defining each section-to-section pair as a distinct market). The x–y pair thus has its consumers' surplus measured before it is aggregated with other x–y pairs. This requires integrating over the range of tolls for each flow, and then integrating all the resulting consumers' surpluses over the relevant spaces. Fortunately, by Fubini's Theorem, so long as a function is continuous over real space, the order of integration of a double (or triple, etc.) integral does not matter. So the results would be the same, independent of how the markets are defined.

PROFIT

Profit or producers surplus (Π_i) is defined below as total revenue from tolls (R_T) minus total (fixed and variable) costs (C_T):

$$\Pi_i = R_T - C_T \tag{6}$$

where:

Π_i = profit to jurisdiction i;
R_T = total revenue from tolls;
C_T = total cost.

Any loss is by definition made up from general taxes, and any profit is used to reduce them. Therefore, the impact of general taxes to support roads on welfare can be measured in terms of the profit or loss of the network operator. Because general taxes and transportation demand are assumed to be independent, taxes do not need to be measured explicitly.

COST

Total costs to the network operator (C_T) are an increasing function of jurisdiction size (C_S), traffic flow (C_ρ), and variable and fixed toll collections (C_{CV}, C_{CF}). The model is linear; there are no (dis-)economies of scale or scope. The assumption of no economies of scale is roughly consistent with Chapter 3.

The first cost category, cost as a function of jurisdiction size, can be considered analogous to a fixed cost. It depends only on the size of the jurisdiction $|b - a|$ and the cost per unit distance (γ) of constructing and operating infrastructure. The second cost category, cost as a function of traffic flow, depends on the vehicle distance traveled in the jurisdiction, which is multiplied by a cost per vehicle distance traveled (ϕ). Because it is assumed the network is sized to ensure a given (uncongested) level of service, the cost as a function of traffic flow is a composite of infrastructure capital and operating and maintenance costs. While the first cost category is determined by the length of the road, the second is determined in part by the width of the road necessary to ensure a particular level of service. The third and fourth cost categories are the variable and fixed costs of collecting tolls. The variable cost depends on the number of toll booths (K_i) maintained by jurisdiction i and flow at each toll booth k, $f(k)$, as well as the cost per collection transaction (θ). The fixed portion simply multiplies a fixed cost per toll booth (κ) by the number of toll booths in the jurisdiction (which is 0 in the case of general taxes and 2 in the case of cordon tolls). The model can be expressed as follows:

$$C_T = C_S + C_\rho + C_{CV} + C_{CF} \tag{7}$$

$$= \gamma|b - a| + \phi\int_a^b f(z)\,dz + \theta\sum_{k=1}^{K_i} f(k) + \kappa K_i$$

where:

C_T = total cost;
C_S = fixed cost of jurisdiction size;
C_ρ = variable cost of traffic flow;
C_{CV} = variable cost of toll collection;
C_{CF} = index for number of toll booths on road;
a,b = cordon boundary locations;
$\gamma, \phi, \theta, \kappa$ = cost coefficients;
z = point on road;
$f(z)$ = traffic flow across point z;
k = index of toll booths in jurisdiction i;
$f(k)$ = traffic flow across toll booth k; and
K_i = total number of toll booths in jurisdiction i.

REVENUE

Revenue depends on the specific instrument chosen, the rate, and the quantity. For instance the revenue from tolls (R_T) collected at toll booths in jurisdiction i (K_i) ($k=1, ..., K_i$) on the road is given below. In the case of jurisdiction-based cordon tolls, $K_i=2$ (a and b).

$$R_T = r_\tau \sum_{k=1}^{K_i} f(k) \qquad (8)$$

where:
  R_T = total revenue (\$);
  r_t = rate of toll (\$/crossing);
  k = index of toll booths in jurisdiction i;
  $f(k)$ = traffic flow across toll booth k; and
  K_I = total number of toll booths in jurisdiction i.

MATHEMATICAL SOLUTION

The discussion to date still leaves some latitude for solving the tactical problem of determining the rate of toll. The issue, in solving for the J_0's toll (r_τ), is what does J_0 assume the other jurisdictions use as a toll (r_τ) when it is known what policy they choose. For convenience, all other jurisdictions are imposing identical policies (either all tax or all toll), although not necessarily the same policy as J_0. A non-cooperative Nash equilibrium for toll-setting, which assumes no collusion (implicit or otherwise) between jurisdictions, is sought. This means that J_0 can do no better by changing its toll given what all other jurisdictions do, while each other jurisdiction can also do no better. This does not necessarily result in the best satisfaction of the objective function, but it is sustainable.

An iterative approach solves this equilibrium, (employing a macro and the solver algorithm of a standard spreadsheet software package). For each iteration, J_0 sets its payoff-maximizing toll as if the tolls in other jurisdictions are fixed. Under that constraint, the best assumption J_0 can make is that the other jurisdictions are using their last posted toll. Their last posted toll happens to be the toll previously solved for by J_0, since all jurisdictions are identical, and simultaneously performing these calculations.

Table 8.2   Model equations by category

Group	Equation
Variable Collection Costs (C_{CV})	
G_{00}	0
G_{0+} G_{-0}	$\theta \delta w^2 v^2 \dfrac{u e^{\alpha\left(r_\tau + r_{\underline{\tau}}\right)}(1-t)^2}{\left(1 - te^{\alpha 2 r_{\underline{\tau}}}\right)}$
G_{-+}	$\theta \delta w^2 v^2 \dfrac{u e^{\alpha 2\left(r_\tau + r_{\underline{\tau}}\right)}\left(-1 - t^2\right)}{\left(1 - te^{\alpha 2\left(r_{\underline{\tau}}\right)}\right)^2}$
Fixed Collection Costs (C_{CF})	
All	$\kappa K_{\underline{\tau}}$
Variable Network Costs (C_r)	
G_{00}	$\varphi \delta w^3 v^3 u(t\ln(t) + \ln(t) - 2t + 2)$
G_{0+} G_{-0}	$\dfrac{-\varphi \delta w^3 v^3 (1+t)(-1 + \ln(t))u e^{\alpha\left(r_\tau + r_{\underline{\tau}}\right)}(1-t)}{\left(1 - te^{\alpha 2 r_{\underline{\tau}}}\right)}$
G_{-+}	$\varphi \delta (b-a) w^2 v^2 \dfrac{u e^{\alpha 2\left(r_\tau + r_{\underline{\tau}}\right)}\left(-1 - t^2\right)}{\left(1 - te^{\alpha 2\left(r_{\underline{\tau}}\right)}\right)^2}$
Fixed Network Costs (C_S)	
All	$\gamma w v \ln(t)$
Toll Revenue (R)	
G_{00}	0
G_{-0}, G_{0+}	$r_\tau \delta w^2 v^2 \dfrac{u e^{\alpha\left(r_\tau + r_{\underline{\tau}}\right)}(1-t)^2}{\left(1 - te^{\alpha 2 r_{\underline{\tau}}}\right)}$
G_{-+}	$2 r_\tau \delta w^2 v^2 \dfrac{u e^{\alpha 2\left(r_\tau + r_{\underline{\tau}}\right)}\left(-1 - t^2\right)}{\left(1 - te^{\alpha 2\left(r_{\underline{\tau}}\right)}\right)^2}$
Consumers' Surplus (U)	
G_{00}	$\delta w^3 v^2 u(1 - t + \ln(t))$
G_{0+}	$\dfrac{-\delta}{\alpha} w^2 v^2 \dfrac{u e^{\alpha\left(r_\tau + r_{\underline{\tau}}\right)}(1-t)^2}{\left(1 - te^{\alpha 2 r_{\underline{\tau}}}\right)}$
G_{-0} G_{-+}	0

where: $v = \dfrac{1}{\psi}$; $w = \dfrac{1}{\alpha}$; $t = e^{\alpha\psi\left|b - a\right|}$; $u = e^{\alpha z}$; *and* $\psi = v + \dfrac{V_T}{Sf}$.

Note: r_τ = toll set by J_0, $r_{\underline{\tau}}$ = toll set by all other jurisdictions.

To translate this into an algorithm: during solution round (i), J_0 assumes that $r_{\underline{\tau}}$ is equal to J_0's toll in solution round $i-1$: $r_{\underline{\tau}}^i = r_\tau^{i-1}$ The algorithm says: given $r_{\underline{\tau}}$ and all the other pertinent variables, J_0 finds the welfare-maximizing r_τ, updates $r_{\underline{\tau}}$, and solves until equilibrium ($r_\tau{}^* = r_{\underline{\tau}}{}^*$).

The reduced-form solutions of the model components are given in Table 8.2. Table 8.3 shows the underlying assumptions about the rate of toll in J_0 (r_τ) and in the other jurisdictions (the environment) ($r_{\underline{\tau}}$) under the various J_0 policy and environment conditions.

In the case of cordon tolls, as the size of jurisdiction J_0 increases the total number of trips crossing cordon a remains the same or increases, and the ratio of non-through to through trips increases. As b gets farther from a, the number of trips crossing both a and b decreases, and the negative effect (finance externality) of a toll at b on traffic crossing a declines. Any trip going the distance $|y-x|$ is more likely to take place if it crosses one toll booth rather than two. Similarly, as jurisdiction size increases, the number of trips originating in or destined for jurisdiction J_0 increase. However, the number of non-local trips approaches a limit (the maximum flow past the cordon), while local trips increase with jurisdiction size.

EVALUATION

The toll which maximizes welfare can be found by solving the welfare maximization problem, that is, by setting the first derivative of the welfare expression to zero and solving for the toll. As can be seen from the slew of equations described above, this is a rather long expression in its full (expanded) form.

Perhaps a more comprehensible way to understand what is going on is by examining some illustrations of how welfare changes as certain factors are altered. The underlying assumptions are given in Table 8.4, developed from empirical studies of travel cost described in Chapter 3. Any changes to those assumptions are discussed in the text. Briefly, the cost of vehicle ownership was estimated directly from the economic value that cars lose as they age and are driven. A value of time of $10 per hour, consistent with other studies, and a free-flow speed of 100 kph, typical of highway travel, were assumed. The variable α was estimated from a gravity model for the Washington DC region (Levinson and Kumar 1995). Toll collection costs were estimated using data from bridges in California. Network costs were estimated based on highway expenditure data collected from the states by the Federal Highway Administration.

Table 8.4   Baseline scenario: empirical values of model coefficients

Variable	Description	Value
Zeta (ζ)	Fixed cost of vehicle ownership ($/veh-trip)	1.23
Psi (ψ)	$v + V_T / S_F$ variable cost of travel ($/vkt)	0.15
Alpha (α)	Coefficient relating demand to price	-1
Delta (δ)	Total demand multiplier (trips)	180
Kappa (κ)	Fixed collection cost ($/toll booth/hour)	$90
Gamma (γ)	Fixed network cost ($/km)	0
Theta (θ)	Variable collection cost ($/vehicle)	0.08
Phi (ϕ)	Variable network cost ($/vkt)	0.018

Figure 8.3 shows how welfare changes in J_0 as it varies its toll, keeping fixed jurisdiction size (at 10 km) and all other factors, and assuming, first, that all other jurisdictions employ a tax, and second, that they all employ a toll. Tolls of zero are computed both with and without collection costs for comparison. Higher welfare is found without collection costs, a toll of value zero is equivalent to a tax policy in the absence of collection costs. Here (with $0.05 increments on the graph), the welfare-maximizing toll can be read as $0.70, lower than the profit-maximizing toll ($1.10). This reflects that consumers' surplus and profit are included in the welfare objective function. The serial (complementary) nature of the network creates interactions that do not necessarily exist in a strictly competitive market analysis. Welfare can remain positive despite the lack of cost recovery, suggesting that, under certain circumstances, welfare maximization may result from a combination of cordon tolls and tax financing used to subsidize roads. At low tolls, costs exceed revenues (at very high tolls, costs exceed revenues as well). Here, however, the optimum toll rate generates a positive profit, which, as explained above, is returned to the jurisdiction's residents through reduced taxes or a direct payout.

In the all-toll environment, the welfare and welfare-maximizing tolls of a given jurisdiction depend upon the tolls of other jurisdictions. The tactical, toll-setting problem is solved by assuming that jurisdictions do not cooperate. This gives the Nash equilibrium toll, which is necessary to find the Nash equilibrium policy. At the Nash equilibrium toll, the tolls set by all jurisdictions will be the same. To find the Nash equilibrium value, it is assumed that all jurisdictions other than J_0 charge the same toll, and find the value for that toll such that J_0's welfare-maximizing toll takes the same value. Observe (by comparing the tax and toll environments) that for any toll level, the welfare attained by J_0 is less when other jurisdictions are charging tolls. At low toll values, the welfare difference is dominated by consumers' surplus, reflecting the payments that J_0's residents are making to other jurisdictions. At high toll levels, profit disparities predominate, since the tolls in other jurisdictions are suppressing lucrative toll crossings at J_0. However the welfare-maximizing toll in the all-tax environment is approximately the same ($0.70) as that in the all-toll environment. This implies that the system is fairly stable, and that tolls in one jurisdiction will not fluctuate significantly as a result of road finance mechanism changes in other jurisdictions.

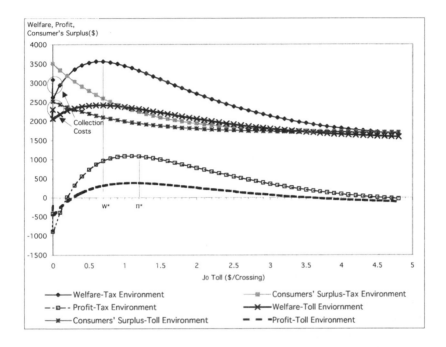

Note: Jurisdiction size = 10 km, baseline empirical values.

Figure 8.3   Welfare in J_0 as a function of J_0 Toll

Under the tax regime, it is fairly clear that to achieve a maximum of local (transportation and non-transportation) welfare while still recovering costs, the rate of taxes must be set such that total revenue equals total costs. The total welfare associated with a tax policy in an all-tax environment thus rises linearly with jurisdiction size. Because the environment and J_0 have identical policies, neither of which affects travel demand, there is no per capita variation in welfare, cost, or consumers' surplus. The horizontal line in Figure 8.4 (denoted by 'W-Tax/km'), which displays the welfare resulting from both tax and toll policies in an all-tax environment, illustrates this.

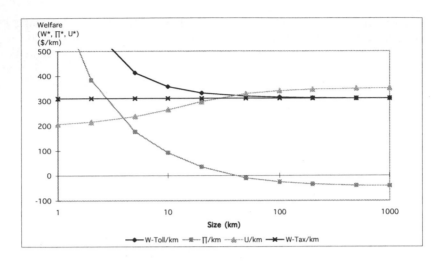

Figure 8.4   Welfare in J_0 at welfare-maximizing tolls versus jurisdiction size in an all-tax environment

Figure 8.4 also shows how welfare (W-Toll), profit (Π), and consumers' surplus (*U*) vary with jurisdiction size under a cordon toll policy in J_0 and an all-tax environment. Total welfare increases simply because the number of trips (and thus consumers' surplus) increases. Per capita transportation consumers' surplus increases with size as the effective price falls (more and more trips are local and thus pay no toll). This happens because the proportion of non-toll-paying local trips increases relative to the toll-paying, boundary-crossing trips. However this increase in consumers' surplus with jurisdiction size does not offset the loss due to a leveling off of revenue and a steady increase in cost. Thus per capita welfare declines despite the increase in total welfare. This graph indicates that small jurisdictions have a higher per capita payoff from tolls than larger jurisdictions, and thus a greater incentive to toll. This policy is profitable for jurisdictions of up to almost 50 km in length, similar in size to a metropolitan area.

A key point to note is that welfare remains positive despite the fact that costs exceed revenue. This indicates that a mixed financing system of taxes and tolls maximizes welfare even when cordon tolls cannot be relied on to finance the roads alone. Total costs increase non-linearly with jurisdiction size because travel demand increases when the share of trips paying tolls decreases. It should be noted further that a toll policy always results in greater per capita welfare than a tax policy in the all-tax environment. To see this, compare the curve denoted '*W*-toll/km' with '*W*-Tax/km'. However, the differences get smaller as jurisdiction size gets larger.

It might be noted that the choice of toll does not affect welfare very much in the neighborhood of the optimum value. This suggests a certain robustness of the results, and the importance of getting the answer nearly rather than exactly right. The robustness follows from the offsetting factors – local welfare and total demand decline with increases in tolls especially in a toll environment but revenue per toll-payer rises. Still, being far from the optimal value will result in significant welfare loss.

Figure 8.5 illustrates the welfare over a range of jurisdiction sizes in a toll environment. The curve denoted 'W-tax/km' illustrates the case when jurisdiction J_0 imposes taxes. While welfare rises with jurisdiction size, it does so at a decreasing rate. This is so because, as jurisdictions get larger, the impact of other jurisdictions on local welfare diminishes, and non-local policies affect a smaller proportion of locally originating trips. So the curves in very large jurisdictions approach those of a tax policy in an all-tax environment. It should be noted that welfare is negative at very small jurisdiction sizes, indicating the cost of the road outweighs its benefits.

The curves representing the welfare (W-toll), consumers' surplus (U), and profit (Π) from a cordon toll policy in an all-cordon toll environment are also shown in Figure 8.5. Welfare is maximized in the largest jurisdictions here, rising continuously at a decreasing rate. The cordon toll policy tracks closely (though is always slightly greater than) the welfare resulting from a tax policy in this environment. Again welfare is negative at very small jurisdiction sizes, though higher than the tax policy case, suggesting a very high finance externality. This scenario is profitable for jurisdictions over a limited range of jurisdiction sizes (from about 2 km to above 20 km). This peaked shape is due to the interaction of jurisdictions. Closely spaced toll booths (found in small jurisdictions) have a much greater finance externality than a farther spacing, so demand for longer trips increases with spacing of toll booths. However, profit declines for larger jurisdictions because revenue reaches a maximum while costs increase steadily. The welfare increase indicates that the rise in consumers' surplus outweighs the decrease in profit.

Comparing the welfare over the range of jurisdiction sizes under the assumptions outlined above for the four strategies, the highest welfare is attained by imposing tolls when others impose taxes (all-tax environment), followed by imposing taxes in the all-tax environment, imposing tolls in the all-cordon toll environment, and imposing taxes in the all-cordon toll environment. In the larger jurisdictions (above 100 km in length) the welfare measurements are very close and almost independent of policy. However, imposing tolls always beats imposing taxes in either environment.

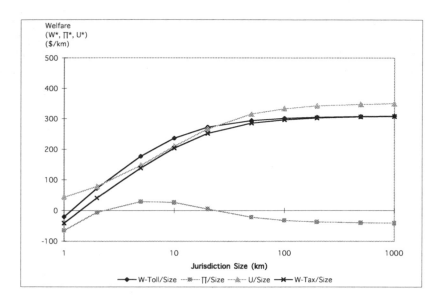

Figure 8.5   Welfare in J_0 at welfare-maximizing tolls versus jurisdiction size in an all-toll environment

POLICY SELECTION

Four cases describe a jurisdiction's possible strategic decision with regard to tax or toll policy:

- always tax;
- always toll;
- mixed (do the opposite): toll when everyone else is taxing, but tax when everyone else is tolling; and
- mixed (do the same): tax when everyone else is taxing, but toll when everyone else is tolling.

Three of the four cases appear in the range of data examined below. Clearly the mixed solution 'do the opposite' is not, in and of itself, stable. If every jurisdiction is supposed to toll when others tax and tax when others toll, they will flail about in their policy selection. Rather, a certain fraction of jurisdictions invoking one policy and the rest the other is more likely to be stable. The solution 'do the same' has at least two stable points, everyone taxing and everyone tolling, although which will be achieved depends on the evolution of the system, or perhaps on which gives higher welfare, depending on the behavior ascribed to the decision-makers and the process they employ.

The fixed collection costs (C_{CF}') are computed to equate tax and toll policies under each environment, where welfare from tolling equals the welfare from taxing under the all-tax environment ($W_{\tau\chi} = W_{\chi\chi}$), and the all-cordon toll environment ($W_{\tau\tau} = W_{\chi\tau}$). The equations in the case of the all-tax environment are given below (the equations in the all-cordon toll environment are similar):

$$W_{\tau\chi} + C_{CF} - C_{CF}' - W_{\chi\chi} = 0 \qquad (9)$$

$$C_{CF}' = W_{\tau\chi} + C_{CF} - W_{\chi\chi}$$

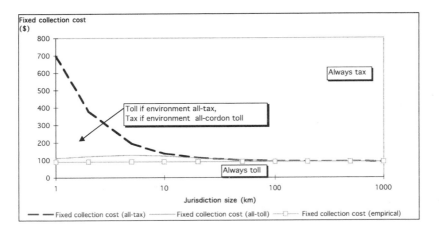

Figure 8.6   Policy choice as a function of fixed collection costs and jurisdiction size

Figure 8.6 illustrates policy selection as fixed collection costs (per jurisdiction) and jurisdiction sizes vary. The figure shows that when fixed collection costs (from both the entry and exit toll booths) are high, jurisdictions should (in the interest of maximizing local welfare as defined here) *always tax* (regardless of what other jurisdictions do); when they are low, jurisdictions should *always toll*. Small jurisdictions, basically below 20 km in length, also have a large mixed solution for collection costs between $100 and $700, of *tax when other jurisdictions toll and toll when other jurisdictions tax*. The exact threshold where a policy shifts from being '*always tax*' to '*tax when other jurisdictions toll and toll when other jurisdictions tax*' varies with jurisdiction size. Two factors influence the location of this threshold. First, large jurisdictions spread fixed collection costs over a larger number of users. Second, small jurisdictions suffer a finance externality from other jurisdictions' tolls. There is a large range of values where the policy choice depends on the behavior of neighboring jurisdictions. Because tolling when everyone else taxes is not a stable equilibrium among identical jurisdictions, the mixed region suggests a mixed set of policies. Thus some proportion of jurisdictions tax and others toll in order to arrive at a stable equilibrium. As jurisdiction size gets larger, the '*always tax*' area gets larger (takes effect at a lower fixed collection cost). The '*always toll*' region is relatively flat with jurisdiction size.

Policy choice as a function of variable collection costs is more complicated than as a function of fixed collection costs. Although tolls are independent of fixed collection costs, they depend on variable collection costs (and thus the variable θ). Similar to the case of fixed collection costs, the variable cost coefficient (θ') where welfare from tolling equals the welfare from taxing under both the all-tax and the all-cordon toll environment must be computed. The equations for the all-tax environment are (the equations in the all-cordon toll environment are similar):

$$Let \quad C'_{CV} = \frac{C_{CV}}{\theta} \tag{10}$$

$$W_{\tau\chi} + C_{CV} - C'_{CV} * \theta' - W_{\chi\chi} = 0$$

$$\theta' = \frac{W_{\tau\chi} + C_{CV} - W_{\chi\chi}}{C'_{CV}}$$

Figure 8.7 shows the results where the welfare is calculated using the collection costs (θ') which are consistent with the welfare-maximizing tolls resulting from those collection costs. This calculation uses a recursion procedure to solve for both the welfare-maximizing toll and the collection costs necessary to equalize the welfare from toll and from tax policies. It was not possible to obtain solutions in all cases, for instance, the points not shown on the figure. Examining the variable collection costs, both curves are downward sloping. The lower the collection costs, the more likely it is that a jurisdiction will toll, but the larger the jurisdiction size, the more likely it will tax. The estimate of collection costs using conventional technology (estimated from California data) falls below the two results for all values of jurisdiction size. This indicates that with the baseline scenario the always toll solution is expected, consistent with the one-shot game described in a previous section and consistent with the results for fixed collection costs. In practice, given equal collection costs, large states are less likely to toll than small states. This result confirms the expectation that the two curves will be downward sloping (the '*always toll*' area gets smaller and the '*always tax*' area gets larger as jurisdiction size increases) for both fixed and variable costs. The figure also shows the tolls consistent with the collection costs necessary to equate the welfare from tax and toll policies. It is interesting that the tolls are decreasing with jurisdiction size.

This is at odds with the previous cases, where the coefficient for variable collection costs did not vary.

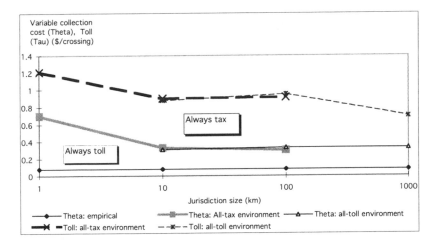

Figure 8.7 Policy choice as a function of variable collection costs and jurisdiction size.

GOVERNMENT HIERARCHY

The information generated permits an examination of the consequences of larger or smaller governments. This is analogous to the serial monopolist problem, where the toll paid by a traveler using two serial monopolists over an area is more than if the area were under the control of a single monopolist.

Table 8.5 summarizes the welfare-maximizing tolls from the analysis above of a toll policy in an all-cordon toll environment as jurisdiction size varies. For instance, traveling 20 km through two 10 km jurisdictions, a traveler pays four tolls of $0.65 ($2.60) each. However, traveling 20-km through one 20 km jurisdiction, the traveler pays only two tolls of $0.68 each ($1.36), much less.

Table 8.5 also summarizes the welfare for the case of a toll policy in an all-cordon toll environment. Here, more total welfare is generated for one government of 20 km than the sum of two 10 km governments. For this case, the consolidation of jurisdictions eliminates a finance externality, and thus increases welfare. However, under a different scenario (for instance lower collection costs), the welfare gains from a reduction in the finance externality may be outweighed by the efficiency gains from a reduction in free riders associated with closer toll booths.

Table 8.5   Comparison of tolls and welfare for different jurisdiction sizes

Jurisdiction Size (km)	Toll ($)	Welfare ($)
10	0.65	2367
2 X 10	1.30	4734
20	0.68	5451

Source: Author's analysis of toll policy for J_0 and all-cordon toll environment

Here there are no diseconomies of scale associated with higher levels of government. However, two particular issues should be kept in mind. First, higher government levels have a broader span of control, so for the same number of managers, each area gets less attention, or more levels of management must be appointed. This can be more costly than local governance. Second, logrolling in a political environment can be a problem when resources need to be allocated centrally to numerous constituencies. Logrolling can lead to inefficient investments, as the incentives for efficiently managing other people's money are less than those for managing one's own. If economies of scale in the provision of networks do exist for a particular facility type, the lower costs with a higher level of government may offset these administrative inefficiencies. The presence of scale economies would thus make it harder to implement tolls.

SENSITIVITY TO MODEL COEFFICIENTS

This section examines the sensitivity of the basic welfare measures to model coefficients, under standardized assumptions of a local welfare maximization objective, a 10 km jurisdiction size, a toll policy and an all-cordon toll environment where jurisdictions employ non-cooperative toll-setting. Each of the variables is examined over a range of coefficient values approximately centered upon the default values developed in Table 8.4. Table 8.6 summarizes the elasticity about the mean for each of the key variables. The elasticity is found by calculating the change in welfare (revenue, cost, consumers' surplus, and profit) over the difference between two values of the variable in question, where one value is the mean, and the other is a 1% increment on the mean.

Table 8.6   Elasticity about mean

	Variable	Welfare	Revenue	Cost	Consumers' Surplus	Profit
|Alpha|	Sensitivity of demand to cost	−3.070	−3.437	-1.758	-2.785	−5.320
Delta	Density of trip origins	1.038	1.000	0.699	1.000	1.337
Zeta	Private fixed costs	−0.424	−1.150	-0.498	-0.239	−1.879
Psi	Sensitivity of demand to trip length	−0.094	−0.143	-0.119	-0.065	−0.156
Gamma	Fixed costs associated with network length	−0.044	0.000	0.250	0.000	−0.596
Phi	Variable cost associated with network use	−0.049	−0.028	0.277	−0.017	−0.251
Theta	variable collection costs	-0.016	-0.013	0.053	-0.009	-0.065

Note: Elasticity of welfare (revenue, cost, consumers' surplus, profit) about mean of alpha (delta, zeta, psi, gamma, phi, theta*).*

First, the sensitivity of demand to cost in general, the variable alpha (α), is evaluated over a range of values (recall the default value of –1). Clearly, as expected from inspection of the model, as alpha increases in absolute value, welfare, revenue, cost, and consumers' surplus drop.

Second, the density of trip origins, the variable delta (δ), is evaluated with a default value of 180. As the density of trips increases, total welfare, consumers' surplus, revenue, and cost rise. Under the model, the more trips, the higher the welfare, because there is no offsetting congestion factor.

Third, private fixed costs per trip, the elasticity for the variable zeta (ζ), is computed with a default value of 1.23. As might be expected, as this cost rises, welfare, costs, revenue, and consumers' surplus drop.

The fourth variable, psi (ψ), which is the sensitivity of demand to trip length |y–x|, has a default value of 0.018. As sensitivity increases, welfare, revenue, cost, and consumers' surplus decrease.

The fifth variable, gamma (γ), is the coefficient on jurisdiction size (in $/km) in the cost equation. Recall that fixed costs equal to zero in the analyses in previous sections. As gamma rises, costs rise (by definition) and welfare falls continuously. However, only as costs approach $100 per linear kilometer per hour do they noticeably influence the welfare indicators. Revenue and consumers' surplus remain unchanged, because this variable does not affect tolls.

The sixth variable, phi (ϕ), reflects the variable cost to the jurisdiction as a function of vehicle flow, with a default value of \$0.018/vkt. As the variable cost increases, per capita cost increases (again, by definition), and welfare, consumers' surplus, and profit fall. Interestingly, revenue peaks at a value of about \$0.10/vkt; as costs rise, so do tolls, but above a certain point, the tolls are sufficiently high to drive away the significant amount of toll-paying (interjurisdictional) traffic.

Finally, consider theta (θ), the variable cost of toll collection as a function of flow past the toll booth, with a default value of \$0.08/trip. As this coefficient increases, welfare and consumers' surplus fall. Costs rise up to \$0.20, and then fall, as the increase in welfare-maximizing tolls drives away more traffic (and thus reduces costs) than the increase in variable collection costs increases costs.

CONCLUSIONS

While many jurisdictions do not actually consider their choice of revenue mechanism, they probably should. Changes in technology and funding sources warrant a reconsideration of the standard financing mechanisms. The purpose of this chapter was to develop a model to explain whether jurisdictions choose to tax or to toll as a function of the length of trips, the size of the jurisdiction, the transaction costs of collecting revenue, demand, and the cost of providing infrastructure. In short, the intent was to help frame the analysis of how jurisdictions have historically considered, albeit in a more complex and less mathematical environment, and may in the future consider, the choice of revenue mechanism.

Large jurisdictions are more likely to impose taxes or a mixed financing policy than only-cordon tolls, because cordon tolls raise insufficient revenues to cover costs, as revenue levels off above a certain point. Similarly, the higher the cost of collecting tolls, the less likely tolls will be the preferred revenue mechanism. The welfare-maximizing toll may not fully recover costs, and still require subsidy. The maximum welfare from taxes may exceed that of tolls under certain circumstances, depending on model parameters. However, if jurisdictions are sufficiently small, demand sufficiently high, and collection costs relatively low, then tolls will be preferred. Chapter 4, which examined the financing behavior of US states, has corroborated the result that small states are more likely to toll. In that work, it was found that states which import proportionately more workers (typically the smaller east coast states) tend to have a higher share of state highway revenue from tolls than other states.

The gains to a jurisdiction of imposing tolls exceed the gains from taxes under certain circumstances. The gains come foremost from residents of other jurisdictions. This problem, a finance externality, is well known in certain cases, for instance the reliance of local governments on some mix of sales, income, and property taxes, each of which are borne by a different set of people, not all of whom are local.

Congestion pricing has long been a goal of transport economists, who argue that it will result in more efficient use of resources. The path for implementing such a system has been strewn with political potholes, as pricing inevitably creates winners and losers. An alternative approach, one that would create the local winners necessary to implement road pricing, is required before congestion pricing can be expected to become widespread. This research suggests one approach, one that would decentralize the decision about whether to tax or toll before attempting to impose road pricing. Road pricing is a necessary prerequisite to congestion pricing. Imposing congestion pricing on already tolled roads is not nearly as difficult a problem as placing tolls on untolled roads in the first place. And tolls are a rational financing mechanism for a sufficiently small jurisdiction, particularly with the advent of electronic toll collection systems.

The prospects for future success of toll roads depend on several factors, including the relative centralization of control of the highway sector and the transaction costs of collecting revenue. Factors that would be conducive to a return to turnpikes are a reduction in collection costs and a decentralization of authority. Should the governance become more decentralized, and collection costs continue to drop, tolls could return to prominence as the preferred means of financing roads for both local and intercity travel.

The analysis presented herein is a simplified representation of reality. The network geometry, while representative of certain stylized cases without parallel competitive roads, certainly does not reflect all conditions. However, it does represent, in a manner, cases such as the northeast corridor of the United States where parallel roads are controlled by the same government. Future research should be directed toward a more general network formulation of the model, where links or sets of links within the network are governed collectively.

The analysis also excludes the effect of tolls on land values. Economic theory dictates that higher tolls will lead to lower property value. Because of the structure this chapter imposes, a jurisdiction's toll falls on residents and non-residents alike. So if a jurisdiction tolls, its immediate neighbors on the network cannot gain a competitive advantage regarding commercial location by not tolling. Tolls will lead to a greater share of local (non-boundary-crossing) trips, and higher tolls will lower consumers' surplus. Still, model extensions should endogenize the changes in property value as an aspect in the toll-setting problem. Other future specific extensions include: congestion and travel times as a function of use, public versus private ownership, multiple owners and different numbers of owners of alternative routes, degrees of vertical and horizontal integration, scale, scope, and sequence economies, and heterogeneous users with different values of time which might lead to a differentiated network.

9. Finance Choice at a Frontier

INTRODUCTION

If tolls ever again become a widely used revenue source, it will not happen overnight. Some locations will be more politically acceptable for new toll collections than others. In particular, jurisdiction boundaries or frontiers, where at least half the crossing vehicles are driven by non-residents, would seem to be among the most politically palatable locations for tolls. However, a frontier, by definition, involves more than one jurisdiction, and the policies of neighbors affect each other.[1]

This chapter considers the welfare implications of tolling at a frontier under alternative behavioral assumptions – different objectives (welfare-maximizing, profit-maximizing, cost recovery), willingness to cooperate on setting tolls – and over different time frames (one-time interactions and repeated interactions). By understanding how tolls, welfare, and profits vary under different behavioral assumptions, both the motivations of jurisdictions and under which behaviors tolls will be most likely can be assessed.

There are two problems that are considered in this chapter, referred to as strategic and tactical decisions respectively. First is the strategic decision: will a jurisdiction tax or toll? Second is the tactical decision: if it tolls, what toll will it set? The decision to toll and the rate of toll set by one jurisdiction affects the welfare of the residents of another jurisdiction, leading to interactions and possible gains to both jurisdictions by cooperating. Game theory, developed by Von Neumann and Morgenstern (1944), presents an analytic approach to explain the choices of multiple actors in conflict with each other, with scope for cooperation, where the payoffs are interdependent.[2]

The focus of this chapter is on the revenue policies and rates of toll which emerge at jurisdiction boundaries under alternative behaviors in the absence of congestion. The model is developed in the next section. Alternative objectives, one aspect of behavioral variation, are then considered. Two different toll setting methods, cooperative and non-cooperative, are investigated, and comprise the second main behavioral variation. After presenting empirical values for the model coefficients, an algebraic solution to the model under the different behaviors is computed.

Then sensitivity tests are conducted and the model applied in the context of a one-shot game. The application is extended into the realm of repeated games, where many outcomes are possible.

MODEL

The model assumes an infinitely long, two-way road covered by two jurisdictions, one ranging from the point $-\infty$ to a boundary point b (jurisdiction J_I), the other covering the area from point b to $+\infty$ (jurisdiction J_J). Both jurisdictions may establish tollbooths at the boundary. Tolls can be collected in either one or both directions. This will affect welfare by a fixed amount associated with establishing toll booths and a variable cost per collection. For convenience we assume tolls in both directions if tolls are collected. There are no internal toll booths. This is illustrated in Figure 9.1.

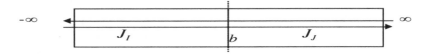

Figure 9.1   Frontier model geometry

This network structure implies four classes of trips, trips staying within J_I (T_{ii}), trips from J_I to J_J (T_{ij}), trips from J_J to J_I (T_{ji}) and trips staying within J_J (T_{jj}). Only trips crossing the boundary matter. By assuming symmetry, the equations for T_{ij} and T_{ji} trips are identical.

Table 9.1   Frontier model equations

Component	Equations	
Flow	$f_b = \omega e^{\alpha(r_I + r_J)}$	(1)
Consumer's surplus	$U_{ij} = \int_{r_\tau + r_J}^{\infty} \omega e^{\alpha(p)} \partial p = -\dfrac{\omega e^{\alpha(r_I + r_J)}}{\alpha}$	(2)
Network use cost	$C_{Nij} = \dfrac{\phi}{\psi} \omega e^{\alpha(r_I + r_J)}$	(3)
Collection cost	$C_{Vij} = \theta \omega e^{\alpha(r_I + r_J)}$	(4)
Revenue	$R_{ij} = r_I \omega e^{\alpha(r_I + r_J)}$	(5)

Note: ω, α, θ, ϕ, ψ = model parameters.

Our model assumes that flow (f_b) across point b on a road is described by a negative exponential model, where demand depends on the toll charged by both jurisdictions (r_I, r_J = the toll charged by jurisdiction J_I, J_J) and can be described by equation (1) of Table 9.1.

Because the jurisdictions are infinite in size, total welfare does not matter, rather only in welfare crossing the boundary point b. The consumers' surplus of local boundary crossing trips (U_{ij}) is measured as the difference between what each consumer would pay and what they do pay. Consumers' surplus can be computed by integrating the demand function over the range of tolls from what they do pay ($r_I + r_J$) to infinity. This is given by equation (2).[3]

Two components comprise cost: network use cost (C_{Nij}) and toll collection cost (C_{Vij}). External costs are excluded because jurisdictions do not generally include them in their decision making. Implicit in this model is that jurisdictions have the obligation of maintaining a level of service with a specific travel speed. Thus 'congestion effects' are ascribed to infrastructure costs which are proportional to traffic flow. To simplify the analysis there are no (dis)economies of scale, there are smoothly and continuously increasing infrastructure costs, and there are zero fixed costs associated with operating the network and collecting tolls or taxes. Equation (3) shows the network use cost (C_{Nij}), which equals the flow multiplied by the average trip length of the portion of the trip in jurisdiction I ($1/\psi$), multiplied by a cost per unit distance (ϕ). Equation (4) provides the cost of toll collection per traveler (C_{Vij}) as the flow multiplied by the collection cost per crossing (θ). Equation (5) shows the revenue from toll collection (R_{ij}) as the rate of toll for jurisdiction I (r_I) multiplied by flow.

OBJECTIVES

Which objective jurisdictions employ will shape the resulting tolls and welfare, and thus perhaps the decision to employ tolls. Four objectives are shown in Table 9.2. When it is assumed that jurisdictions have the objective of local welfare maximization, welfare is defined narrowly as the sum of profit (loss) from administering the road and consumers' surplus for its residents.

The profit maximization objective excludes all consumers' surplus. This represents conditions when the toll booth is privately controlled, for instance, to compare the consequences of unfettered private control with the public control of the network. To the extent that the welfare losses associated with private control are not excessive, it may be a reasonable organizational form for jurisdictions to consider.

Table 9.2   Objectives

Objective	Function
Local welfare	$\max\limits_{r_i} \quad W_L = U_{ij} + 2*R_{ij} - 2*C_{Nij} - 2*C_{Vij}$
Profit	$\max\limits_{r_i} \quad \Pi = 2*R_{ij} - 2*C_{Nij} - 2*C_{Vij}$
Cost recovery	$\max\limits_{r_i} \quad W_{LCR} = U_{ij}$
	$s.t. \quad 0 = 2*R_{ij} - 2*C_{Nij} - 2*C_{Vij}$
Global welfare	$\max\limits_{r_i} \quad W_G = 2*U_{ij} + 4*R_{ij} - 4*C_{Nij} - 2*C_{Vij}$

The objective of local welfare maximization is analysed using a cost recovery constraint. This objective requires that tolls be high enough to recover the costs imposed by those crossing the toll booth but that toll revenue cannot be raised in excess of costs.

If both jurisdictions (J_I and J_J) were under single control, and if that government imposes tolls, it will require only a single toll booth, so collection costs will remain the same as those of a single jurisdiction. On the other hand, it will consider consumers' surplus of all frontier-crossing trips and the network costs they impose on both jurisdictions' roads.

TOLL SETTING

The discussion to date still leaves some latitude in how to solve the tactical problem of toll setting. The issue, in solving for the toll of jurisdiction *I* (r_I), is what toll (r_J) does jurisdiction *I* assume that jurisdiction J will use when it is known what policy jurisdiction *J* chooses. Two approaches can be considered: non-cooperative and cooperative equilibria.

First, with no collusion (implicit or otherwise), there is a non-cooperative Nash equilibrium for toll setting. This means that jurisdiction *I* can do no better by changing its toll given what jurisdiction *J* does, while jurisdiction *J* can also do no better. This does not necessarily result in the best satisfaction of the objective function, but is sustainable. This is solved by keeping the two toll variables: r_I and r_J, separate and not necessarily equal.

It may be possible to attain higher overall welfare (profit) than using a non-cooperative approach. However it will be to the advantage of any jurisdiction to cheat (that is, raise tolls) if the other jurisdiction does not cheat or retaliate but retains the cooperative tolls resulting from this solution. The cooperative solution is sustainable as an equilibrium in indefinitely repeated games.[4] Simply, the issue again is how does jurisdiction I treat r_J. To attain this cooperative solution, each jurisdiction includes both its own and the other jurisdiction's tolls as variables in its objective satisfaction calculations. (Under the non-cooperative equilibrium, the other jurisdiction's toll could be treated as a constant.) The overall payoff-maximizing result can be achieved by setting $r_J = r_I$ in the equations, and solving for the equilibrium toll ($r^* = r_J = r_I$).

Economic theory argues that, when jurisdictions are welfare-maximizing, cooperation should result in a rate of toll equal to the marginal cost of travel for those paying the toll, that is, the network cost, which is the average trip length of the portion of the trip in jurisdiction I ($1/\psi$) multiplied by a cost per unit distance (ϕ) plus the cost of toll collection (θ). In fact, this is the case, as will be seen in the next section.[5] In the absence of fixed costs, and where average costs equal marginal costs, this implies that cost recovery is satisfied.

SOLUTIONS

Figure 9.2 shows how welfare and profits change as tolls ($r_I = r_J$) vary. Table 9.3 shows algebraic solutions for each scenario (combining objective and toll setting methodology), assuming that jurisdictions do employ tolls. These results were simplified by assuming the demand coefficient $\alpha = -1$ (a special case that simplifies the analysis). The final column shows the mathematical result assuming the empirical values developed in Chapter 3.[6]

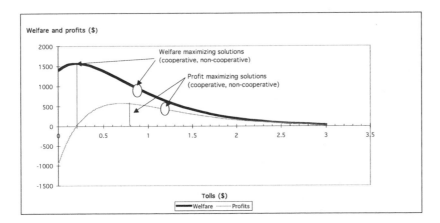

Figure 9.2   Welfare and profit as tolls change by scenario

Table 9.3   Tolls by scenario

Scenario (Objective: maximize; toll setting)	Solution	Result ($)
Local welfare, non-cooperative (W_n)	$r_I = \dfrac{2\phi + \psi + 2\theta\psi}{2\psi}$	0.70
Local welfare, cooperative (W_c)	$r_I = \dfrac{\phi + \theta\psi}{\psi}$	0.20
Local profit, non-cooperative ($\prod_n$)	$r_I = \dfrac{\phi + \psi + \theta\psi}{\psi}$	1.20
Local profit, cooperative ($\prod_c$)	$r_I = \dfrac{2\phi + \psi + 2\theta\psi}{2\psi}$	0.70
Local welfare, cost recovery (CR)	$r_I = \dfrac{\phi + \theta\psi}{\psi}$	0.20
Global welfare (W_g)	$r_{IJ} = \dfrac{2\phi + \theta\psi}{\psi}$	0.32*

Note: Solution obtained by setting $\alpha = -1$. The * indicates tolls in case of global welfare maximization, which should be halved for comparison with other scenarios.

The first thing to note is that the tolls resulting from the non-cooperative welfare-maximizing scenario (r_I^{WN}) are the same as cooperative profit-maximizing tolls ($r_I^{\prod C}$). As mentioned in the previous section, welfare-maximizing cooperative tolls (r_I^{WC}) do equal the marginal costs of travel across the frontier.   Also, because there are no fixed costs here, the tolls and welfare from the cost recovery objective is the same as welfare-maximizing with cooperative toll setting. The global welfare-maximizing objective also has tolls equal to marginal costs, except that, with fewer toll booths, marginal costs are lower.

There are some other interesting relationships in the analysis, independent of the empirical values of the model coefficients:

- Profit-maximizing cooperative tolls ($r_I^{\prod C}$) are always \$0.50 higher than welfare-maximizing cooperative tolls (r_I^{WC}).
- Profit-maximizing non-cooperative tolls ($r_I^{\prod N}$) are always \$0.50 higher than welfare-maximizing non-cooperative tolls (r_I^{WN}).
- Welfare-maximizing non-cooperative tolls (r_I^{WN}) are always \$0.50 higher than cooperative tolls (r_I^{WC}).
- Profit-maximizing non-cooperative tolls ($r_I^{\prod N}$) are always \$0.50 higher than cooperative tolls ($r_I^{\prod C}$); and therefore
- Profit-maximizing non-cooperative tolls ($r_I^{\prod N}$) are always \$1.00 higher than welfare-maximizing cooperative tolls (r_I^{WC}).

Finance Choice at a Frontier 153

These relationships are summarized below:

$$r_I^{WC} + \$1.00 = r_I^{WN} + \$0.50 = r_I^{\Pi C} + \$0.50 = r_I^{\Pi N}$$

In contrast to the usual application of cooperative equilibria for analysing industrial organization of competitive markets, the best repeated game (cooperative) equilibrium toll is lower than the Nash equilibrium (non-cooperative) toll. Furthermore, the lower toll results in higher welfare and profit. The main reason for this is that these are dealing with complementary rather than substitute goods in the revenue mechanism game. Thus, cooperation with lower tolls allows higher welfare in an application similar to serial monopolists raising profits by cooperating to lower tolls (Chamberlin 1933). A second reason is that the objective function includes not just profit, but also consumers' surplus.

NON-COOPERATIVE GAME THEORY

Non-cooperative game theory is employed to analyse the strategic interactions between two jurisdictions under various conditions and objectives. Two decisions are considered: first, the strategic choice of revenue mechanism (tax or toll); and second, the tactical selection of the rate of tax or toll given the strategic choices by jurisdiction J_0 and the other jurisdictions (the environment).

The application of game theory requires acceptance of certain assumptions about the behavior of actors (in this case, jurisdictions) and their level of knowledge. First, it is assumed that actors are instrumentally rational, that is, they express preferences (which are ordered consistently and obey the property of transitivity) and act to best satisfy those preferences. Second, it is assumed that there is common knowledge of rationality (CKR), which means that each actor knows that each other actor is instrumentally rational, and that each actor knows that each actor knows, and so on. Third, it is assumed that there is a consistent alignment of beliefs (CAB), such that that each actor, given the same information and circumstances, will make the same decision – no actor should be surprised by what another actor does. Last, it is assumed that all players know the rules of the game, including all possible actions and the payoffs of each for every player. These four assumptions are used in the analysis of a highly stylized game between two jurisdictions that have clear objectives.

The payoff to each jurisdiction depends on the policy (tax or toll), objective (welfare or profit), and the toll setting equilibrium (cooperative or non-cooperative) taken by both itself and the other jurisdiction. The source of interaction between jurisdictions derives from residents of one jurisdiction traveling on the roads of the other. Thus the revenue and the pricing policy of one jurisdiction alters the demand for the roads of both jurisdictions. The payoffs to jurisdictions are shown in Tables 9.4 and 9.5, representing welfare- and profit-maximizing respectively.

Table 9.4 shows the Nash equilibrium solution to the one-shot game, that is the solution where J_I cannot improve its position given what J_J is doing, and vice versa, for welfare-maximizing jurisdictions. The tolls from the non-cooperative, local welfare-maximizing scenario produce the Nash equilibrium. For all J_J policies, J_I maximizes welfare by choosing this policy, similarly for J_J. However, a number of scenario pairs, denoted in italics, have higher overall welfare, and both jurisdictions together would be better off if somehow they could choose any of those pairs. Assuming toll policies, welfare would be maximized by each jurisdiction choosing the lower tolls of cooperative toll setting, while overall, a [tax, tax] scenario pair (with no tolls) has the highest overall welfare. Similarly, examining Table 9.5, where both jurisdictions are profit-maximizing, the Nash equilibrium is to employ the tolls assuming profit-maximizing, non-cooperative toll setting. Again, a number of scenario pairs have higher overall payoffs.

Table 9.4   Payoffs for welfare-maximizing jurisdiction

J_J J_I	∏ Non-Coop.	W Non-Coop.	W Coop.	Tax
∏ Non-Coop.	[636, 636]	[1049, 699]	[1822, 577]	[2226, 535]
W Non-Coop.	[699, 1049]	[1153, 1153]*	[1901, 951]	[2322, 883]
W Coop.	[577, 1822]	[951, 1901]	[1567, 1567]	[1914, 1455]
Tax	[535, 2226]	[883, 2322]	[1455, 1914]	[1777, 1777]

Table 9.5   Payoffs for profit-maximizing jurisdictions

J_J J_I	∏ Non-Coop.	W Non-Coop.	W Coop.	Tax
∏ Non-Coop.	[424,424]*	[699, 350]	[1246, 0]	[1521,-169]
W Non-Coop.	[350, 699]	[577, 577]	[951, 0]	[1161, -279]
W Coop.	[0, 1246]	[0, 951]	[0, 0]	[0, -459]
Tax	[-169,1521]	[-279, 1161]	[-459, 0]	[-561, -561]

Notes: [payoff to J_I, payoff to J_J]; *: Indicates Nash equilibrium in one-shot game; *italics* : indicates higher payoff scenario pair; *underline italics* : indicates highest stable non-cooperative repeated game payoff pair with toll policy; *double-underline italics* : indicates highest payoff pair. W-non-coop. solution equals ∏-coop; w-coop solution = cost recovery.

INFINITELY REPEATED GAME

Tables 9.4 and 9.5 represent a number of payoffs, but at their heart lies a complex prisoners' dilemma, with multiple cooperative and non-cooperative strategies. The tables show that the Nash equilibrium solution does not have the highest overall payoff. In a repeated game, the payoff-maximizing solution may also be an equilibrium when some mechanism to enforce cooperation is in place. Cooperation has two advantages. First, cooperation protects local citizens from the negative effects of other jurisdictions' pricing policies. Second, cooperation eliminates the finance externality that reduces demand for local roads from non-local residents and then hurts profits. Other mixed policies (alternating [tax, toll] and [toll, tax], for instance) may also achieve higher results, especially since they reduce collection costs and the negative effects of a serial monopoly relative to a single monopoly (Chamberlin 1933). Enforcement mechanisms include the ability to 'punish' and 'reward' neighbors in a repeated game, a government in the case of many players (jurisdictions), or a negotiated treaty, contract, or compact.

This dissonance between individual and collective payoffs in a one-time game may disappear in a repeated game. While both the one-shot and the finitely repeated prisoners' dilemma give unique solutions, the indefinitely repeated prisoners' dilemma does not ensure a unique solution. The 'Folk Theorem' demonstrates that in infinitely and indefinitely repeated games, any of the potential payoff pairs in repeated games can be obtained as a Nash equilibrium with a suitable choice of strategies by the players. There are always multiple equilibria in an indefinitely repeated game, although some strategies have higher collective payoffs than others. Given various discount rates, different solutions will result in the highest repeated game payoff.

The question is how cooperation between jurisdictions can be achieved. A mechanism that can result in strategic cooperation without actual negotiation is the enforcement available in repeated games. In an indefinitely repeated game, one jurisdiction's behavior can be disciplined by another. Cheating on an agreement (for instance, tolling when taxing was agreed to) by jurisdiction J_I in one round (year) can be punished in the next period by jurisdiction J_J, which would also toll, thereby hurting the payoff to jurisdiction J_I. This section applies the mathematics underlying repeated games, and computes the necessary discount factors for cooperation to be stable between rational jurisdictions.

To begin, consider the conventional two-strategy, one-shot game, represented in Table 9.6 (after Taylor 1987), of the payoffs for two strategies of the two-player prisoners' dilemma game, where the traditional prisoners' dilemma strategy of cooperation is associated with taxing and the defect strategy with non-cooperative toll setting. (A similar construction could be made between either of these two policies and a cooperative toll setting policy). As noted, above non-cooperative toll setting is a Nash equilibrium in this one-shot game. The letters w, x, y, and z are used to denote the payoffs in this section, as shown in the table.

Table 9.6   Welfare of trips crossing frontier of two welfare-maximizing jurisdictions

	J_J Tax	Non-cooperative tolls
J_I		
Tax	$[x, x] = [1777, 1777]$	$[z, y] = [883, 2322]$
Non-Cooperative Tolls	$[y, z] = [2322, 883]$	$[w, w] = [1153, 1153]$

Note: where: $y > x > w > z$, numeric values indicate payoff from model.

Payoffs from repeated games (or a supergame) can be thought of as the summation of a series of payoffs from one-shot games, discounted so that the present period's game is more valuable than the next and so on. If the discount factor for jurisdiction i is a_i (and a discount rate: $1 - a_i$), then the supergame payoff (X) can be computed from a strategy which results in the payoff x on every turn as $X = x(a_i + a_i^2 + a_i^3 + ...)$, or $X = x(a_i / (1 - a_i))$, and similarly for any other payoffs (w, y, z). It should be noted that $1 \geq a_i \geq 0$, and other values are invalid (suggesting either that future payoffs are more valuable than the present if ones $a_i > 1$, or that future payoffs are negative in value if $0 > a_i$). It should also be noted that the discount factor can vary for different jurisdictions.

Strategies in a sequence of games can be formulated that result in stable equilibria for each player and higher payoffs. Consider four supergame strategies: tax on every round (χ^∞), toll on every round (τ^∞), conditionally tax with initial trust (B), and conditionally tax with initial distrust (B'). The first conditional strategy (B), (also called *'tit for tat'*) begins by cooperating (imposing a tax) on turn 1, and then on all subsequent turns does what the other player did in the previous turn. A variation on this strategy (B') is also *tit for tat*, but begins by defecting (imposing a toll) on turn 1, and then doing what the other player did.

In the repeated game, the strategy pair of both jurisdictions choosing to toll on every round, independent of what the other player is doing, $[\tau^\infty, \tau^\infty]$, is an equilibrium. Neither player can improve their position if the other plays τ^∞. However, this is not necessarily the best equilibrium. The strategy of taxing every round, again independent of what the other players are doing (χ^∞), is never an equilibrium. If your opponent is playing χ^∞, there is always a gain possible from any other strategy. The conditional

supergame strategies, where the policy employed by one jurisdiction
depends on what other jurisdictions did on a previous turn, are more
complicated.

Table 9.7 shows the reformulated game in terms of supergame
strategies. The three supergame strategies which are sometimes equilibria
(B, B', τ^{∞}) can be played by jurisdiction J_I and J_J. The cells in the table
show which conditions (of Table 9.8) hold for the supergame strategy to be
a repeated game equilibria. It can be shown (Taylor 1987) that the results
shown in the first column of Table 9.8 hold when the conditions in the
second column are borne out.

Table 9.7   Conditions for supergame strategies to be equilibria

$J_0 \backslash J_1$	B	B'	τ^{∞}
B	(1) and (2) for J_0, J_1 $[1 \geq a_i \geq 0.60]$	(3) and rev. (2) for J_0, J_1 $[0.60 \geq a_i \geq 0.23]$	Never equilibrium
B'	(3) and rev. (2) for J_0, J_1 $[0.60 \geq a_i \geq 0.23]$	(4) and rev. (3) for J_0, J_1 $[0.30 \geq a_i \geq 0]$	(4) and rev (3) for J_J $[0.30 \geq a_i \geq 0]$
τ^{∞}	Never equilibrium	(4) and rev (3) for J_1 $[0.30 \geq a_i \geq 0]$	Always equilibrium

Note: rev. denotes reversing the $\geq$ in the equation (that is, making it $\leq$). Conditions
are defined in Table 9.8. [ ] indicates results of conditions for game.

Table 9.8   Conditions for supergame strategies, and results from equations

Result	Condition	Value of RHS
(1) B is superior to τ^{∞} if	$a_i \geq \dfrac{y-x}{y-w}$	0.46
(2) B is superior to B' if	$a_i \geq \dfrac{y-x}{x-z}$	0.60
(3) B' is superior to τ^{∞} if	$a_i \geq \dfrac{w-z}{y-w}$	0.23
(4) Mutual B' is stable if the reverse of condition (3) holds and	$a_i \leq \dfrac{w-z}{x-z}$	0.30

The final column of Table 9.8 gives the value associated with the right-
hand side of the condition in the table. Applying those conditions to the
strategy pairs in Table 9.7 gives us the solution to the repeated game
equilibria, shown by the range of discount factors in square brackets in that
table. If there are multiple equilibria in the game, jurisdictions will choose

the one which results in the highest welfare to them so long as it results in the highest welfare to other players. Just as in the one-shot game, if there is one stable equilibrium which does provide the highest welfare to all players, it can be anticipated to be chosen. Several policy pairs are valid (repeated game equilibria). Significantly, for discount factors in the range $1 \geq a_i \geq$ 0.60 (or discount rates between 0% and 40%, where typical government interest rates are well under 10% in the United States), mutual cooperation $[B, B]$ is a stable equilibrium, and since it has the highest payoff, it would be the selected equilibrium.

This alternating policy pair $[B', B]$ or $[B, B']$ emerges as stable for the range of discount factors $0.60 \geq a_i \geq 0.23$ (or discount rates between 40% and 77%). Implicitly this assumes that toll booths can be constructed and removed at no loss, or at least result in no charge during the turn when tolls are turned off, though the extent to which this is true is empirical. A similar policy is for one jurisdiction to always play cooperate and the other defect, so long as revenues are shared equally between them. Whether this can actually be enforced depends on the institutional arrangements between the jurisdictions. However, if these jurisdictions can cooperate at that level, it is unclear why they would select the alternating policy pair unless it had a higher payoff.

A range of discount factors $(0.30 \geq a_i \geq 0)$ –discount rates between 70% and 100% – allows the policy pair of $[B', B']$ to be stable, which in practice is the equivalent of mutual defection $[\tau^{\infty}, \tau^{\infty}]$. Similarly $[\tau^{\infty}, B']$ and $[B', \tau^{\infty}]$ are stable when one or the other jurisdiction has such a low discount factor $(0.30 \geq a_i \geq 0)$. These policies are also the equivalent of mutual defection $[\tau^{\infty}, \tau^{\infty}]$.

This exercise can be undertaken for other profit and welfare-maximizing policy couplets. The key point is that cooperative equilibria are stable for a wide variety of realistic interest rates for indefinitely and infinitely repeated games.

CONCLUSIONS

This chapter has examined the question of what happens when jurisdictions have the opportunity to establish toll booths at the frontier separating them. Clearly, tolls are more likely at frontiers than at internal locations, if only because a greater percentage of the toll falls on non-residents. Nevertheless, for larger jurisdictions, frontier toll booths still raise nearly half their revenue from residents.

If welfare-maximizing jurisdictions behave non-cooperatively, they are likely to toll. However if they can arrange to cooperate, they will employ lower tolls or agree not to toll. Cooperation is easier the fewer jurisdictions are involved. A border between two large jurisdictions essentially involves traffic from only those two jurisdictions. However, that same border along small jurisdictions will serve traffic from many different jurisdictions.

If all jurisdictions hope to maximize profit, they will toll, even if they do cooperate. However if they cooperate (by means such as forming a single toll or road authority), they will charge lower tolls and even eliminate one toll booth between them (so that they share revenue while lowering operating costs). Profit maximization is more likely under private sector than public sector management. So if tolling is a desired policy outcome, privatization will be more likely to achieve it than public control.

There are several ways in which the analysis could be extended. First would be the inclusion of congestion costs. Congestion pricing is often cited as the main benefit from road pricing, but its benefits cannot be understood with the model in the absence of delay due to excess demand. Second, this chapter has assumed that travelers are identical except in their reservation price. Congestion pricing is most meaningful when demand is heterogeneous, that is, different travelers have different values of time and differ in their disutility from congestion. Third, all fixed costs have been neglected. This simplifies the analysis, particularly under cost recovery behavior, but is not necessarily a realistic approach.

NOTES

1. To quantify the importance of frontiers, of 133 major countries existing prior to the fall of the Soviet Union, there were 500 international boundaries between them, with each boundary containing multiple crossings (source: author's calculations). This does not include sub-national frontiers (state, provincial, county, or city boundaries, for instance).
2. See also: Axelrod 1984; Hargreaves-Heap and Varoufakis 1995; Osborne and Rubinstein 1994; Rapoport 1970; Taylor 1987.
3. By symmetry, the consumers' surplus in each direction is identical, and by symmetric trip tables, half the flow in each direction is made by residents, therefore only the total consumers' surplus in one direction is needed rather than half in both directions.
4. The Nash equilibrium conditions state that when all jurisdictions are identical, each jurisdiction will try to achieve the highest welfare for themselves, recognizing that other jurisdictions will do the same. However in an indefinitely repeated prisoners' dilemma game, strategies which enforce cooperation by punishing 'defection' can be employed to maximize overall welfare.
5. In an infinitely repeated games context, this is the best result that jurisdictions can attain over the long term, and though other solutions are also equilibria, no other solution improves on this one overall (though a single jurisdiction raising tolls - violating the equal tolls provision, may have a higher individual welfare or profit).
6. The model does not have much real-world meaning without understanding typical values for the model coefficients. The table below gives some values developed in

Chapter 3 and from earlier research by the author. The first two variables, α and ω, describe demand. The variable α is set to -1, this value makes consistent what is known about the user costs of highway travel developed from Chapter 3 and a gravity model's decay function (Levinson and Kumar 1995). This variable must be less than zero to ensure that demand falls when prices rise. The second demand variable ω describes the number of trips when the total monetary price $r_I + r_J = 0$. Clearly this is a scalar and does not affect tolls or the ultimate decision to tax or toll in this analysis. To keep this analysis consistent with the previous chapter, it is set at 2338, which is a value derived from a more complex version of the model (considering multiple jurisdictions). The variable network cost is the cost that a jurisdiction faces for every vehicle kilometer traveled, estimated in Chapter 3 from a database of state highway expenditures and vehicle travel. The variable collection cost (θ) was estimated from toll collection costs on California bridges. Average trip length ($1/\psi$) within the jurisdiction was calculated from the multiple jurisdiction model, which required a factor for which trips were sensitive to distance traveled, ($\psi=\$0.15/km$).

Table: Empirical values of model coefficients

Variable	Description	Value
Alpha (α)	Coefficient relating demand to price	-1
Omega (ω)	Demand multiplier (trips at price = 0)	2338
phi (ϕ)	Variable network cost ($/vkt)	0.018
1/psi ($1/\psi$)	Average trip length in jurisdiction (km)	6.67
Theta (θ)	Variable collection cost ($/vehicle)	0.08

10. Congestion Pricing

INTRODUCTION

Explaining the advantages of congestion pricing to a non-technical or even non-economist audience is difficult. The task is made more difficult by the choice of graphs and the assumptions used in the explanation. Often, the graphs do not permit the use of standard economic tools such as consumers' surplus. The difficulty lies with the use of generalized cost and a revealed demand curve, rather than the use of a money cost and the multiple underlying demand curves reflecting different demands for road use at different levels of service. This chapter seeks a more straightforward development of the justification for congestion pricing from a graphical perspective. It then develops a more microscopic understanding, which will be important when considering compensation in the next chapter.

Game theory has been applied to a number of issues involving the financing of transportation. In previous chapters, game theory was used to help understand how jurisdictions choose to finance their roads. This chapter considers its application to congestion and congestion pricing. While congestion is normally thought of as a phenomenon involving hundreds or thousands of vehicles, at its most basic, it simply involves two. Those two may want to use a facility that can only accommodate one at any given time, forcing the other to wait. If there were no penalty for arriving early or late, the individuals might coordinate their actions to arrive at different times. However, if there is an advantage to arrive a particular time (the cost of being early or late exceeds the cost of delay), congestion may be a natural consequence.

First this chapter elaborates on the conventional explanation of congestion pricing. It next describes a game theoretic model of congestion. Then congestion pricing is incorporated. The chapter concludes with suggestions for extending this approach.

CONVENTIONAL CONGESTION PRICING MODEL

The conventional explanation of road pricing found in various sources uses a variation of Figure 10.1. On the y-axis is a measure of generalized cost (for example, price plus monetized time). On the *x*-axis is flow in vehicles per hour. In the absence of any toll, equilibrium occurs at (Q_o, P_o), where demand intersects the short-run average cost curve. Any traveler who values a trip at more than P_o will travel; anyone who does not do so will not travel. The shaded area on the graph is considered the welfare loss, the benefit lost when tolls are not imposed. The loss is due to the difference between the cost a driver imposes on society (the short-run marginal cost) by making everyone else's trip take a little bit longer, and the cost that driver bears personally which is spent in traffic congestion due to all the other cars on the road (short-run average cost). The imposition of a marginal cost toll moves the equilibrium to (Q^*,P^*) and eliminates the welfare loss due to the congestion externality.

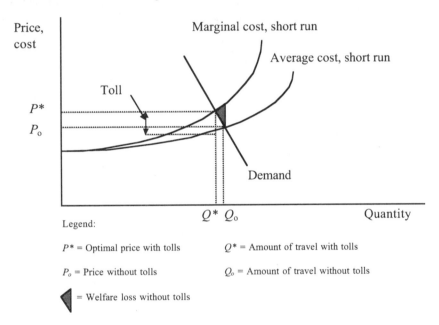

Figure 10.1   Optimal congestion toll and welfare loss without toll

However, the use of a single demand curve on the graph confuses the issue. Moving from short-run average cost to short-run marginal cost has a welfare implication; raising the price lowers the demand, and thus the area that is conventionally thought of as consumers' surplus gets smaller. But whether consumers' surplus gets larger or smaller depends on how individuals value the time savings. The conundrum results because individual drivers would pay more for a better level of service (LOS). In actuality, the movement from short-run average cost to short-run marginal cost implies a movement from a demand curve with poor LOS (D_F) to a demand curve with a better LOS (D_A).

The demand for a graded commodity at a given price depends on the quality of that commodity. In the case where the commodity in question is road use, the grade is the level of service, the time it takes to traverse the road. At better levels of service (lower travel times), the demand will be higher at the same money price than at lower levels of service. We will describe LOS as ranging from S_A to S_F, with S_A being best.

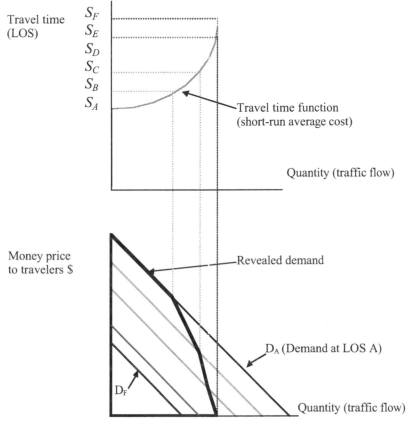

Figure 10.2 (A) Time versus flow; (B) implicit and revealed demand versus price

Suppose that there is some money price (a toll) charged by the agent managing the road, such that, even if the travel time is zero, the quantity demanded will be very small or zero. At a zero price, even if the travel time is small or zero, the quantity of travel will be limited. Similarly, there is a travel time at which demand will be small or zero, even at zero price. This is represented by the Figure 10.2.

The top part of Figure 10.2 shows schematically the travel time (short-run average cost) a driver faces at a bottleneck resulting from various approach flows (approach flow is the traffic accumulating at the back of the queue, departure flow is the traffic leaving the front of the queue; which is constrained by capacity). The travel time function relates travel time (or delay) and approach traffic flow. The greater the approach flow, the higher the travel time. At flows below capacity (level of service A (S_A) or B (S_B)), traffic flows smoothly, while at high approach flows, those above capacity, traffic is stop and start and is classified as level of service E (S_E) or F (S_F).

The bottom part of Figure 10.2 shows schematically the implicit demand for travel on a link as a function of the travel time. All else equal (for instance, the price charged to users), demand to travel on a link at level of service A (D_A) is higher than demand at level of service F (D_F). However, the demand and the travel time on a link are not independent, as shown in the top of Figure 10.2. So the implicit demand and revealed demand are not identical, but rather, the revealed demand is formed by projecting the travel time at a given flow onto the implicit demand curves. So for instance, when the charged price users is high, the revealed demand coincides with the implicit demand at level of service A (D_A). As the prices are lowered, the revealed demand crosses the implicit demand curve at level of service B (D_B), then D_C, D_D, D_E and finally at a zero money price it crosses D_F. While the actual prices that generate specific demand levels vary from place to place with local circumstances, demand preferences, and market conditions, the general trend (higher prices gives lower approach flow gives better level of service) is simply an application of the law of demand from economics along with traffic flow theory.

In other words, the change in welfare with and without congestion pricing depends not only on the change in both price and quantity, but also on the change in reservation price, the price travelers would be willing to pay at a given level of service. And at better levels of service, travelers (and potential travelers) have a higher reservation price.

The movement along the revealed demand curve follows the shape of the curve shown above because of the relationship between traffic flow (quantity demanded) and travel time. Assume, for instance, that each level of service category represents a one minute increase in travel time from the immediately better travel time. So, in the graph, let the level of service for a one-minute trip be denoted S_A, and for a six-minute trip, S_F. The amount of traffic necessary to move from one minute to two minutes exceeds the amount to move from two to three minutes. In other words, there is a rising average (and thus marginal) cost in terms of time.

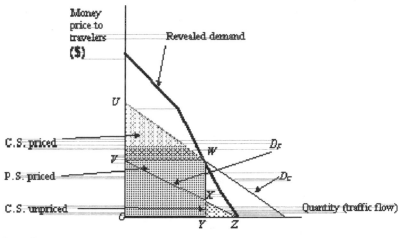

Legend:

Consumers' surplus priced = *UVW*   Producer's surplus priced = *OVWY*
Consumers' surplus unpriced = *VOZ*   Producer's surplus unpriced = 0

Figure 10.3   Welfare analysis with and without pricing

The concepts in Figure 10.2 can be used to develop the welfare analysis shown in Figure 10.3. There are several areas of interest in Figure 10.3. The first is defined by the lower left triangle (*VOZ*) which is the consumers' surplus when the road is unpriced. The second is the producer surplus (profit) to the road authority when the road is priced, illustrated by the rectangle formed in the lower left (*OVWY*). The third is the consumer surplus when the road is priced, shown in gray (*UVW*). This consumer surplus represents a higher reservation price than the other because the level of service is better when flow is lower. That first area needs to be compared to the sum of the second and third areas. If the sum of the second and third areas (*OUWY*) is larger than the first (*OVZ*), then pricing has higher welfare than remaining unpriced. Similarly, two price levels can be compared. In other words, the welfare gain from pricing is equal to the area (*VUWX*) minus the area (*XYZ*). In this particular figure, consumers' surplus is maximized when the good is free, but overall welfare (including producer's surplus) is not. Whether consumers' surplus is in fact higher in a given situation depends on the slopes of the various demand curves.

Welfare is maximized by maximizing the sum of the producer's surplus rectangle and the consumers' surplus 'triangle' (it may not be a true triangle), recognizing that the hypotenuse of the consumers' surplus triangle must follow an underlying demand curve, not the revealed demand curve.

Differentiating the level of service (for instance, providing two different levels of service at two different prices) may result in higher overall welfare (though not necessarily higher welfare for each individual).

How welfare is measured and how it is perceived are two different things. If the producer's surplus is not returned to the users of the system somehow (through rebates of other taxes or reinvestment in transportation), the users will perceive an overall welfare gain as a personal loss because it would be acting as an additional tax. It should be noted that the entire argument can be made in reverse, where consumer and producer surpluses are measured in time rather than money, and the level of service is the monetary cost of travel. This, however, has less practical application.[1]

GAME THEORETIC CONGESTION MODEL

The previous argument is macroscopic in nature, and atemporal. It should be possible to describe congestion from first principles, using simple vehicle interactions. In its simplest form, this game theoretic model requires three variables and some assumptions. First, we need to define a penalty for early arrival (E) and for late arrival (L). There is also a penalty for being delayed (D). There are two players, or vehicles. Each (vehicle 1 and vehicle 2) has the option of departing early, departing on time and departing late. If both individuals depart at the same time, there will be congestion.

- If both individuals depart early, one will arrive early and one will be delayed but arrive on time. We can say that each individual has a 50% chance of being early *or* being delayed.

- If both individuals depart on time, one will arrive on time and one will be delayed and arrive late. Each individual has a 50% chance of being delayed *and* being late.

- If both individuals depart late, one will arrive late and one will be delayed and arrive very late. Each individual has a 50% change of being delayed *and* being very late.

We can compute expected values for each of the nine choice pairs, shown in Table 10.1. The equilibrium solution clearly depends on the values of E, L, and D. Payoffs are shown here as costs, so users are trying to minimize the values in the cells. Total social costs for a strategy pair are the sum of the values of vehicles 1 and 2.

Table 10.1   Payoff matrix

		Vehicle 2		
		Early	On time	Late
Vehicle 1	Early	[0.5*(E+D), 0.5*(E+D)]	[E,0]	[E,L]
	On time	[0,E]	[0.5*(L+D), 0.5*(L+D)]	[0,L]
	Late	[L,E]	[L,0]	[L+0.5*(L+D), L+0.5*(L+D)]

Note: [Vehicle 1 payoff, Vehicle 2 payoff].

In example 1 (Table 10.2), we assume that the early arrival penalty is one unit, the late arrival penalty is also one unit, but there is no penalty for delay. In this case, the Nash equilibrium is both vehicles departing on time. If vehicle 1 departs on time, vehicle two can do no better than depart on time as well, and vice versa. This results in congestion, but not necessarily a social loss compared with other non-congested scenarios such as [on time, early].

Table 10.2   Example 1

E, D, L		Vehicle 2		
1, 0, 1		Early	On time	Late
	Early	[0.5,0.5]	[1,0]	[1,1]
Vehicle 1	On Time	[0,1]	[0.5, 0.5] *	[0,1]
	Late	[1,1]	[1,0]	[1.5, 1.5]

Note: * indicates Nash equilibrium.

In example 2 ($E = 3$, $D = 1$, $L = 4$), the equilibrium is the same strategy pair [on time, on time]. But now the total welfare (-5 units) is no longer as good as the best socially optimal choice [on time, early] or [early, on time] with a welfare of -3 units. Other scenarios are given in note 2. Most of them do not result in a congested outcome. Many of the scenarios have multiple equilibria. Empirical investigation is necessary to determine the most plausible values.

Table 10.3   Example 2

E, D, L		Vehicle 2		
3, 1, 4		Early	On time	Late
	Early	[2,2]	[3,0]	[3,4]
Vehicle 1	On time	[0,3]	[2.5, 2.5] *	[0,4]
	Late	[4,3]	[4,0]	[6.5, 6.5]

Note: * indicates Nash equilibrium.

The model can also be extended to deal with congestion pricing as shown in Table 10.4. We need to add a pricing term to the cells on the diagonal where congestion occurs (P_e, P_o, P_l for early, on time, and late departure prices respectively). Congestion is contingent on the demand, so congestion prices are similarly contingent. If congestion prices occur only when there is actual congestion, in six of the nine off-diagonal positions no congestion prices are actually imposed, but are simply used as a threat.

Table 10.4   Payoff matrix with congestion pricing

		Vehicle 2		
		Early	On time	Late
	Early	[0.5*(E+D) + P_e, 0.5*(E+D) + P_e]	[E,0]	[E,L]
Vehicle 1	On Time	[0,E]	[0.5*(L+D) + P_o, 0.5*(L+D) + P_o]	[0,L]
	Late	[L,E]	[L,0]	[L+0.5*(L+D)+ P_l, L+0.5*(L+D) + P_l]

A question remains as to what the appropriate 'marginal cost' price is. The value of time in the vehicle is not the only cost that the congested vehicle suffers. The vehicle also bears a late penalty associated with being delayed. This suggests that $P_o = P_l = 0.5*(L+D)$. The case of delay because both vehicles depart early is subtler, as here a vehicle is early *or* delayed, but it is only the delay that is imposed by the other vehicle. Further, that second vehicle avoids the early arrival penalty. This suggests $P_e = 0.5*(D)$. A vehicle does, however, have effects on the other vehicle, even in the absence of congestion. Displacement in time is one example; if the equilibrium is moved (so a traveler now departs early rather than on time), a vehicle's utility may diminish. Returning to Example 1, but including congestion prices, now gives us a revised Example 1, shown in Table 10.5.

Table 10.5   Example 1 with congestion prices

E, D, L 1, 0, 1		Vehicle 2		
		Early	On time	Late
Vehicle 1	Early	[0.5,0.5]	[1,0]*	[1,1]
	On time	[0,1]*	[1,1]*	[0,1]*
	Late	[1,1]	[1,0]*	[2,2]

Note: * indicates Nash Equilibrium

Now, rather than a single equilibrium, we have multiple equilibria, and we might suggest that [on time, on time] is somewhat more likely than otherwise if there is any risk of misplay by the other travelers. So marginal cost congestion prices may not always eliminate congestion. On the other hand, under some conditions, it will. Looking at the case example 2 case, as illustrated in Table 10.6 we see that congestion prices will move either vehicle 1 or vehicle 2 to an early departure. This eliminates congestion (and so no congestion prices need be collected).

Compared with the original example 2, one of the vehicles is now better off by 2.5 units, and the other is worse off by 0.5 units. Whether there should be additional compensation for this displacement is a political question, and will be addressed in Chapter 11.

Table 10.6   Example 2 with congestion prices

E, D, L 3,1,4		Vehicle 2		
		Early	On time	Late
Vehicle 1	Early	[2.5,2.5]	[3,0]*	[3,4]
	On time	[0,3]*	[5,5]	[0,4]
	Late	[4,3]	[4,0]	[9,9]

Note: * indicates Nash Equilibrium

CONCLUSIONS

This chapter has developed a new way of viewing congestion and congestion pricing in the context of game theory. Simple interactions among players (vehicles) affect the payoffs for other players in a systematic way. Based on the value of time for various activities (time at home, at work, or on the road), departure times, and consequently congestion, will vary for the players. Under some range of values congestion will occur between non-cooperative players, even if both would be better off making a different decision. A prisoners' dilemma is one of many possible outcomes. Congestion is an outcome of individually rational, and sometimes globally rational behavior, under certain preferences. Where there is a difference between the individual and global rational outcomes, congestion pricing can be used, which in some cases eliminates congestion. The actual early, late, and delay penalties depend on the individual's value of time, and it is easy to extend the model to handle differentiated values of time.

NOTES

1. In low volume situations, those that are uncongested, it is unlikely that the revenue from marginal cost congestion pricing will recover long-term fixed costs. This is because the marginal impacts of an additional car when volume is low is almost zero, so that additional revenue which can be raised with marginal cost pricing is also zero. Imagine a road with one car – the car's marginal impact is zero, a marginal cost price would also be zero, its revenue would thus be zero, which is less than the fixed costs. Add a second car, and marginal impacts are still nearly zero – a phenomenon which remains true until capacity is approached.
2. Eight cases from the basic model are given below.

E, D, L
0,0,0

Vehicle 2

		Early	On time	Late
	Early	[0,0]*	[0,0]*	[0,0]*
Vehicle 1	On time	[0,0]*	[0,0]*	[0,0]*
	Late	[0,0]*	[0,0]*	[0,0]*

E, D, L
0,0,1

Vehicle 2

		Early	On time	Late
	Early	[0,0]*	[0,0]*	[0,1]
Vehicle 1	On time	[0,0]*	[0.5, 0.5]	[0,1]
	Late	[1,0]	[1,0]	[1.5, 1.5]

E, D, L
0,1,0

Vehicle 2

		Early	On time	Late
	Early	[0.5,0.5]	[0,0]*	[0,0]*
Vehicle 1	On time	[0,0]*	[0.5, 0.5] *	[0,0]*
	Late	[0,0]*	[0,0]*	[0.5, 0.5]

E, D, L 1, 0, 0		Vehicle 2		
		Early	On time	Late
	Early	[0.5,0.5]	[1,0]	[1,0]
Vehicle 1	On time	[0,1]	[0,0]*	[0,0]*
	Late	[0,1]	[0,0]*	[0,0]*

E, D, L 1, 1,0		Vehicle 2		
		Early	On time	Late
	Early	[1,1]	[1,0]	[1,0]
Vehicle 1	On time	[0,1]	[0.5, 0.5]	[0,0]*
	Late	[0,1]	[0,0]*	[0.5, 0.5]

E, D, L 1, 0, 1		Vehicle 2		
		Early	On time	Late
	Early	[0.5,0.5]	[1,0]	[1,1]
Vehicle 1	On time	[0,1]	[0.5, 0.5]*	[0,1]
	Late	[1,1]	[1,0]	[1.5, 1.5]

E, D, L 0, 1, 1		Vehicle 2		
		Early	On time	Late
	Early	[0.5,0.5]	[0,0]*	[0,1]
Vehicle 1	On time	[0,0]*	[1,1]	[0,1]
	Late	[1,0]	[1,0]	[2,2]

E, D, L 1, 1, 1		Vehicle 2		
		Early	On time	Late
	Early	[1,1]	[1,0]*	[1,1]
Vehicle 1	On time	[0,1]*	[1,1]*	[0,1]*
	Late	[1,1]	[1,0]*	[2,2]

Note: * indicates Nash equilibrium [Vehicle 1 payoff; Vehicle 2 payoff]
Early arrival penalty (*E*), Delay penalty (*D*), Late arrival penalty (*L*).

11. Compensation

INTRODUCTION

The equity issues facing congestion pricing are an impediment to its adoption. In part there is resistance due to people's dated perceptions of how toll roads operate; they still envision stopping at toll booths and paying the toll, a situation where the toll road causes more delay than it relieves. Electronic toll collection, discussed in Chapter 12, will obviate some of these concerns. There is additional resistance to the idea of paying twice for the same thing. If gas taxes have already paid for the road, why should tolls now be put in place? A third criticism is the idea of so-called 'Lexus lanes', the idea that toll roads (in parallel with free roads) are only for the wealthy, so that they can bypass congestion while poor and middle-class citizens are stuck in traffic. Research on the operations of SR91 in southern California suggests that income effects are weak. While logic argues that the rich do have a higher value of time than the poor, and so would in general be more willing to pay a toll, working-class individuals may have a greater penalty for being late to work or pick up a child from day care. A related criticism, and one that gets very little attention, is that not only does a toll road enable some to buy their way out of congestion, they do so at the expense of others if the toll lanes operate as queue jumpers – that is, they may make others wait longer so that they can avoid delay. They, along with the toll road authority, are in a sense stealing time from those who do not pay.

What to do with the revenue is a critical question that needs to be answered before toll roads will become widely adopted. This chapter investigates the issue of compensation and several possible alternatives. One is the 'delayer pays' principle. It also examines high occupancy toll lanes and some suggested alternatives. This provides a contrast with the efficiency arguments for marginal cost pricing put forward in the previous chapter.

STEALING TIME

Since as early as 1975, a number of environmentalists have called for the imposition of a '*Polluter pays principle*'. The polluter pays principle argues that the parties who impose environmental costs should either pay to avoid pollution or compensate those who suffer because of it.

Any social cost requires at least two parties, for instance the polluter and the polluted upon. In the absence of either one, no economic externality would take place. The party responsible for mitigating the externality depends on the circumstances. Two examples illustrate the point.

- If a new (previously unplanned) airport is built in an existing community, can the airport make as much noise as it wants to?
- If an airport has long been located in the middle-of-nowhere, and then a new subdivision moves in, should the new neighbors be able to require the airport to become quieter?

The 'common-sense' answer to both these two questions is 'no', there is an existing status quo that is disrupted by a change. It is the disrupter who creates the externality. In contrast to the polluter pays principle, one could establish a *'disrupter pays principle'* to deal with externalities.

What happens on a highway? Congestion, like air pollution, noise, and other externalities, results from a lack of well-defined property rights. In the absence of property rights, there is a first-come, first-served priority system. First-come, first-served (FCFS) is an arrangement brought about by the technology and the social norms applied to it. Vehicles line up in narrow lanes. Vehicles arriving at the back of the queue rarely drive to the front while other cars are still ahead of them. One occasionally sees cheaters (people driving on shoulders) who violate this norm. Roads with clearly striped lanes thus differ from the mob behavior seen in other bottleneck environments (for example, a crowded elevator). Transit passengers have different customs in different locations; for instance, everyone is well behaved boarding San Francisco's BART but not on Washington DC's Metro.[1]

On a roadway with a queue, the vehicle in front delays the vehicle at the back. According to the 'polluter pays principle', the front vehicle should compensate the vehicle at the back for the delay. On the other hand, the vehicle in front was there first (that is why they are in the front), and the vehicle in the back disrupted the status quo. So, according to the common-sense 'disrupter pays principle', it is the vehicle at the back that brings the delay on itself by arriving later – and of course it already bears the costs in terms of congestion and time lost.

Most congestion-pricing proposals argue that because vehicle A delays vehicle B, a government authority should be able to impose tolls on vehicle A (or on both vehicles A and B). It is as if person A robs person B and the police captures person A and keep the loot for themselves. This robbery example is socially unacceptable because there is a well-defined system of property rights and clearly the stolen property originally belonged to B. Who does stolen time belong to? Is B complicit in its delay, or is it solely the responsibility of A? In the case of the crime, is it possible that B was 'asking for it', by walking around and flashing money in a well-known crime-infested area? If the government authority gets the money, what does it do with it?

The Coase Theorem famously argues two points assuming rational behavior, no transaction costs, and bargaining (Coase 1992). First, the efficiency hypothesis posits that, regardless of how rights are initially assigned, the resulting allocation of resources will be efficient. Second, the invariance hypothesis suggests that the final allocation of resources will be invariant to how rights are assigned (Medema and Zerbe 1998). Coase shows how it takes two to have positive or negative externalities, and how, depending on one's view of the property rights, the prices, taxes, costs, or negotiations will differ. Traffic manifests high transaction costs, no property rights, and little bargaining, perhaps explaining the lack of efficient outcomes

If property rights are to be assigned, and a low transaction cost exchange mechanism is to be established (for instance, electronic toll collection), perhaps a more efficient and equitable outcome could be achieved. An efficient outcome suggests maximizing net social benefit, which will consider the weighted sum of delay, scheduled delay, and out-of-pocket costs for users, the costs of providing the infrastructure, and the social costs of externalities. Any analysis must assess the appropriate weights – different individuals have different values of time and different types of delay are perceived differently. An equitable outcome is less clear, perhaps equalizing the weighted sum of delay, schedule delay, and out-of-pocket costs for all members of some group (say, people who want to use the facility at a given time).

In the absence of private roads, consider two alternatives regarding the initial distribution of rights:

1. Everyone has the right to free (unpriced) travel.
2. Everyone has the right to freeflow (undelayed) travel.

If everyone has the right to free (no monetary cost) travel, then the mechanism for more efficient travel requires the delayed to pay the delayers not to delay (a congestion prevention mechanism). Alternatively, if everyone has the right to freeflow (undelayed) travel, then the burden is on the delayers to compensate the delayed (a congestion damages mechanism). These comport with the *disrupter pays* and *polluter pays* principles respectively. Whether drivers impose costs on those behind them depends on one's point of view vis-à-vis property rights.

A major difficulty is that traffic and congestion externalities are time-sensitive. By the time the delayed vehicle arrives, it is too late to pay the delaying vehicle not to be there. Furthermore, the delayer delays multiple vehicles, and so if the delayed tried to pay the delayers not to be there, they may pay significantly more than their own benefit would warrant. These dynamics suggest that conventional economic arguments concerning externalities cannot be simply applied. If the delayer pays scheme were in effect, then those behind would be imposing a cost (the price or the tax or the fine or whatever you want to call it) on those in front, in contrast with the traditional first-come, first-served approach.

There is also the issue of the behavioral response of the paid driver. If I am compensated for not doing something, I won't do it. But what if I weren't going to do it initially? For instance, as a non-smoker, I will gladly take any compensation you want to give me for not smoking. Under a compensation regime, I may threaten to smoke just to extort money from you. Similarly, as a driver, I may make the threat to drive on a congested route just to be paid not to. Table 11.1 categorizes alternative payment and compensation schemes.

Table 11.1   Alternative monetary payment and compensation schemes

Delayer	Delayed	Road	Label
0	0	0	First-come first serve (unpriced)
Paid	Pays	0	Disrupter pays
Pays	Paid	0	Polluter pays
Pays	0	Paid	\
0	Pays	Paid	- 'Marginal cost pricing'
Pays	Pays	Paid	/

These difficulties in internalizing the delay externality are, in part, associated with treating the road as a common, and trying to give rights to drivers, rather than having the road owner have the right to charge for use. However, private ownership does not guarantee an absence of delay. This chapter does not consider private roads.

REIMBURSING TIME: DELAYER PAYS

The first system is a variation on the polluter pays scheme applied to congestion. Imagine a cumulative arrival and departure pattern as in Figure 11.1. This is represented numerically in Table 11.2, where the numbers 1–9 indicate the first through ninth vehicle. Each row is a time increment (or turn), for instance a two-second headway, reflecting the capacity of the roadway of 1800 vehicles per hour.[2] Vehicle 1 delays nobody. However after that first vehicle, the arrival rate exceeds the departure rate (say 3600 vehicles per hour for several seconds). As a consequence, vehicle 2 delays vehicle 3 by one turn. Vehicle 3 delays vehicles 4 and 5 by 1 turn. Vehicle 4 delays vehicles 5, 6, and 7 by 1 turn and so on. The direct payments and income from such a system are shown the right-hand columns of Table 11.2.

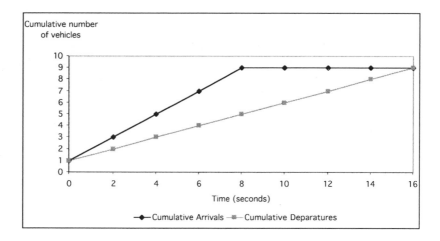

Figure 11.1   Cumulative arrival and departures, base case

Table 11.2   Short-run marginal cost payment scheme with all vehicles.

Time (seconds)	Queue	Vehicle	Payment	Income	Net Income
0:00	1	1	0	0	0
0:02	23	2	1	0	−1
0:04	345	3	2	1	−1
0:06	4567	4	3	1	−2
0:08	56789	5	4	2	−2
0:10	6789	6	3	2	−1
0:12	789	7	2	3	1
0:14	89	8	1	3	2
0:16	9	9	0	4	4
Total			16	16	0

Note: Vehicle 1 arrives and departs before vehicle 2 arrives.

This *short-run* marginal cost is defined as the change in the *short-run* total cost, because only information about the present (the number of vehicles in the queue at the time a vehicle leaves) is known, not the full consequences of delay on vehicles yet to join the queue. The short-run marginal cost scheme above would then charge one unit of toll to vehicles 2, 3, and 6. It would charge two units of toll to vehicles 4 and 5. Vehicles 7, 8, and 9 would get refunds of 1, 2, and 4 units of toll respectively. If everyone has the same value of time, which can be monetized in units of tolls, this seems fair.

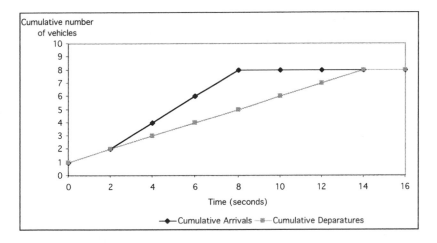

Figure 11.2 Cumulative arrival and departures, in the absence of vehicle 2

Table 11.3 Payment scheme in the absence of vehicle 2

Time (seconds)	Queue	Vehicle	Payment	Income	Net Income
0:00	1	1	0	0	0
0:02	3	3	0	0	0
0:04	45	4	1	0	-1
0:06	567	5	2	1	-1
0:08	6789	6	3	1	-2
0:10	789	7	2	2	0
0:12	89	8	1	2	1
0:14	9	9	0	3	3
Total			9	9	0

However, the short-run marginal costs imposed by a vehicle are not its only costs. Rather, a vehicle's presence has a reverberation much longer in time. For instance, in the absence of vehicle 2, the queue looks like the cumulative arrival and departures given in Figure 11.2, shown numerically in Table 11.3. Note that the total difference in costs with and without vehicle 2 is now 16 – 9 = 7, implying a true marginal cost for vehicle 2 of seven units, rather than the one unit shown above.

The long-run marginal costs of vehicle 3 are again only nine units, while those of vehicle 4 are 10 units. But those savings are not additive. That is, initially there were 16 units of cost, the savings from vehicle 2 is seven units, from vehicle 3 is also seven units and from vehicle 4 is six units. Yet, one cannot add 7 + 7 + 6 to obtain 20, which would be greater than the total delay. Rather, the total cost is four units and only 16 – 4 = 12 units are saved. So even eliminating vehicles 2, 3, and 4 does not completely eliminate congestion. The long-run marginal cost of a vehicle depends both on how many other vehicles there are and when each vehicle arrives.

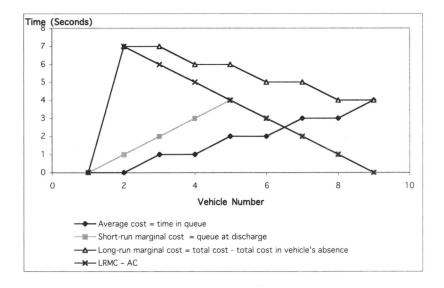

Figure 11.3   Average and marginal effects of delayer pays principle

Charging the long-run marginal cost (rather than the short-run marginal cost), and paying people the amount of their delay, would produce the results shown in Figure 11.3. The figure shows that more money is paid in than paid out. This discrepancy is because eliminating a vehicle will sharply reduce delay, but to the delayed vehicle, it matters not which vehicle ahead is eliminated, as any one of them will reduce delay significantly. Thus using long-run marginal cost accounting will generate surpluses.

This can be described mathematically through the equations and description given in Table 11.4.

Table 11.4   Mathematical model of delayer pays compensation schemes

Cost and income variables	Expression
S_v = Own cost	$S_v = A_v - D_v$
$T_{[\,]}$ = Total cost [for arrival pattern containing vehicles in bracket]	$T_{[\,]} = \sum_{[\,]} S_v$
J_v = Short-run marginal cost	$J_v = Q(D_v) - 1$
M_v = Long-run marginal cost	$M_v = T_{[1..V]} - T_{[1..v-1,v+1..V]} - S_v$
R_v = Reimbursement income	$R_v = S_v / \mu$
N_v = Net income	Short-run marginal cost
	$N_v = J_v - R_v$
	Long-run marginal cost
	$N_v = M_v - R_v$

Notes: Subscript $_v$ denotes vehicle v. A_v = Arrival time (at back of queue). D_v = Departure time (from front of queue). $Q(t)$ = Number of vehicles in queue at time t. μ = Service time (headway between vehicles departing queue).

If people vary in their values of time, people with a high value of time may not be fully compensated, while those with a low value of time would get more dollars back than the value of the time that was wasted. This may induce more travel by clever people with low values of time trying to scam the system; however, clever people rarely have low values of time for long.

Moreover, the system would send price signals back to drivers, who would then change their departure times in some fashion, probably smoothing out their behavior. A new, less-peaked, arrival pattern would then come about. So after equilibration between price and demand, the system would have a lower price and lower net turnover than suggested by Table 11.2.

One can imagine problems with this scheme, as getting on a queue becomes a gamble that there is not a large platoon of vehicles behind you. Can the technical 'gamble' problem be solved? Yes, but it will require implementing a detailed traffic-monitoring system, as illustrated in Figure 11.4.

Strictly speaking, the long-run marginal cost is unknown until some time after the driver exits (the front) of the queue, but some approximations can be made. The charge depends not only on how many vehicles are behind the driver at the time the driver exits, but also on how many vehicles are behind those vehicles – that is, on how much delay that vehicle actually caused. Figure 11.4 represents a freeway with an on-ramp and an off-ramp just before a bottleneck. If the mainline traffic flow, on-ramp flow and off-ramp flow are known, the expected price can be posted at the variable message sign (VMS) just before the bottleneck. This will not be strictly accurate, as the mainline flow may suddenly spike upward, and the actual price would drop. Or the off-ramp may suddenly get more traffic (and the actual price would drop). But with experience, the forecasting system would become more and more accurate.

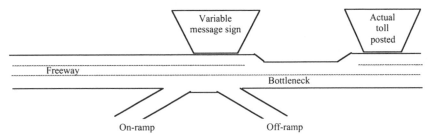

Figure 11.4   Detailed monitoring system

This leads to a modified strategy that would distribute the revenue back to the delayed, but would only charge drivers based on what they were promised at the VMS. In this case the toll authority would assume the risk of under- or over-forecasting, and someone would monitor it to ensure it behaved well.

The delayer pays scheme, using short-run marginal cost, enables a straightforward solution to 'what to do with congestion pricing revenue' – return it directly to those who were delayed, almost instantly. The system can be perfectly revenue-neutral, stay within the roadway sector, and be economically efficient. Overall, the amount of revenue collected equals the amount distributed. But those who delay others the most pay the most, while those who are delayed more than they impose delay on others are compensated for their delay.

BUYING TIME: HOT LANES

In 1998 the Congestion Pricing Policy Project at the Humphrey Institute of the University of Minnesota released a short video entitled *Buying Time*. It argued that individuals with a high value of time, perhaps because of a business meeting, a doctor's appointment, late departure for the airport, or the need to pick up a child at day care, should be able to buy into a toll lane that moves faster than the freeway it parallels. It is well established that high-occupancy vehicle (HOV) lanes are often underutilized (Dahlgren 1998). While Dahlgren's argument suggests that most HOV lanes should revert back to general purpose lanes, an alternative has emerged in recent years. High-occupancy/toll (HOT) lanes are an innovative solution, suggested by Fielding and Klein (1993) to implement what is now called 'value pricing' by selling the available HOV lane capacity to those willing to pay extra. Those who pay to use the HOT lanes save time. Other HOV travelers do not noticeably lose time because the additional flow is managed to keep sufficiently below capacity. What happens to traffic in the general purpose lanes (serving low-occupancy vehicles, or LOVs), however, depends on the geometric configuration of the roads.

Baseline with bottleneck

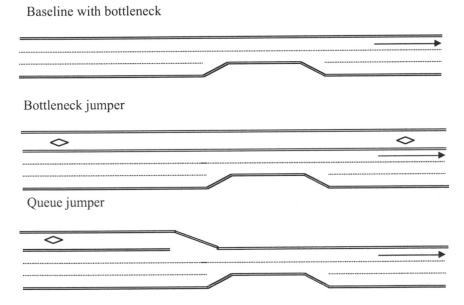

Figure 11.5   Baseline and two types of diamond lanes

Figure 11.5 illustrates two cases of special (diamond) lanes which are used for HOV traffic and might be used as HOT lanes. In the first case, the bottleneck jumpers, the diamond lane traffic does not interfere with the regular LOV traffic, and avoids the queue entirely. The presence of the additional lane provides a net benefit to regular traffic, by taking cars out of the stream and thus reducing total delay.

In the second case, queue jumpers, the diamond lane traffic simply moves to the head of the queue, displacing the regular LOV traffic (making regular cars wait longer). The total delay in the second case is the same as the baseline, and regular traffic views it as a net loss unless it is compensated. These two outcomes have very different equity implications.

Assume that the diamond lanes allow toll users to buy in. Like a corrupt *maître d'hôtel* at an expensive restaurant, the toll authority receives payment for allowing the bribers to pass the honest.[3]

Compensation is required to make the situation fair. Assume that the toll payers have a higher value of time than the no-toll traffic, otherwise they would not pay the toll. The maximum payment that should or could be made to the no-toll traffic is the price of the toll. If the payment were too high, however (congested no-toll travelers were paid more than their extra delay would warrant), travelers would be induced by the compensation payment to travel more. People with low values of time would drive to generate income. To avoid this kind of scheming, a two-tier pricing system must be established. Part 1 would be a fixed cost assessed to all travelers to pay for maintenance and operation of the roads, as well as other non-delay externalities, part 2 would be a premium to avoid congestion. The part 2 revenue collected from toll-payers could offset the part 1 charge, but should not exceed it.

BORROWED TIME

Patrick DeCorla-Souza (2000) has put forward an idea he has called 'fair lanes'. Noting that congested facilities often have lower throughput than uncongested facilities, he would separate currently free, but congested, freeway lanes into two sections: toll lanes (diamond lanes) and 'credit' lanes. Electronically tolled express lanes would bear tolls dynamically set to maximize throughput.   Electronic credits, funded from tolls, would be given to travelers in the credit lanes where congestion continued.   The credits could be spent on the toll lanes or on other priced transportation goods (for example, transit fares or parking), or could be taken as cash. DeCorla-Souza claims credit lane travelers would benefit in two ways. With better traffic traffic management, the toll lanes now have a higher throughput than they did previously, indicating less congestion on the other lanes. Second, credit lane travelers receive credits to compensate them for their frustration and for seeing free lanes converted to tolls. While this might again induce travelers with low values of time to drive just to receive credits, perhaps some control could be placed on that. Also, the claim of higher throughput needs to be established empirically.

SHARING TIME

A Pareto-efficient outcome is one where some people are better off while no one is made worse off. Unless revenues are returned to drivers, conventional congestion pricing or marginal cost pricing is not Pareto-efficient. Hau (1991) speaks of the tolled or tolled-on and the tolled-off. The wealthy minority with a very high value of time clearly benefit from congestion pricing, but others lose. Losers are either those who pay a toll but would prefer the congestion to the toll, or those who are tolled-off and do not pay the toll. Further, some people will switch routes to avoid the toll, making the individuals onto whose route they switch worse off. To overcome such difficulties, Daganzo and Garcia (1998) suggest drivers should take turns. By combining rationing (some fraction of users get a free pass every day) with tolling (the remaining users pay a daily toll that depends on the length of the queue), a Pareto-efficient outcome results, even if revenues are not returned to the original drivers. Their analysis considers commuters driving through a single bottleneck during the morning commute, each with a desired arrival time, and early and late penalties if they miss that time. Each commuter selects an arrival time at the bottleneck to minimize the weighted sum of tolls, queuing time and deviation from the desired passage time. This system is Pareto-efficient where others are not because everyone alternates in paying the toll and receiving the benefits of others paying the toll. Unless the benefits of traveling faster are shared among the entire population, congestion pricing benefits some (those with a high value of time) at the cost of others, who either pay the toll and save time, but not enough to make it worth while, or who defer the trip altogether.

CONCLUSIONS

Equity and efficiency form the two pillars on which transportation decisions should be made. However, determining what is efficient, much less what is equitable, is far from simple. When considering whether and how to compensate for congestion pricing, there are a number of alternatives:

* continue with first come, first served, using delay as the cost of travel – the 'no-toll' option;
* introduce marginal cost pricing during peak times, without compensation;
* implement a delayer pays scheme and charge based on the actual congestion caused;
* split the difference between delayer and delayed;

- convert HOV lanes to HOT lanes;
- convert general purpose lanes to 'fair' lanes; or
- construct a toll and rationing system.

Who owns the right to travel on the roadway? Currently the system is first-come, first-served. Unfortunately, the conventional marginal cost pricing approach described in Chapter 10 ignores traffic dynamics and tends to treat time in large discrete blocks rather than continuously. How significant a problem this is depends on the conditions of the case. The delayer pays scheme outlined in this chapter implies that everyone has a right to free-flow traffic conditions, and the individuals who deny that right to others are the ones who should pay. So is delayer pays a good idea? This depends on answers to two questions, the first empirical and the second technical:

- What will the magnitude of cheating/gaming the system be?
- What is the cost of the added data collection and toll redistribution?

There are also several key philosophical questions that need to be addressed. These very much parallel the fundamental question of whether people should be guaranteed equality of opportunity or equality of outcome. Congestion externalities require two actors, the delayer and the delayed. If both parties have equal opportunity to arrive, than one should not compensate the other. But to guarantee an equal outcome in terms of a combination of time and money, those who save time should pay more money and those who spend more time should be paid by those causing their delay.

Congestion pricing generates revenue that can substitute for conventional transportation financing (such as the gas tax). Few argue against substitution, as it makes sense as a demand management measure. However, what to do with excess congestion pricing revenue has been a hurdle for its adoption. In the absence of private roads, this is a political problem. Suggestions range from the government keeping the money, to building more roads, to providing transit, to compensating the poor (redistributing the money by income class). There is a clear alternative, however that is fair, namely returning the excess congestion-pricing revenue to those who are congested, in the form of cash or credits, in such a way as to avoid encouraging gaming the system or driving for dollars.

NOTES

1. On San Francisco's BART the transit agency has put black pads on the station platforms adjacent to where the train doors open, but on Washington DC's Metro the train doors open at seemingly random locations along the platform.

2. The idea of delayer pays scales up to a much longer time period than the 18 seconds represented by nine vehicles, it is just unwieldy to draw in detail.

3. The mention of expensive restaurants suggests the theoretical ideal known as *reservation pricing*. If only n vehicles can depart in a given time slot, why should more than n vehicles arrive during that same period? Logically, all other arrivals involve wasted time. If properly implemented, reservation pricing would ensure no delay. Just like restaurant reservations, bottleneck reservations would be made. Obviously guaranteeing arrival in a 2-second time window is impossible, but with a larger time block and multiple vehicles, the total amount of queueing will be short and random. The driver would arrange to arrive at a bottleneck at a given point in time (say a time window such as between 5:00 and 5:05 p.m.). The system managers would ensure there was sufficient capacity to handle the assigned reservations during that period. If drivers were able to accurately predict when they could show up, such a system could ensure no or minimal delay. A bottleneck management system would be required that took reservations and ensured that only reserved vehicles would be allowed to enter the bottleneck. Reservations could be auctioned off, or priced in any other efficient manner. At peak times the price to travelers for a reservation would be highest, trailing off to the shoulders of the peak. To make such a system revenue neutral, you would need negative prices in the off-peak, or some other way to compensate travelers.

12. Deploying Electronic Tolls

INTRODUCTION

Electronic toll collection (ETC) systems save bridge, tunnel, and turnpike operators' staffing costs while cutting delay for travelers. However, such systems are not yet ubiquitous, and not all users buy into the system. There is a lag both on the part of toll collectors, who must become familiar with the technology, and users, who must expend some effort to obtain the transponder and establish accounts. To accelerate deployment, some portion of the benefits could be returned to users in the form of a discount. The intent of this chapter is to inform decisions that tolling agencies must make regarding discounting tolls and dedicating lanes to ETC. This chapter therefore considers the speed with which lanes should be converted to ETC and what discount for using ETC would be socially optimal.[1]

A model for dynamic optimization over a wide choice set must be developed. This model will depend on what share of the initial reluctance to switch to electronic tolls is fixed by the individual, what share depends on exposure, and what share is simply random. An agency's decision to deploy ETC lanes in one year will affect the market conditions it faces in the next.

This chapter begins by discussing deployment theory and the interrelationship of technology and demand. A dynamic payment choice model describing how users choose between manual and electronic tolls is proposed. The benefits and costs to society and users' payment choice, which vary with demand and the number of ETC lanes, need to be determined in order to find the best combination in the optimization exercise. The welfare maximization model is applied to the Carquinez Bridge case and a series of sensitivity analyses varying the capacity assumptions are performed. Finally, some conclusions are drawn about the pace of deployment of electronic toll collection.

DEPLOYMENT THEORY

Electronic toll collection can be considered a network in the financial and communication sense of the word. Electronic transactions take place between nodes – transponders and collection points – both tied back to the rest of the financial network. Electronic toll collection, like many complex networks, entails economies of scope, joint and common costs, spillovers, externalities, and cross-subsidies. The use of an ETC system depends on decisions made by travelers and toll agencies, while user demand for ETC depends on the environment, including other ETC locations. This system exhibits several sources of positive feedback.

One source of positive feedback is network externalities: a network becomes more valuable the more members (users, destinations and so on) it has. In principle, a single transponder may be used for multiple toll plazas and parking garages. Additional uses become increasingly viable the more uses and users that already exist, and make acquiring a transponder that much more valuable. Recently, transponders have been used at drive-through fast food outlets and at service stations. Incompatible adjacent systems add unnecessary costs and decrease overall ETC share, while compatible systems following the same standards exhibit positive network externalities.

The longer a system is deployed, and the more users it has, the more confidence a non-user will have in it. They trust others' judgment that the system is reliable (it doesn't overcharge or violate their privacy), that it works, and that it is easy to use. Furthermore, the more users there are, the more opportunities for learning exist. A non-user will be more likely to take a ride with a user as the number of users increases and as time progresses. This learning will decrease the predisposition against ETC. Also, the longer the system is around, the more opportunities a potential user has to choose the system. With each day that a potential user has some probability of telephoning to sign up, the greater the cumulative likelihood of such a call.

A related source of positive feedback is the process of cumulative causation and historical path-dependence. The longer a particular technological path is followed, the harder it is to switch, as more and more new technologies reinforce the old; technology adoption decisions assume a certain market environment. Finally, endogenous growth creates market niches and opportunities as the network expands, which reinforces that growth. The success of ETC deployment depends on these conditions.

However, positive feedback growth is not inexhaustible, and diminishing marginal returns tend to set in after a point. S-curves, introduced in Chapter 2 concerning the deployment of turnpikes, describe how a given technology is deployed over time, showing the gestation period, take-off, and saturation of a technology. The S-curve shows the cumulative amount of a technology as a share of its total potential market. The idea of the S-curve can be seen as an application of network externalities. In the case of electronic toll collection, the theoretical maximum of users is 100% of the market. This market is constrained locally by demand for a transportation facility and globally by society's willingness to toll roads.

One underlying constraint behind technological advances in complex systems is the requirement of 'co-evolution', that is, interdependent complementary technologies. Understanding this interdependence is critical to understanding the pitfalls of deploying a new technology or redeploying an old one. Co-evolution is an example of the network externality phenomenon. Complex elements require the proper environment (network of related technologies) in which to work, and so cannot emerge in isolation. The environment here is defined broadly, to include the entire socio-technical system outside of the technology element in question. Electronic tolls only became viable when all of the related component technologies (including communications, electronic miniaturization, and finance) also became individually feasible in the 1990s. In economic terms, the environment needed for a technology to be viable can be considered as a hidden fixed cost of that technology.

DYNAMIC PAYMENT CHOICE MODEL

The dynamic payment choice model predicts the share of each payment mechanism in any given year, recognizing that travel time, ideal lane configuration, optimal discount, and payment choice decision are all interdependent. Details on the benefit–cost analysis and key assumptions are given in Appendix A12.1.

Payment Choice

The choice of payment mechanism (manual or electronic) by travelers depends on the out-of-pocket cost, travel time, and fixed costs associated with the alternatives. For convenience, only the difference in fixed costs between manual and ETC is considered. The ETC-specific cost is expected to have a negative sign since travelers have to go through a non-effortless process to obtain transponders and open an ETC account. The logit functional form was chosen for its clarity of results rather than because of theoretical precepts related to the expectations of the error distribution (Train 1986). In addition, the linear utility function implies complete substitutability between the travel time and out-of-pocket costs. Individuals using manual payment re-evaluate their payment mechanism each time there is a change in circumstances (in this case, growth, a change in the lane configuration, and discount policy), assumed to be once per year. Clearly, a more frequent cycle of user re-evaluation would entail a change in the model.

This model estimates payment choice among those who are presently users of manual lanes. An irreversibility assumption means that ETC users do not revert to manual transactions. However, there is a survival rate, so that ETC users who change commutes away from the Carquinez Bridge (because they change jobs, homes, or both) are replaced by new, manual users who are then subject to choosing ETC. The fraction of those who stay with the same commute from year to year is dubbed the 'survival rate' (R). This value is taken to be 84% based on previous research evaluating the survival of commutes between the same home and workplace (Levinson 1997). All replacements for non-survivors are placed in the pool of users who may choose their payment each year.

The model is given by:

$$S_{e,n,x} = R\left(S_{e,n-1} + \left(S_{m,n-1}\right) \cdot \frac{e^{U_{e,n}}}{e^{U_{e,n}} + e^{U_{m,n}}} \right) \tag{1a}$$

$$S_{m,n,x} = R\left(\left(S_{m,n-1}\right) \cdot \frac{e^{U_{m,n}}}{e^{U_{e,n}} + e^{U_{m,n}}} \right)$$

The model for replacement commuters is given by:

$$S_{e,n,w} = \left(1 - R\right) \cdot \frac{e^{U_{e,n}}}{e^{U_{e,n}} + e^{U_{m,n}}} \tag{1b}$$

$$S_{m,n,w} = \left(1 - R\right) \cdot \frac{e^{U_{m,n}}}{e^{U_{e,n}} + e^{U_{m,n}}}$$

such that:

$$S_{e,n,w} + S_{m,n,w} + S_{e,n,x} + S_{m,n,x} = 1$$

The market shares for new commuters (traffic growth) are implicitly assumed to be:

$$S_{e,n,v} = S_{e,n,w} + S_{e,n,x} \tag{1c}$$

$$S_{m,n,v} = S_{m,n,w} + S_{m,n,x}$$

such that:

$$S_{e,n,v} + S_{m,n,v} = 1$$

where:

R	= survival rate of commutes;
$S_{e,n,x}$ $S_{m,n,x}$	= share of existing ETC, manual users in year n;
$S_{e,n,w}$ $S_{m,n,w}$	= share of replacement ETC, manual users in year n;
$S_{e,n,v}$ $S_{m,n,v}$	= share of new ETC, manual users in year n;
$U_{e,n}$	= utility of ETC in year $n = \alpha_0 + \alpha_1 T_e + \alpha_2 P_e$;
$U_{m,n}$	= utility of manual tolls in year $n = \alpha_1 T_m + \alpha_2 P_m$;
T_e T_m	= travel time in ETC, manual lane (min);
P_e P_m	= toll in ETC, manual lane (dollars/veh); and
α	= model parameters.

The baseline scenario coefficient on time was borrowed from previous studies on the sensitivity of choice to travel time ($\alpha_1 = -0.03$) (Ben-Akiva and Lerman 1985). From this and the value of time, the coefficient on price is computed. Using base-year data and these values, an alternative specific constant is estimated.

The coefficient on price (α_2) was computed with the following expression, assuming a weighted value of time (V_T) of \$17.41 per vehicle-hour in the benefit–cost analysis (Gillen et al. 1999).

$$\alpha_2 = \frac{60 \bullet \alpha_1}{V_T} = -0.1034 \qquad (2)$$

In the first year (FY97/98), the share of travelers using electronic toll collection (S_e) was 6%. Using base-year traffic data, a time difference between an average ETC user and a manual user ($T_e - T_m$) of -35 seconds is estimated. Moreover, a discount of \$0.15 was introduced to ETC users in the first year. The α_0 that would result in the model returning the first year values for share of ETC users (S_e) is solved with the following expression:

$$\alpha_0 = \ln\left(\frac{S_{e,1}}{1 - S_{e,1}}\right) - \alpha_1 \cdot \left(T_e - T_m\right) - \alpha_2\left(P_e - P_m\right) = -3.08 \qquad (3)$$

The magnitude of the ETC-specific coefficient is much greater than for the other parameters. This implies a significant amount of savings in time and money is needed to overcome the hurdle to adopt ETC technology. When the time and cost savings are small, travelers would rather endure a slightly longer travel time than go through the process of obtaining a transponder.

Changing Dispositions toward ETC and Network Externalities

The constant (α_0) can be interpreted as a fixed cost associated with acquiring transponders, implicitly a predisposition against switching from manual to ETC. However, this disposition may change over time. There are several parallel but offsetting processes going on.

In the first year some drivers select ETC. These early adopters must have a smaller than average predisposition against the technology, that is, their constant (α_0^{adopt}) is smaller in absolute terms. Thus those who do not adopt in the first year must have a greater than average value of the constant ($\alpha_0^{notadopt}$). In the second year, the average predisposition against adoption rises even more among those who haven't adopted (all other things being equal). Unfortunately, the existing data cannot tell us how much higher the predisposition is, because there are many unknowns affecting payment choice in addition to variations in the constant (α_0).

However, the willingness to try ETC may increase with the rate of adoption if there exist any network externalities, as suggested earlier in this chapter. As noted before, several sources of those network externalities may explain why it is that the more people who have transponders, the more willing non-users will be to choose ETC. As a baseline, α_0 is reduced from its base-year value to zero in year 20 linearly.

POLICY VARIABLES: CAPACITY AND DISCOUNT

According to the choice model, the toll agency can affect the evolution of ETC share in two ways. One is to provide a discount exclusively for ETC users, and the other is to impose congestion in the manual lanes by supplying more ETC capacity than needed and reducing the capacity of manual lanes. In the basic 'myopic' model, the toll agency decides the number of ETC lanes every year according to the forecast ETC share that maximizes the overall social welfare, such that ETC delay is less than manual delay. By adding more ETC lanes and closing manual lanes, travelers will switch to ETC and its market share will grow. This may result in greater benefits in the end, despite deviating from the short-run optimal. This issue would be eliminated if the model could solve the optimization problem simultaneously over 20 years rather than sequentially year by year. Due to the size of the problem, an exact, non-heuristic, solution for the multi-year optimization is not feasible.[2]

Given the number of ETC lanes, annual traffic volume, and the dynamic payment model, the optimal discount that maximizes overall social welfare in any given year is found. For each year from year 2 through year 20, an optimal combination of ETC lanes and discount is chosen to maximize the overall social welfare so long as the net benefit of the toll agency is non-negative. This constraint encourages the toll agency to accelerate deployment of ETC.

MODEL SYSTEM

Knowing the number of ETC lanes, a discount policy and annual traffic volume, the ETC market share is estimated from the payment choice model. The costs incurred and benefits gained for each class are calculated. An iterative procedure searches for the optimal combination of ETC lane configuration and discount policy to maximize total social welfare given the market demand function.

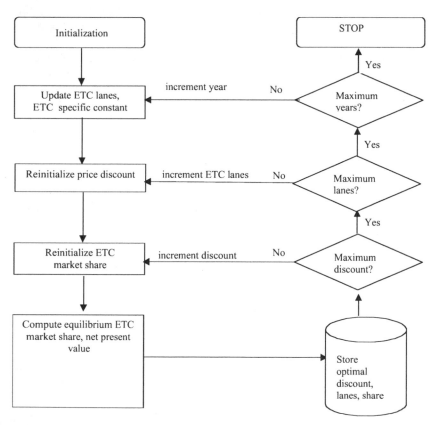

Figure 12.1   Flowchart of the basic ETC optimization model

Figure 12.1 illustrates how the model works. In the initialization stage, the base-year configuration of the toll plaza, survival rate, payment choice parameters, and optimal discount are all established using the initial assumptions. The equilibrium market share is computed using a grid search, establishing a market share that would return traffic delays that result in the same market share, given a discount and lane configuration. If the net present value from that configuration is better than all previous net present values for that year, the lane configuration and discount are stored as optimal; otherwise, the previous optimal combination is retained. If the discount is not at a maximum, it is incremented, and the process is repeated. If the number of lanes for ETC is not at a maximum, it is increased incrementally, and the process is repeated. At the end of a year's trial, the information for that year is recorded, and the model is run for the next year, through year 20.

RESULTS

Historical traffic and financial data for the Carquinez Bridge in northern California are used to illustrate the procedure to determine an appropriate pace of ETC deployment and discount policy. The Carquinez Bridge was selected as the ETC pilot implementation in the Bay Area because it has sufficient capacity to accommodate current traffic (Gillen et al. 1999). There are 12 lanes going through the toll plaza. A dedicated ETC lane has been opened to travelers with transponders since August 1997. In addition, two lanes were opened for mixed ETC/manual toll collection. Since vehicles equipped with ETC suffer delay when the driver of the leading vehicle pays the toll manually in mixed use lanes, the gains from mixed payment lanes are expected to be marginal and are thus neglected in the model. Mixed lanes are treated as manual lanes so that all vehicles equipped with transponders use the ETC dedicated lane only.

For this study's baseline assumptions, the overall net present value is about $61 million dollars. The benefit–cost ratio for the toll agency is much less than 1.0 (0.24), indicating that the agency does not have any reason to proceed with the project if it chooses to ignore community welfare. However, for society overall, benefits greatly exceed costs (benefit– cost ratio of 28.43, internal rate of return of 51.5%), primarily because of delay reductions.

If travelers were forced to switch to ETC payment as early as possible, overall social welfare over the 20 years should be greater. By forcing travelers to switch earlier, future benefits would be realized earlier at the expense of lower welfare in the earlier years. In this simulation, one and two more lanes are added to the number of ETC lanes computed from the myopic optimization rules. The results for evolution of ETC share under different capacity rules are shown in Figure 12.2. Again, the results confirm the observation that the earlier additional ETC lanes are deployed, the greater the overall net present value is gained over the 20-year period. Increasing from $61 million in the base to $74 million with a +1 lane optimization, and $89 million with +2 lanes optimization

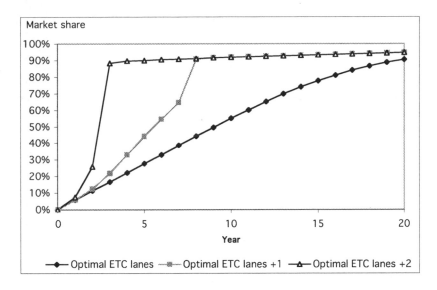

Figure 12.2   Evolution of ETC market share for different capacity rules

Finally, the number of ETC lanes in two-year, three-year, and four-year bundles are optimized, where otherwise all assumptions are the same as the original model. Figures 12.3 depicts the results. The longer time span taken into account, the better the overall results compared with the myopic optimization rules. A four-year optimization will be superior to the two-year optimization. The three-year bundle model is almost identical with the two-year bundle model. The gap between the two-year, three-year, and four-year model is not as much as between the myopic and two-year model. The net gains of the four-year optimization ($89 million) is slightly better than the gains from a two-year optimization ($84 million), though both are much larger than the $61 million in the base one-year optimization case. The improvements obtained by optimization over longer time spans is limited, and faces diminishing marginal returns.

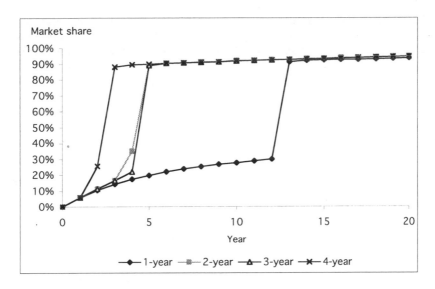

Figure 12.3   Evolution of ETC market share under different optimization rules

CONCLUSIONS

The conversion of conventional toll plazas to electronic toll collection is seemingly inevitable. How quickly it occurs remains to be seen. This chapter has identified a process that may explain the speed of this conversion if public toll agencies strive to improve the welfare of all, but are constrained by myopia. It is clear that government policy – opening ETC lanes faster or slower – can drive user adoption of ETC. Overall welfare is improved the greater the ETC market share, and the sooner that share is achieved. Longer-term decision-making, as expected, will result in higher overall welfare than myopic decisions, although the penalty for myopia (as high as 50%) depends on other assumptions. Many of the gains can be achieved by simply looking two years out; there are diminishing returns to optimizing with an increasing number of years, while modeling costs rise.

This chapter developed a schematic model and applied it to a particular case. As a matter of course, there are some questions that cannot be answered, but which are critical when trying to strategically deploy network technologies such as ETC. In particular, it is unclear whether individuals face positive network externalities associated with the technology or whether their reluctance to make the leap runs deeper. While the second year of data for the Carquinez Bridge suggests the latter, those data are associated with little marketing as the agency attempts to ensure the technology is working smoothly. A more concerted marketing strategy to reduce the barriers to entry could easily shift preferences. Furthermore, deployment of ETC on other Bay Area bridges should also create a positive externality. Alternatively, use of automatic vehicle identification, such as is used on Highway 407 in Toronto, which eliminates the transponder buy-in, may be an option. Clearly, more empirical research is needed on user preferences for this and other new technologies, to ascertain which deployment scenario is most reasonable.

NOTES

1. For previous research on ETC, see Al Deek et al. 1997; Burris and Hildebrand 1996; Friedman and Waldfogel 1995; Hensher 1991, Lin and Su 1994; Sisson 1995; Zarillo et al. 1997.
2. To illustrate the size of the problem, for one year the operator chooses between 1 and 11 lanes (along with discounts). To optimize for two years, the choice is over 11 X 11 lanes (the number of lanes in each year), so for 20 years, in principle, there are 11^{20} possible choices to optimize simultaneously (rather 11 X 20 as in the myopic optimization). Assumptions such as irreversibility reduce this number, it is nevertheless a much larger problem to solve.

APPENDIX A12.1: BENEFITS AND COSTS OF ELECTRONIC TOLL COLLECTION

To estimate the costs and benefits of electronic toll collection, a number of basic assumptions are made. These include overall traffic growth, toll transaction time by type of payments, travel speed, and design configuration of the Carquinez Bridge, as well as the annual inflation rate and interest rate. The main assumptions are listed in Table A12.1 and are explained below.

This framework that identifies benefit and cost categories for Travelers (Time, Vehicle Operating Costs), Agencies (Fixed & Operating Costs of Toll Collection, Revenue), and the Community (Pollution). While this measure of overall net present value (NPV) ignores transfers, they are considered for the net present value of each user class. Transfers include tolls paid (a transfer from the user to the toll agency), or interest on prepaid ETC credit accounts (lost to travelers but accrued to the agency)

Costs and benefits for each class (travelers, the toll agency, and the community) can be estimated separately. The overall social welfare (W) is defined as:

$$W = B_T - C_T + B_A - C_A + B_C - C_C \tag{A1}$$

where:

B_A, B_C, B_T = benefits for toll agency, the community, and travelers; and
C_A, C_C, C_T = costs for toll agency, the community, and travelers.

Travelers

Travelers are divided into two classes, referred to as 'manual' and 'electronic'. Cost savings for electronic travelers come from reduced delay due to higher through-put on ETC lanes, and elimination of acceleration and deceleration processes associated with manual toll collection. For convenience of analysis, it is assumed that the value of time, the mode split (car, truck, bus), and the average vehicle occupancy do not vary over the period of analysis.

In general, delay can be decomposed into three categories: random (or overflow) delay, stop delay, and delay due to acceleration/deceleration. The random delay stands for the stochastic nature of the arrival traffic streams and manual toll collection times. When the number of arriving vehicles exceeds service capacity temporarily during some period, vehicles must wait to pay the toll. The generalized delay model suggested by Fambro and Rouphail (1997) for the new *Highway Capacity Manual* (TRB 2000) is employed to estimate delay. The model is solved separately for manual and electronic lanes. The delay is only computed for peak hours, no delay is assumed outside of the peak period.

$$D_R = 900 T_{peak}\left[(\rho - 1) + \sqrt{(\rho - 1)^2 + \frac{8\rho}{Tm\mu}}\right] \tag{A2}$$

where:
  D_R = average random delay (sec);
  T_{peak} = duration of peak period (hrs);
  μ = capacity of one lane (veh/hr);
  m = number of lanes;
  λ = total arrival rate during the peak period (veh/hr); and
  ρ = degree of saturation, $\rho = \lambda/m\mu$

The stop delay is the time required by a manual user to pay the toll. For manual lanes, mean transaction time is the weighted transaction time multiplied by payment type split. The service capacity is then the inverse of the mean transaction time. For ETC lanes, transaction time is assumed to be 0 seconds, and the capacity is determined by the minimum headway, 2.4 seconds (1500 vehicles per hour) in the Carquinez Bridge case (which retrofits ETC lanes to an older toll plaza design).

In order to make a complete stop at the toll plaza, a manual user experiences acceleration/deceleration delay. The distance traveled during this process is the length of ramps from and leading to the toll plaza. Drivers are assumed to accelerate and decelerate at a constant rate, and thus the average travel speed is equal to one-half of the normal travel speed. The acceleration delay is estimated by dividing the length of the ramp leading to the toll plaza by this average travel speed. The same estimate is applied to the deceleration process. Electronic users escape both stop delay and acceleration–deceleration delay.

ETC users also benefit from a reduction in vehicle operating costs, mainly in fuel consumption. In general, engines need more fuel during acceleration than at other times. Thus, only fuel consumption during acceleration is considered. Fuel costs are estimated as follows:

$$C_{GTn} = T_{plaza,n} \cdot G_a \cdot C_G \cdot (1 + I_f)^n \tag{A3}$$

where:
  C_{GTn} = total gasoline costs in year n (dollars);
  G_a = gasoline consumption during acceleration (gal/hr);
  I_f = annual inflation rate;
  $T_{plaza,n}$ = time to travel the length of toll plaza ramps in year n, (hr/yr);
  C_G = cost of gasoline in base-year (excluding taxes) (dollars/gal).

It is expected that all ticket users will switch to ETC gradually over the 20 years. Furthermore, fuel usage is assumed to be independent of vehicle type. To estimate the future peak hour-volume, the base-year ratio of average annual daily traffic (AADT) to peak-hour volume (PHV) through the toll plaza is computed and assumed to stay constant over time. During the evening peak hour, this ratio is 0.0995, and during the morning peak hour it is 0.0277 for the Carquinez Bridge. (The toll booth is located on eastbound I-80, which is outbound from San Francisco and Oakland).

Agency

The agency has both one-time and continuing operating costs. One-time costs are expended to establish new systems, while operating costs are incurred daily to operate the system. Among the one-time costs, some are spent at the beginning of the project, and are independent of the number of lanes open and the level of traffic. The costs of installing additional ETC lanes and purchasing transponders are allocated to the year associated with the incremental increase in the number of ETC users.

The operating costs can be divided into three categories: staffing, hardware/software, and other. Staffing is comprised of employees in information technology, accounting, and toll collection. Personnel costs for information technology (P_I) and accounting (P_A) are assumed constant over time (California Department of Transportation 1995a, b). Only the numbers of toll collection personnel (P_{Tn}) vary with traffic volume, so those are estimated by the model. A promising cost savings for the toll agency from adopting the ETC alternative is the reduction in toll collection staff, proportionate to the number of manual lanes. Staff costs are estimated by multiplying the number of personnel needed for each alternative by the cost per person. The number of persons needed for toll collection can be estimated given forecast annual traffic volume and ETC market share. The costs of staffing can be obtained as follows:

$$C_{PTn} = C_P \cdot (P_A + P_I + P_{T_n}) \cdot (1 + I_f)^n \tag{A4}$$

where:
  C_{PTn} = total personnel cost in year n (dollars);
  C_P = person year costs in base-year (dollars/yr); and
  P_A, P_I, P_{Tn} = person years for accounting. information, toll collection in year n.

The number of toll collection staff is balanced with the traffic level in the base-year. Furthermore, all manual lanes are open during the peak hour, and the personnel needed during the off-peak period is proportional to the number of manual transactions during the off-peak. Off-peak traffic is estimated by subtracting projected annual peak traffic from the projected annual traffic volume. In the model, the ETC share is the same during the peak and off-peak periods. However, it might be more realistic to expect that the ETC share will be higher during the peak hours when significant time may be saved, and because peak travelers are more regular users of the system. Hardware/software costs for information technology and other program costs are estimated from the ATCAS report (California Department of Transportation 1995a).

Community

The primary benefit of ETC systems to communities at large is the reduction of NOx, HC, and CO emissions during idling and acceleration. Total emissions of pollutant p from idling in year n ($E_{idleT,p,n}$), (in gm) are estimated as follows.

$$E_{idleT,p,n} = T_{idle,n} \cdot E_{idle,p} \cdot 60 \qquad \text{(A5)}$$

where:

$T_{idle,n}$ = time idling in year n (hrs); and
$E_{idle,p}$ = emission rate for pollutant type p during idling (gm/min).

Total emissions of pollutant p from acceleration in year n ($E_{accT,p,n}$) (in gm) are:

$$E_{accT,p,n} = (T_{plaza,n}) \cdot G_a \cdot E_{acc,p} \qquad \text{(A6)}$$

where:

$E_{acc,p}$ = emission rate of pollutant type p during acceleration (gm/gal);
G_a = fuel consumption rate during acceleration (gal/hr).

Table A12.1 Assumptions

Item	Value
Annual traffic growth rate	3%
Seconds/cash transaction	7.5
Seconds/ticket transaction	4.5
Seconds/ETC transaction	2.4
Normal travel speed (mph)	55
Ramp distance to toll plaza (mile)	0.2
Annual discount rate	6%
Annual inflation rate	3%
Average miles/gallon	25
Pre-tax fuel price (excluding taxes) ($/gal)	$0.74
Costs per personal year ($/PY)	$65,000
Unit cost of ETC lanes	$62,361
Unit cost of transponders	$28.85
Person years needed for information technology	0.11
Person years needed for accounting	0.46
Average number of transponders per ETC account	1.35
Average annual times an account is used	160

Modal use assumptions	Auto	Truck	Bus
Mode split	94.76%	5.11%	0.13%
Average vehicle occupancy	1.258	1.1	20
Value of time per passenger	$12.75	$33.41	$12.75

Pollution	NOx	HC	CO
Emission rate during the acceleration (gm/gallon)	24.7	9.5	209.0
Emission rate during the idling (gm/minute)	0	0.15	2.5
Cost of air 0ollution ($/kg of pollutant)	$1.275	$1.275	$0.0063

Payment Split	Cash	Ticket (credit card)
Baseline	83% in base-year; 83% in year 20	17% in base-year; 17% in year 20
ETC alternative-Manual users	83% in base-year; 100% in year 20	17% in base-year; 0% in year 20
ETC alternative-ETC users	64% in base-year; 64% in year 20	(36% in base-year; 36% in year 20)

Source: *ATCAS Feasibility Report* (California Department of Transportation 1995a); Gillen et al (1999) pp.13, 21, 22, A-13, Table B-1,B-2, C-2; Small and Kazimi (1995); ETTM on the web; *Highway Statistics 1996* (FHWA 1997); Cicero-Fernandez and Long, (1993); Older cars (IEPA 1993).

13. Summary and Conclusions

INTRODUCTION

A reconsideration of the existing highway revenue mechanisms, in particular the gas tax, is in order. The original decision to utilize the gas tax for highway finance relied upon certain underlying fundamental conditions. This book's introductory chapter identified several key changes under way that challenge the assumptions that were in place when the decision to employ gas taxes was made. These changes include the increasing importance of social costs, the shift in the vehicle fleet toward alternative fuels or electric power, the rise of congestion, the scarcity of financial resources and resistance to general taxation, the emergence of new, intelligent transportation technologies and electronic toll collection, and changing priorities (from construction to maintenance) associated with a mature technology while America's highway finance system favors ribbon cutting to repairs.

The prospects for the future success of toll roads depend on several factors, in particular the relative centralization of control of the highway sector and the costs of collecting revenue. This book has shown that if the governance were to become more decentralized, and collection costs continue to drop, tolls could return to prominence as the preferred means of financing roads for both local and intercity travel. Success further depends on the choices about what to do with toll revenue, whether they are in lieu of existing revenues or in addition to them.

Proposals to price road use for infrastructure financing, congestion mitigation, or air quality improvement have been surfacing regularly over recent years. Congestion pricing has long been a goal of transportation economists, who argue that it will result in a more efficient use of resources. Outside transportation economics, road pricing is seen mainly as an alternative financing mechanism. The path for implementing road pricing has been strewn with political potholes because pricing, particularly congestion pricing, inevitably produces winners and losers. An alternative approach, one which would create the local winners necessary to implement road pricing, is required before it can be expected to become widespread.

This research suggests one approach, one that would decentralize the decision about whether to tax or to toll rather than attempting to impose road pricing from the central government. This research shows that in certain cases tolls are the only rational financing mechanism to produce a stable equilibrium. This is especially true for sufficiently small jurisdictions, particularly with the advent of electronic toll collection systems.

Road pricing ties revenue to need more closely and directly than a tax system can. It should result in more efficient, and less political, road financing decisions, with less waste due to the log rolling and pork-barrel politics which infests current infrastructure spending. It is easier to raise revenue for transportation from user fees, which directly result in better service, than general taxes. Just as gas taxes substitute more efficiently for general taxes, direct road pricing could substitute for gas taxes.

Road pricing is a necessary prerequisite to the economists' goal of congestion pricing. One can reasonably argue that it is not nearly as difficult to vary rates once tolls are in place, as it is to place tolls (varying or fixed) on untolled roads in the first place. Over time, direct road pricing can be structured to provide off-peak discounts, and can thus be converted to time-of-day pricing, which is more efficient than 'one size fits all' pricing. Congestion pricing requires peak-period road users to pay for the additional capacity that travel during the peak requires, while not requiring off-peak users to pay for the excess capacity they don't need. However, it is clear that the acceptance of toll roads is required before time-of-day differentiation, much less dynamic pricing, can be deployed.

This chapter first summarizes the key findings of this book. Some general trends suggest the growing importance of road pricing, including a reduction in transactions costs, decentralization, deployment of new advanced highway infrastructure, privatization, and federal rules on toll roads. Deployment scenarios for electronic toll collection, new toll roads, and the conversion of existing roads to toll roads are offered. Any change from one financing system to another cannot take place instantaneously, nor is it likely to take place universally.

SUMMARY

Chapter 2 examined the history of priced roads, including both their initial deployment and the subsequent disturnpiking. The first significant wave of turnpikes, which began in the 1700s and peaked in the early to mid-1800s, saw turnpikes under the control of local companies and trusts. Rationales for tolling included the rise of long-distance trade and difficulties in the then-existing system which utilized statutory labor for maintaining roads. In this pre-automobile era, roads were financed with tolls when it was recognized that they served non-local residents. Non-residents neither pay local taxes nor perform statutory labor to maintain local roads, and thus would act as free riders without tolls. Local residents often received discounts or paid lump sum charges to use the roads rather than being inconvenienced by the tolls. The early 1900s saw the first significant deployment of smooth paved roads. In the United States most roads were financed by states, and later the federal government, by means of a gas tax. With the relatively slow speed of highway travel during the early automobile era, most trips remained within states; through trips were not as significant as they were to become later in the twentieth century. However, a number of excludable parkways were toll-financed.

Another significant wave of toll financing arrived with the deployment of grade-separated highways. As both vehicles and highways improved, trips of longer distances could be made in the same time and trip lengths increased. This in turn implied more trips between states, and the emergence of the free-rider problem when the basis over which roads were financed (taxes or tolls) did not coincide with the use of the system. Since financing was at the state level, turnpikes were effective for collecting revenue from all users and mitigating the potential free-rider problem. But when national financing became dominant, the definition of 'local' changed to include everyone in the nation, and the revenue mechanism with lower collection costs (that is, the gas tax) was preferred to tolls, especially when the goal was simply cost-recovery rather than profit. As a result, few new toll roads were constructed in the United States during the interstate era, although international experience varies. Furthermore, unlike earlier roads, grade-separated roads are easily excludable, that is, the number of entrances is limited and tolls can be cost-effectively assessed at each. The same is not true of roads without grade separations.

Finally, upon completion of the interstate system in the United States, the financing of new roads has largely become a local problem again, and new toll roads are being constructed, including some private roads. Because of the length of trips, and because of the ease with which tolls can be collected on these excludable roads, as well as a reduction in toll collection transaction costs on both the government and traveler side with electronic toll collection, tolls are again a feasible option. Road-pricing proposals now assume electronic toll collection. Further, cordon tolls are being placed around a number of cities internationally, to collect revenue from non-local residents for traveling on urban streets. The cordons establish excludability for use of a network from outside, though not for any particular link once the network is entered. Where cordons can easily be established, such as on river crossings and ring roads, it is feasible for localities to switch the road-financing burden to suburban residents. Ironically, the attempts of localities, often subject to obsolete political boundaries, to finance infrastructure for the 'wrong' reason – the offloading of costs on non-residents – creates opportunities to achieve a more efficient infrastructure pricing and financing system.

Highway transportation financing involves the public costs of building and operating infrastructure, the private costs of owning and operating a vehicle, and other costs borne by society. While the public costs of infrastructure and the private costs of vehicle operations are generally understood, social or external costs are hidden to the users and operators of the transportation system. The first element in the full cost model are vehicle costs borne by users. Estimates for average unit costs and marginal cost imply that, for a 1000 km trip, the average cost for the automobile user is \$130, but the marginal cost is only \$49. The second component in the full cost model is infrastructure costs. Long-run marginal costs exceed average costs for automobiles, suggesting diseconomies of scale in infrastructure provision. Trucks impose higher costs than automobiles, due to increased pavement damage, and so pay higher charges. Creative ways to charge for pavement damage using advanced technologies and refined tolling schemes would be appropriate. Collection costs depend on the technology used to collect tolls. Data for manual collection on California's toll bridges suggest that the fixed costs of collection amount to \$0.03/vehicle, compared with variable costs of \$0.085/vehicle. Delay costs rise steeply as roads become congested, suggesting marginal cost pricing as a viable remedy. Accident costs also depend on traffic flow and distance, arguing perhaps for alternatives to fixed-rate insurance schemes. Noise costs, which are internalized by homeowners in lower property values or by infrastructure providers who supply noise walls, really depend on traffic levels. Pollution costs depend on emissions, and should be considered in financing transportation, as the hidden costs are paid by society rather than the polluters.

While tolls may be seen as efficient user charges, as states provide a service in exchange for payment of a toll, in practice they are at present more analogous to tariffs. Because out-of-state residents cannot vote in a state's election, toll policies will be more prevalent in states that import labor, as it enables them to raise revenue from non-voters. In labor-exporting states, the burden of tolls (collection costs and all) falls disproportionately on residents. Small states are more likely to import workers, and thus more likely to toll. Therefore, a way to increase the likelihood of tolling is to decentralize the financial responsibility and governance of highways to more local agencies (for instance, by eliminating federal funding and moving authority from states to sub-metropolitan areas and counties). This has the potential to lead in the direction of marginal cost pricing.

The hierarchy of roads separates the function of access from that of through movement, and a link's economic properties further helps explain that hierarchy. Typically, the hierarchy of roads is constructed such that links with high free-flow speeds and high flows are at the top of the hierarchy, while slow and low flow links are at the bottom. Networks can be divided into two basic structures, trees and webs. Trees are local monopolies, while webs are competitive. These suggest the organizational structure that is most appropriate for each. Broadly, three classifications emerge: local roads, which serve neighborhood collection and distribution of traffic, arterial roads, which connect neighborhood roads with other arterials, and limited-access highways. Local roads, which don't become congested, are akin to club goods, and require different types of highway financing than arterials or intercity highways.

Local jurisdictions must balance present and future needs against costs when financing infrastructure, and have relied on pay-as-you-go financing, impact fees, and bonds in different circumstances. In general, average fixed costs decline with additional users, but average variable costs rise. At low demand levels, average fixed costs dominate; at higher levels of demand, variable costs are more significant. When average costs are rising, marginal cost pricing can pay for the costs of infrastructure. However, when average costs are falling, each additional user has little impact on existing users. This is the problem faced by local road infrastructure. If these roads are paid for in a pay-as-you-go scheme, existing users are disadvantaged compared with future ones. A continuous recovery approach can alleviate this problem. Unlike conventional impact fees, which are used to expand facilities, the recovery fee allows development to buy into existing excess capacity provided by the community. The total capital cost of the facility is allocated proportionately to existing and future households. Unfortunately, existing capital cost recovery approaches fail to return the funds directly to the residents who paid for it.

Roads higher up the hierarchy are more susceptible to toll financing. The preference for taxes or tolls as revenue sources or financing mechanism can be considered a function of trip length, jurisdiction size, and collection costs. In the case of tax-only financing, travelers from outside the taxing jurisdiction do not pay taxes to support the construction, operation, and maintenance of the road. In the case of toll-only financing, travelers entering and exiting the network within the toll cordon pay nothing. The gains to a jurisdiction of imposing tolls exceed the gains from taxes under certain circumstances. The gains come from residents of other jurisdictions. This problem is modeled on a beltway using simple arithmetic to ascertain some basic relationships.

Then a more sophisticated model is developed. A community's residents use both local and non-local network links, and the local links are used by both local and non-local residents. Cordon tolls (tolls placed on jurisdiction boundaries) by themselves are economically unsustainable as jurisdictions become large. Large jurisdictions are more likely to impose taxes or a mixed financing policy than cordon tolls only because cordon tolls alone raise insufficient revenues to cover costs. Toll revenue levels off above a certain point. In uncongested conditions with low variable costs, use of interior (non-cordon) tolls does not enhance local welfare, as any additional revenue raised compared with cordon tolls comes from local residents, except to the extent that the tolls reduce overuse and social loss. Similarly, the higher the cost of collecting tolls, the less likely it is that tolls will be the preferred revenue mechanism. The welfare-maximizing toll may not fully recover costs, and thus may still require subsidy (thus toll-only financing may be unsustainable). The maximum welfare from taxes may exceed those of tolls under certain circumstances, depending on model parameters. However if jurisdictions are sufficiently small, demand sufficiently high, and collection costs relatively low, then tolls will be preferred. Hence collection costs need to be fairly high before no tolls is a better solution than some tolls. The gains to a jurisdiction from imposing tolls exceeds the gains from taxes under certain circumstances. The gains come foremost from residents of other jurisdictions. This problem, a finance externality, is well known in certain cases, for instance the reliance by local governments on some mix of sales, income, and property taxes, each of which is borne by a different set of people, not all of whom are local.

The problem is considered in the context of a repeated game with multiple possible objectives. Profit-maximizing behavior is more likely to lead to tolls than welfare-maximizing behavior; cooperation is more likely to lead to taxes, or lower tolls, than non-cooperation; re-evaluation of the decision periodically is more likely to lead to cooperation (taxes) than a one-time decision. This comports with the notion that privatization of various kinds and consideration of roads as a market good will influence financing in favor of tolls.

Then congestion and congestion pricing were considered. Conventional arguments for congestion pricing use what is called 'generalized cost'. It would be better to represent behavior as if people have a money demand curve at each level of service. Imposing congestion prices raises both the money price for travel, but also the quality of the trip being received, that is, people are no longer paying for the same good. Moving from the short-run average cost to short-run marginal cost has a welfare implication; raising the price lowers the demand, and thus the area that is conventionally thought of as consumer surplus gets smaller. In actuality, the movement from short-run average cost to the short-run marginal cost implies a movement from a demand curve with poor level of service to a demand curve with a better level of service.. At better levels of service (lower travel times) the demand will be higher at the same money price than at lower levels of service. Game theory was applied to congestion and congestion pricing. In the model, each vehicle may depart during one of three time slots: early, on-time, or late. If both depart at the same time, there will be congestion. Depending on the value of time in delay, arriving early, or arriving late, congestion may or may not be a stable equilibrium. And the stable equilibrium may or may not be welfare-maximizing. However, there is a set of prices which will eliminate congestion.

If congestion pricing is such a great idea, why isn't it here already? In part, there is resistance to tolls due to dated perceptions of how toll roads operate (and also because of toll operators, sluggishness in adopting advanced technologies); people still envision stopping at toll booths and paying a toll, a situation where the toll road causes more delay than it relieves. But perhaps more significantly, if gas taxes have already paid for the road, why should tolls now be put in place? In particular, if A delays B, why should C (the government) collect the revenue? Several scenarios have been developed to return congestion pricing revenue to travelers which, if implemented, might reduce some of the opposition that will inevitably accompany road pricing.

The use of an electronic toll collection (ETC) system depends on decisions made by travelers and toll agencies while user demand for ETC depends on the environment, including other ETC locations. A model to analyse the ETC deployment problem suggests that the toll agency needs to push deployment to maximize overall welfare.

GENERAL TRENDS

From a positive perspective, many general trends can be cited which suggest road pricing will become more rather than less likely in the future. Some key trends (a reduction in transaction costs, decentralizing decisions, deploying new infrastructure technologies, privatization of roads, and implementation of new federal rules) are discussed in turn.

An important result was that the lower the transaction costs for collecting tolls, the more likely toll collection becomes. How likely is it that toll collection will become less costly? Electronic toll collection is a set of technologies which automates the manual, in-lane, toll collection process so that drivers do not have to stop and pay cash at a toll booth, thereby reducing the cost to the user of transacting the collection of tolls. Three major technologies are employed: automatic vehicle identification, automatic vehicle classification, and video enforcement (ETTM 1997). It can also be expected that the variable costs (if not the fixed costs) of ETC will be lower than is the case with traditional toll booths, which require labor. Friedman and Waldfogel (1995) estimate significant welfare gains from switching to electronic toll collection using data from New Jersey and Massachusetts. Including the reduction in vehicle delay, $5,000 a day would be saved by using ETC. Fourteen ETC systems were operational by the end of 1995, and since then, numerous others have been deployed. It seems reasonable to suppose that ETC, if appropriately pushed by toll agencies as described in Chapter 12, will become a standard feature of toll roads in the future.

To the extent that decentralization is applied to roads, it indicates an increased likelihood of toll financing. Several chapters showed that small jurisdictions have a strong temptation to toll. How likely is it that roads will be governed by more local jurisdictions? There is a broad though not universal trend toward shifting authority from the central government to the more local entities. In different contexts, this is called decentralization, devolution, or the new federalism. The best-known recent example of devolution of power is in the United Kingdom, where the power over local policies for Scotland and Wales have been shifted from London to Edinburgh and Cardiff following recent referenda. In the United States, the term 'New Federalism' denotes the shift in the balance of powers and responsibilities among localities, the states, and the federal government. The intent is to administer government programs more effectively by playing to the strengths of each governmental level (Urban Institute 1997). At the core of the shift is the belief that the federal government (and, to a lesser extent, each state's government) is rigid, and that its 'one size fits all' notion is not the most effective way of implementing policies, whereas states, counties, and cities are closer to the needs of their citizens and are thus more able to respond flexibly to local needs. Welfare reform is the programmatic change which has received the most notice, although the federal government has handed many programs to the states to administer, under more general block grants rather than specific rules. Similarly, a significant amount of transportation-planning and decision-making authority has been shifted from states to metropolitan planning organizations in the most recent highway bills. To the extent that this trend continues, road pricing becomes more probable, especially the implementation of urban or metropolitan toll cordons.

This research has shown that cross-subsidies from voters to road users become less likely when the road users and voters comprise an increasingly distinct population. Two cases where they are distinct groups are when road users live out of district, or when the users of a particular facility are a small sub-population of the voting population. The second case has direct bearing on the deployment of new intelligent transportation systems such as automated highway systems. Automated highway systems are supposed to result in vehicles being driven without the active participation of drivers for at least part of the journey. While the degree of centralization of control versus autonomy for the automobile is not certain, the system may require separate facilities for automated vehicles and the existing fleet to take advantage of automation (tighter spacing and higher speeds). These facilities will not be free and will not, at first, serve the entire population. In particular, the first users are likely to be a self-selected wealthy sub-group willing to pay for advanced technology. Some special-purpose financing mechanism, such as tolls or a subscription, is likely to be necessary to build these facilities.

An unregulated private firm operating the road can be expected to employ an objective such as profit maximization. It was found that for large jurisdictions, a cooperative profit-maximizing firm (typical of a vertically integrated road) generated the same overall welfare (distributed differently) as a non-cooperatively toll-setting, welfare-maximizing jurisdiction (typical of local public sector ownership at the city or town level or larger). Private toll roads, if properly organized and regulated, may be able to serve as a substitute for public sector ownership. How likely are private toll roads? As noted in Chapter 2, there are a number of private road facilities throughout the world. The deployment of private (usually toll-financed) roads appears to be a growing trend. Several models of privatization are used, including build–operate–transfer (BOT) and design–build–finance–operate (DBFO), and variations on these with forms of public subsidy. In recent years, following the BOT model, the private Northumberland Strait Crossing and the Highway 104 Western Alignment Tollway in Nova Scotia were opened in Canada. In Britain, the DBFO model, including shadow tolls rather than real tolls, has been employed on some recent private roadways. Shadow tolls involve payment from the government (rather than travelers) to the road operator, in proportion to the amount of traffic. In 1996, eight DBFO franchises were awarded in Britain. France and Germany have also authorized recent projects, France a $2.2 billion 10-kilometer tunnel in the Paris ring road. Portugal is considering selling the state-owned toll authority and has approved several private toll road projects. Eastern European countries including Hungary, Croatia, Poland, and Romania are progressing in plans to use the BOT model for new roads. Several projects in Latin America are in the planning stage (Poole 1997). Clearly the use of the private sector to finance, build, and operate toll roads is an increasing trend.

Just as smaller governments have a strong incentive to impose tolls, larger governmental units have an incentive to use more general financing mechanisms. In general, the United States federal government has had a long-standing prohibition against funding toll facilities. Four major exceptions to prohibitions on federal toll funding have been identified (Gittings 1987). First, in 1927 the government permitted tax funding of tolled bridges and their approaches and connections to the federal aid highway system. Second, in 1956, approaches to toll roads on the interstate system were able to receive federal support. Third, also in 1956, pre-existing toll roads incorporated into the interstate system could receive funding. And finally, in 1978, federal Interstate 4R funds could be applied to interstate system toll roads. However, in the first, second, and fourth cases, upon the retirement of bonded debts, the tolls had to be removed. This has happened in several states (Connecticut, Kansas, and New York). On the other hand, roads may be converted to toll status once all contributed federal money for the road's construction and maintenance has been repaid. This repayment requirement is the principal cost of converting existing roads from untolled to tolled. The construction of toll barriers has been estimated at about one-twentieth the cost of repayment (Gittings 1987). To the extent that new federal rules are more sympathetic to both decentralization of power and more experimentation on the part of the states, road pricing will be more widely seen on the federally funded interstate highway systems.

SPECULATIONS ON THE DEPLOYMENT OF PRICED ROADS

Physical networks require long lead times to construct, and are extremely durable. The deployment of a new transportation technology is unlikely to take place quickly for both political and technical reasons. Perhaps the ultimate application of road-pricing technology will require advanced highway systems. In an era of smart cars and smart roads, one can conceive of quasi-competitive highways dynamically altering their tolls in response to demand (and travel time), while drivers (or pre-programmed cars) select routes in response to the posted prices and their individual value of time. However, in the interim, a path for deploying the currently available road-pricing and electronic toll collection technologies is needed. Three different road-pricing deployment problems are identified and discussed in turn: deployment of ETC on existing roads, construction on of new toll roads, and conversion of existing untolled roads to toll roads.

The first issue concerns the deployment of ETC on existing turnpikes, and on toll roads, bridges and tunnels. As noted in the section on general trends, toll facilities are presently converting from human toll operators and automatic coin deposit boxes to ETC systems. However, different systems use different technologies. While this may suffice for the vast majority of local trips, and may be a necessary interim step to winnow out technological winners and losers, over the long term some standardization is necessary before road pricing becomes widespread. With the provision of compatibility between regions, users can use multiple toll facilities, each under different management, while only having one ETC device in their vehicle. As many individuals use different toll facilities from time to time, the presence of an ETC unit in the vehicle will become common, at least in certain parts of the country. Thus, the transaction costs (such as delay due to stopping, labor costs, and construction of toll booths) associated with implementing tolls on a new facility could be minimized if new facilities were tolled using a standard ETC system. The costs of ETC should decline as the fixed costs of development and initial deployment are spread over a wide number of users. Network externalities can be exploited by the adoption of a standard ETC mechanism by special facilities which are already tolled, such as tunnels, bridges, turnpikes, selected new highways, parking garages, and high-occupancy/toll (HOT) lanes.

A second issue is the construction of new toll roads. Since the completion of the interstate highway system, new highway construction has been relatively sparse. In some sense, applying the idea of the S-curve, the mature limited access highway network has reached saturation.   Much of the new, albeit limited, highway construction is being toll-financed because of scarce resources.   First, finding financing from a higher level of government for local projects is difficult in the absence of a national road-building program. Second, roads paid for by one jurisdiction serve both local and non-local residents – generating revenue from non-local residents requires a mechanism such as tolling.

Furthermore, the dearth of new construction implies that travel speeds on highways will decrease, as current roads became saturated with traffic which continues to grow. Proposals to construct automated highway systems (AHSs), which promise both higher travel speeds and smoother traffic flow, will require a new financing mechanism to be implemented. As these systems will, at least initially, only support a subset of the vehicle fleet, it seems reasonable to suppose that a special financing mechanism (tolls) will be preferred to a more broadly based mechanism (funding out of general revenue). If AHS were to become a dominant technology, it can be expected to bring tolling back as the primary revenue mechanism. The toll collection mechanism for these roads should be consistent with the technology used elsewhere, so that users need only support one in-vehicle toll communication device.

This research suggests that under certain circumstances, including vertical integration of monopoly road segments, new roads can be financed by the private sector without significant welfare losses compared with uncoordinated local roads. As the welfare losses are small or non-existent, the opposition to new toll roads will be less strong than might be expected if losses were large. As the construction of new private roads becomes increasingly common, as suggested in the trends section, toll roads will impose themselves as a significant component of the transportation landscape.

The third and hardest case is the tolling (or re-tolling) of presently unpriced, publicly controlled roads, presumably utilizing electronic toll collection. The idea of local welfare maximization under decentralized decision making should be employed. It was shown that the more decentralized the decision-making, the more likely that tolls would be employed.

The following is a scenario of how tolling might be deployed on the existing 'free' network. Central cities would establish cordon rings in lieu of or in addition to other financing mechanisms so long as the dollars collected remain within the transportation sector. This is akin to a commuter tax, which several cities already assess on individuals working but not living within their boundaries. The idea of cordon rings is not as unlikely as it seems. Already several cities (Singapore, Oslo, Bergen, and Trondheim) have imposed explicit cordon rings. Other places, such as Manhattan, have implicit cordon rings: one cannot enter that island from most directions without paying tolls. Similarly, San Francisco has a partial cordon ring from the north and east, though the revenue collected remains with the bridge authorities rather than being used for city streets. Cordons can be established at convenient locations, most often natural barriers such as bodies of water, but also artificial barriers such as beltways. Whether these are imposed by central cities or by metropolitan areas, the point remains that those inside the ring are distinct from those outside, although both groups may have to cross from time to time.

In response, suburbs (or exurbs) would likely establish cordons to toll city residents at convenient boundaries. It would be perceived as unfair that suburban residents pay tolls to enter the city, but city residents can drive on suburban roads without a similar charge. Whether the suburban cordons would require separate facilities from the city cordon, or simply share the revenue from those crossing the cordon, is a secondary issue to its presence.

Once they are initially constructed, cordon rings can be made more efficient as they get drawn tighter and tighter over time. The smaller the area enclosed within a cordon, the more direct the pricing of the network, and the more use and revenue coincide. For a very tight cordon, this method approaches link-specific tolls, particularly on excludable facilities. The traditional downside of 'perfect' tolls on excludable facilities is that spacing between exits is increased, so backtracking and slowtracking costs are increased. However, with low transaction costs associated with ETC, this problem need not arise.

It should be emphasized that these tolls primarily substitute for existing road-financing systems (gas tax and general revenue), a substitution which is more efficient because it directly collects revenue from users of a specific facility and thereby can be used to provide incentives to reduce the welfare loss associated with excess use (where marginal cost exceeds marginal benefit). Of course, the burden associated with tolling will shift, but if decision-making is sufficiently decentralized, the shift will be politically palatable because the burden shifts from local to non-local residents.

At first, pricing would likely be applied to limited-access links dedicated to longer-distance movement. These roads have a cost structure where users face increasing costs as demand rises. Cordons around sub-areas, networks used mainly for access and short movement, are the second candidate for road pricing – although this would mainly be to recover fixed costs and some maintenance costs rather than to increase the size of the local network or reduce congestion. Local streets are more likely to be operating on the left side of the U-shaped cost curve, the area of declining average costs.

Alternatively, road pricing could be forced by an unexpected source. The adoption of new fuel sources for automobiles (such as fuel cells, batteries, or hybrid vehicles) may steadily reduce gas tax revenue network-wide, and force jurisdictions to find a new source of money. If the road pricing alternative is fully developed and just sitting on the shelf waiting to be deployed, it has a good shot at being implemented as a replacement for dwindling gas tax revenues.

Bibliography

American Automobile Association (AAA) (1993), *Your Driving Costs*, Rochester, Wisconsin: Runzheimer International.

Albert, William (1979), 'Popular Opposition to Turnpike Trusts in Early Eighteenth Century England', *Journal of Transport History* 2:5:1: pp. 1–17.

Al-Deek, Haitham A. Essam Radwan, A.A. Mohammed and J.G. Klodzinski (1996), 'Evaluation of the Improvements in Traffic Operations at a Real-life Toll Plaza with Electronic Toll Collection', *ITS Journal*, 3(3), pp. 205–223.

Al-Deek, Haitham, A.A. Mohamed and A. Essam Radwan (1997), 'Operational Benefits of Electronic Toll Collection: Case Study', *Journal Of Transportation Engineering*, 123(6) pp. 467-477.

Altshuler, Alan and José Gomez-Ibañez (1993), *Regulating for Revenue: The Political Economy of Land Use Exactions*, Washington, DC: Brookings Institution.

Axelrod, Robert (1984), *The Evolution of Cooperation*. New York: Basic Books.

Baer, Christopher, Daniel Klein and John Majewski (1993), 'From Trunk to Branch: Toll Roads in New York, 1800-1860', *Essays in Economic and Business History*, pp. 191-209.

Bauman, Gus and William Ethier (1987), 'Development Exactions and Impact Fees: A Survey of American Practices', *Law and Contemporary Problems,* 50(1), pp. 51–68

Ben-Akiva Moshe and Stephen Lerman (1985), *Discrete Choice Analysis*, Cambridge, Massachusetts: MIT Press.

Bernstein, D. and J. Muller (1993), 'Understanding the Competing Short-run Objectives of Peak Period Road Pricing', *Transportation Research Record,* 1395, pp. 122–128.

Bobrick, Benson (1986), *Labyrinths of Iron: Subways in History, Myth, Art, Technology, and War*, New York: Henry Holt.

Boske, Leigh (1988), 'Alternative Formulations of the Federal Highway Administration's Bid Price Index for Highway Construction', *Logistics and Transportation Review*, 24(2), pp. 165–174.

Buchanan, B.J. (1990) 'The Turnpike Roads: A Classic Trap?', *Journal of Transport History*, 3:11:2, pp. 60–72.

Buchanan, James M. and Gordon Tullock (1962), *The Calculus of Consent, Logical Foundations of Constitutional Democracy*, Ann Arbor: University of Michigan Press. <http://www.econlib.org/library/Buchanan/buchCv3c10.html>.

Bureau of Census (1993), *The Statistical Abstract of the United States*, Washington, DC: Bureau of Census.

Bureau of Transportation Statistics (1994), *1994 Annual Report*, Washington. DC: US Department of Transportation.

Bureau of Transportation Statistics (1995), *American Travel Survey*. Washington, DC: US Department of Transportation. <http://www.bts.gov/programs/ats/>.

Bureau of Transportation Statistics (1999), *National Transportation Statistics*, Washington, DC: US Department of Transportation.

Burris Mark and Eric Hildebrand (1996), 'Using Microsimulation to Quantify the Impact of Electronic Toll Collection', *ITE Journal*, 66(7), pp. 21–24.

Button, Kenneth (1994), *Alternative Approaches Toward Containing Transport Externalities: An International Comparison*, *Transportation Research A* 28(4), 289-305.

California Air Resources Board (1991), *Methodology to Calculate Emission Factors for On-Road Motor Vehicles*, Sacramento, CA: CARB, July.

California Air Resources Board (1996), *Memorandum of Understanding with Automakers*.

California Air Resources Board (1997), ZEV Incentives <http://arbis.arb.ca.gov/msprog/zevprog/zev2.htm> .

California Department of Transportation (1995a), *Advanced Toll Collection and Accounting System (ATCAS) Feasibility Study Report*, TIRU Project no. 2400-146.

California Department of Transportation (1995b), *Annual Financial Report: State Owned Toll Bridges*.

California Highway Patrol (1993), *Annual Report of Fatal and Injury Motor Vehicle Traffic Accident*.

Caro, Robert (1974), *The Power Broker*, New York: Alfred Knopf Publishers.

Casson, Lionel (1974), *Travel in the Ancient World*, London: Allen and Unwin.

Chamberlin, Edward (1933), *The Theory of Monopolistic Competition: A Re-orientation of the Theory of Value*, Cambridge Massachusetts: Harvard University Press.

Chapman, Graham, John Cleese, Terry Gilliam, Eric Idle, Terry Jones and Michael Palin. (1989), *The Complete Monty Python's Flying*

Circus All the Words, Volume One. New York: Pantheon Books, p. 196.

Chevallier, Raymond (1976), *Roman Roads* (translated by N. H. Field), Berkeley: University of California Press.

Clean Air Action Corporation (1993), *'Proposed General Protocol for Determination of Emission Reduction Credits Created by Implementing an Electronic Pike Pass System on a Tollway'*, Study for the Northeast States for Coordinated Air Use Management, December.

Coase, Ronald (1992), *'The Problem of Social Cost, and Notes on the Problem of Social Cost'*, reprinted in *The Firm, The Market and the Law*, Chicago: University of Chicago Press.

Copeland, John (1963), 'An Essex Turnpike Gate', *Journal of Transport History*, 1:6:2: pp. 87–94.

Cornes, Richard and Todd Sandler (1996), *The Theory of Externalities, Public Goods, and Club Goods*, Cambridge, England: Cambridge University Press.

Cupper, Dan (1990), 'The Road to the Future', *American Heritage*, May/June pp. 103–111.

Daganzo, Carlos and Reinaldo Garcia (1998), 'A Pareto Improving Strategy for the Time-Dependent Morning Commute Problem', *Transportation Science*.

Dahlgren, Joy (1998), 'High Occupancy Vehicle Lanes: Not Always More Effective than General Purpose', *Transportation Research*, 32A(2) pp. 99-114.

de Palma, Andre and Robin Lindsey (1998), 'Private Toll Roads: A Dynamic Equilibrium Analysis', Paper presented at the Western Regional Science Association Meeting Monterey, CA., February.

Deakin, Elizabeth (1989), 'Toll Roads: A New Direction for US Highways?', *Built Environment* 15 (3/4): pp. 185–194.

DeCorla-Souza, Patrick (2000), Making Value Pricing on Currently Free Lanes Acceptable to the Public with 'Credit' Lanes, unpublished manuscript, <http://pdecorla.tripod.com/lane3.htm>.

Delucchi, Mark (1991), *Emissions of Greenhouse Gases from the Use of Transportation Fuels and Electricity: Volume 1 Main Text*, Washington, DC: US Department of Energy.

Delucchi, Mark (1996), *The Annualized Social Cost of Motor-Vehicle Use in the United States, based on 1990–1991 Data*, (UCD-ITS-RR-96-3), Davis, California: Institute of Transportation Studies, University of California at Davis.

Dilts, James (1992), *The Great Road: The Building of the Baltimore and Ohio, The Nation's First Railroad, 1828-1853*, Stanford, California: Stanford University Press.

Downs, Anthony (1957), *An Economic Theory of Democracy*. New York: Harper Collins Publishers.

Downs, Anthony (1992), *Stuck in Traffic: Coping with Peak-Hour Traffic Congestion*, Washington, DC: Brookings Institution.

Duckham, Baron (1984), 'Road Administration in South Wales: The Carmarthenshire Roads Board, 1845–89', *Journal of Transport History*, 3:5:1: pp. 45–65.

Dupuit, Jules (1849), 'On Tolls and Transport Charges', reprinted in *International Economic Papers,* 1962, 11: pp. 7–31.

Durrenberger, Joseph (1931), *Turnpikes: A Study of the Toll Road Movement in the Middle Atlantic States and Maryland*, Valdosta Georgia, Ann Arbor: University Microfilms.

Electronic Toll Collection and Traffic Management (ETTM) (1997), Electronic Toll Collection <http://www.ettm.org>.

Encyclopedia Britannica (1999), 'Toll', *Encyclopedia Britannica*. Standard CD.

Energy Information Administration (1994), *Emissions of Greenhouse Gases in the United States 1987-1992*, Washington: US Department of Energy.

Environmental Protection Agency (1988), *Procedures for Emission Inventory Preparation, Volume IV: Mobile Sources*, Research Triangle Park, NC: Office of Air Quality Planning and Standards, US Environmental Protection Agency: December.

Fambro, Daniel and Nagui Rouphail (1997), 'Generalized Delay Model for Signalized Intersections and Arterial Streets', *Transportation Research Record* 1572 pp. 112-121.

Federal Aviation Administration (1983), *Airport Capacity and Delay* (AC 150/5060 -5), Washington, DC: US Department of Transportation.

Federal Aviation Administration (1989), *Economic Value for Evaluation of FAA Investment and Regulatory Programs*, June, Washington, DC: US Department of Transportation.

Federal Highway Administration (1982), *Final Report on the Federal Highway Cost Allocation Study: Report of the Secretary of Transportation to the United States Congress.* Washington, DC: FHWA.

Federal Highway Administration (1993), *Highway Statistics 1992*, Washington, DC: Office of Highway Information Management.

Federal Highway Administration (1994), *Price Trends for Federal Aid Highway Construction, Fourth Quarter 1993*, p. 7, Washington, DC: Federal Highway Administration.

Federal Highway Administration (1996), *Highway Statistics 1995,* Washington, DC: Office of Highway Information Management.

Federal Highway Administration (1999), *Highway Statistics 1998*, Washington, DC: Office of Highway Information Management.

Fielding, Gordon and Daniel Klein (1993a), *High Occupancy Toll Lanes: Phasing in Congestion Pricing a Lane at a Time*, Reason Foundation Policy Study No. 170, November.

Fielding, Gordon and Daniel Klein (1993b), 'How to Franchise Highways', *Journal of Transport Economics and Policy*. May, pp. 113–130

Flink, James (1990), *The Automobile Age*, Cambridge, Massachusetts: MIT Press.

Friedman, David and Joel Waldfogel (1995), 'The Administrative and Compliance Cost of Manual Highway Toll Collection: Evidence From Massachusetts and New Jersey', *National Tax Journal*, 48(2), pp. 217–228.

Fuller, John, Barry Hokanson, John Haugard and James Stoner (1983), *Measurements of Highway User Interference Costs and Air Pollution and Noise Damage Costs*, (NS 83-817), Iowa City, Iowa: Institute of Urban and Regional Research, University of Iowa.

Gifford, Jonathan (1983), *An Analysis of the Federal Role in the Planning, Design, and Deployment of Rural Roads, Toll Roads, and Urban Freeways*, Dissertation UCB-ITS-DS-83-2, Berkeley: Institute of Transportation Studies, University of California, Berkeley.

Gillen, David, Mark Hansen, Shomik Mehndiratta and Todd Soderberg (1994), 'The Impact of Air Transportation Technology on Aggregate and Sectoral Economic Efficiency and Growth in California', UCB-ITS-RR-94-18: Berkeley: Institute of Transportation Studies, University of California, Berkeley.

Gillen, David, Jianling Li, Joy Dahlgren and Elva Chang (1999), *Assessing the Benefits and Costs of ITS Projects: Volume 2: An Application to Electronic Toll Collection*, UCB-ITS-PRR-99-10, Berkeley: Institute of Transportation Studies, California PATH Program, University of California, Berkeley.

Gittings, Gary (1987), 'Some Financial, Economic, and Social Policy Issues Associated with Toll Finance', *Transportation Research Record* 1102 pp. 20–30.

Goddard, Stephen (1994), *Getting There: The Epic Struggle Between Road and Rail in the American Century*, New York: Basic Books.

Gomez-Ibañez, José and John Meyer (1993), *Going Private: The International Experience with Transport Privatization*, Washington, DC: Brookings Institution.

Goodrich, Carter (1960), *Government Promotion of American Canals and Railroads: 1800–1890*. Westport Connecticut: Greenwood Press Publishers.

Gray, Ralph (1967), *The National Waterway*, Urbana, Illinois: University of
    Illinois Press.
Gwilliam, Kenneth and Harry Geerlings (1994), 'New Technologies and
    Their Potential to Reduce the Environmental Impact of
    Transportation' *Transportation Research A*, 28A(4), pp. 307–319.
Hall, Kermit (1992) (ed.) *The Oxford Companion to the Supreme Court of
    the United States*, Oxford, England: Oxford University Press.
Hargreaves-Heap, Shaun and Yannis Varoufakis (1995), *Game Theory: A
    Critical Introduction*, New York: Routledge.
Hau, Timothy (1991), *Economic Fundamentals of Road Pricing: A
    Diagrammatic Analysis*, Washington, DC: World Bank
Hau, Timothy (1992), *Congestion Charging Mechanisms: An Evaluation of
    Current Practice*, Washington, DC: World Bank
Heath, David, Glenn Kreger, Glenn Orlin, and Meg Riesett (1989), 'Traffic
    Impact Fees' in Arthur C. Nelson (ed.), *Development Impact Fees*,
    Chicago IL.: APA Press, pp. 188–203.
Hensher David (1991), 'Electronic Toll Collection', *Transportation
    Research Part A*, 25(1), pp. 9–16.
Hensher, David (1995), 'Value of Travel Time Savings in Personal and
    Commercial Automobile Travel',   Paper prepared for the
    Conference on Social Cost–Benefit Analysis, sponsored by the US
    Bureau of Transportation Studies, Irvine, California, July 6–8.
Hilton, George and John Due (1960), *The Electric Interurban Railways in
    America*, Stanford, California: Stanford University Press.
Hood, Clifton (1993), *722 Miles: The Building of the Subways and How
    They Transformed New York*, New York: Simon and Schuster.
IBI Group (1995), *Full Cost Transportation Pricing Study: Final Report to
    Transportation and Climate Change Collaborative*, Ottawa: IBI
    Group.
INFRAS IWW (1995), *External Effects of Transport*, International Union of
    Railways, IWW Karlsruhe University, INFRAS Consultants.
INRETS (1993), *Impact des Transports Terrestres sur l'Environment:
    Méthodes d'Evaluation et Couts Sociaux*, Report no. 23, Institut
    National de Recherche sur les Transport et Leur Securité,
    September, p. 61.
Keeler, Theodore and Kenneth Small (1977), 'Optimal Peak-load Pricing,
    Investment, and Service Levels on Urban Expressways', *Journal of
    Political Economics* , 85(1), pp. 1–25.
Keeler, Theodore, Kenneth Small, and Associates (1975), *The Full Costs of
    Urban Transport, Part III: Automobile Costs and Final Intermodal
    Cost Comparisons*, Monograph no. 212, Berkeley: Institute of
    Urban and Regional Development, University of California at
    Berkeley.

Klein, Daniel (1990), 'The Voluntary Provision of Public Goods? The Turnpike Companies of Early America', *Economic Inquiry*, March, pp. 788-812.

Klein, Daniel and Chi Yin (1996), 'Use, Esteem, and Profit in Voluntary Provision: Toll Roads in California, 1850 - 1902,' *Economic Inquiry*, October 1996, pp. 678-692.

Klein, Daniel and John Majewski (1994), 'Plank Road Fever in Antebellum America: New York State Origins', *New York History*, January, pp. 39–65.

Lay, Maxwell (1992), *Ways of the World: A History of the World's Roads and of the Vehicles That Used Them*, Camden, New Jersey: Rutgers University Press.

Lee, Douglas (1989), 'Evaluation of Impact Fees Against Public Finance Criteria', in Arthur C. Nelson (ed.), *Development Impact Fees*, Chicago: APA Press, pp. 290–312.

Levinson, David (1997), 'Job and Housing Tenure and the Journey to Work', *Annals Of Regional Science* 31(4), pp. 451–471.

Levinson, David (1998), 'The Limits to Growth Management', *Environment and Planning* b 24, pp. 689–707.

Levinson, David and Ajay Kumar (1995), 'A Multi-modal Trip Distribution Model', *Transportation Research Record* No. 1466 pp. 124–131.

Li, Jianling, David Gillen and Joy Dahlgren (1998), 'An Illustration of Benefit-Cost Method for the ETC System At Carquinez Bridge', PATH Program, Institute for Transportation Studies, University Of California, Berkeley.

Li, Jing, Nagui Rouphail, and Rahmi Ak Helik (1985), 'Overflow Delay Estimation For A Simple Intersection With Fully Actuated Signal Control', *Transportation Research Record*, 1457, pp.73–81.

Lin, Feng-Bor and Cheng-Wei Su (1994), 'Level-of-Service Analysis of Toll Plazas on Freeway Main Lines.' *Journal Of Transportation Engineering*, 120(2), pp. 246–263.

Linowes, David (1988), *Privatization: Toward More Effective Government*, Chicago: University of Illinois Press.

Lo, Hong, Mark Hickman and Maura Walstad (1996), *An Evaluation Taxonomy for Congestion Pricing*, UCB-ITS-PRR-96-10, Berkeley: University of California at Berkeley.

Loveland Colorado (2000), Web Page: <http://www.ci.loveland.co.us/INSIDE/finance/budget.htm>.

Mackenzie, James, Roger Dower and Donald Chen (1992), *The Going Rate: What it Really Costs to Drive,* Washington, DC: World Resources Institute.

Maggi, Rico (1994), Environmental Implications of Missing Transport Networks in Europe, *Transportation Research A* 28A(4), pp. 343–350.

Majewski, John, Christopher Baer and Daniel Klein (1993), 'Responding to Relative Decline: The Plank Road Boom of Ante-bellum New York', *The Journal of Economic History*, 53(1) pp. 106–122.

Martin, Albro (1992), *Railroads Triumphant: The Growth, Rejection, and Rebirth of a Vital American Force*, Oxford, England: Oxford University Press.

McCarthy, Patrick and Richard Tay (1993), 'Economic Efficiency vs. Traffic Restraint: A Note on Singapore's Area License Scheme', *Journal of Urban Economics* 34, pp. 96–100.

McCormack, John and Robert Rauch (1997), 'Initial Thoughts on the Mexican Toll Road Restructuring', BradyNet Inc., <http://www.bradynet.com/n036.html>.

McShane, Clay (1994), *Down the Asphalt Path: The Automobile and the American City*, New York: Columbia University Press.

McShane, William and Roger Roess (1990), *Traffic Engineering*, Englewood Cliffs, New Jersey: Prentice Hall.

Medema, Steven and Richard Zerbe, Jr. (1998), 'The Coase Theorem', in *The Encyclopedia of Law and Economics*, <http://allserv.rug.ac.be/~gdegeest/0730art.htm>.

Miller, Eric and Kai-Sheng Fan (1992), 'Travel Demand Behavior: Survey of Intercity Mode-split Models in Canada and Elsewhere' in *Directions: The Final Report of the Royal Commission on National Passenger Transportation*, Vol. 4, Ottawa, Canada: Ministry of Supply and Services.

Miller, Peter and John Moffet (1993), *The Price of Mobility: Uncovering the Hidden Costs of Transportation,* San Francisco: National Resources Defense Council, October.

Miller, Ted (1992), *The Costs of Highway Crashes,* FHWA-RD-91-055, Washington, DC: US Federal Highway Administration.

Mitretek Systems Inc. (1999), *'Intelligent Transportation Systems Benefits: 1999 Update'* Washington, DC: Mitretek Systems Inc.

Modra, J. D. and D.W. Bennett (1985), 'Cost-Benefit Analysis of the Application of Traffic Noise Insulation Measures to Existing Houses', *Forum Papers of 10th Australian Research Forum*, vol. 1, 13–15 May 1985, Melbourne, pp. 63–86.

Mohring, Herbert (1970), 'The Peakload Problem with Increasing Returns and Pricing Constraints', *American Economic Review*. 60, pp. 693–705.

Mohring, Herbert (1976), *Transportation Economics*, Cambridge, Massachusetts: Ballinger Press.

Mohring, Herbert and Mitchell Harwitz (1962), *Highway Benefits: An Analytical Framework*, Evanston, Illinois: Northwestern University Press.

Monroe, Elizabeth (1992), 'Charles River Bridge v. Warren Bridge, in Kermit L. Hall (ed.) *The Oxford Companion to the Supreme Court of the United States*, New York: Oxford University Press, p. 135-6.

National Safety Council (1993), *Accident Facts: 1993 Edition*, Washington DC: National Safety Council.

National Transportation Safety Board (1992), *Annual Review of Aircraft Accident Data: US Air Carrier Operations Calendar Year 1992*, Washington, DC: US Department of Transportation:

Nelson, Arthur C. (ed.) (1989), *Development Impact Fees*, Chicago IL.: APA Press.

Nelson, Jon (1982a), 'Airports and Property Values: A Survey of Recent Evidence', *Journal of Transport Economics and Policy*, January, pp. 37-52.

Nelson, Jon (1982b), 'Highway Noise and Property Values: A Survey of Recent Evidence', *Journal of Transport Economics and Policy*, May, pp.. 117-138.

Newell, Gordon (1980), *Traffic Flow on Transportation Networks*, Cambridge, Massachusetts: MIT Press.

Nicholas, James, Arthur C. Nelson and Julian C. Juergensmeyer (1991), 'A Practitioner's Guide to Development Impact Fees', Chicago: APA Press, Ch. 13.

Nijkamp, Peter (1994), 'Roads Toward Environmentally Sustainable Transport', *Transportation Research A* 28A(4), pp. 261–272.

Nordhaus, William (1994), *Managing the Global Commons,* Cambridge Massachusetts: MIT Press.

OECD (1975), *The Polluter Pays Principle: Definition, Analysis, Implementation.* Paris: OECD.

Olson, Mancur (1965), *The Logic of Collective Action: Public Goods and the Theory of Groups*: Cambridge, Massachusetts: Harvard University Press.

Osborne, Martin and Ariel Rubinstein (1994), *A Course in Game Theory*, Cambridge, Massachusetts: MIT Press,

Ottinger et al. (1990), *Environmental Costs of Electricity*, Buffalo: Pace University Center for Environmental and Legal Studies.

Owen, Wilfred and Charles Dearing (1951), *Toll Roads and the Problems of Highway Modernization*, Washington, DC: The Brookings Institution.

Pawson, Eric (1977), *Transport and Economy: The Turnpike Roads of Eighteenth Century Britain*, New York: Academic Press.

Payne, Peter L. (1956), 'The Bermondsey, Rotherhithe and Deptford Turnpike Trust: 1776-1810', *Journal of Transport History*, 1:2:3: pp. 132–143.

Philip, Davy and Walter Schramm (1997), *'Cashless Tolls Mean Money Saved'* Reprinted from *Traffic Technology International* for Hughes Transportation Management Systems, Canada.

Phillips, A.D.M. and B.J. Turten (1987), 'Staffordshire Turnpike Trusts and Traffic in the Early Nineteenth Century', *Journal of Transport History*, 3:8:2: pp. 126–146.

Pickrell, Donald (1995), 'The Global Warming Problem', Presentation to the Transportation Science Seminar, Institute of Transportation Studies, University of California at Berkeley, March 22.

Pietrzyk, Michael C. and Edward A. Mierzejewski (1993), *'National Cooperative Highway Research Program Synthesis of Highway Practice 194: Electronic Toll and Traffic Management (ETTM) Systems'* Washington, DC: National Academy Press, pp.23–29.

Pigou, A.C. (1932), *The Economics of Welfare, 4th ed.* London.: Macmillan and Co, originally published in 1920.

Pollakowski, Henry and Susan Wachter, (1990), 'The Effects of Land Use Constraints on Housing Prices', *Land Economics* 66(3), pp. 315–324.

Poole, Robert (1997), 'Banner Year For Highway Privatization (Part I)' *Privatization Watch* no. 242, February 1997.

Poole, Robert and Yuzo Sugimoto (1994), 'Congestion Relief Toll Tunnels', *Transportation Quarterly,* 48(2), pp. 115–134.

Popper, Frank (1988), 'Understanding American Land Use Regulation since 1970: A Revisionist Interpretation', *Journal of the American Planning Association,* 54(3), pp. 291–301.

Pritchett, William (1980), *Studies in Ancient Greek Topography Part III (Roads),* University of California Publications in Classical Studies Vol. 22, p. 183. Dec., Berkeley: University of California Press.

Public Roads Administration (PRA) (1996), *The Automatic Toll Ring in Trondheim,* Oslo: Directorate of Public Roads.

Quinet, Emile (1990), *The Social Cost of Land Transport* O E C D Environment Monograph no. 32, April, Paris: OECD.

Rae, John (1971), *The Road and Car in American Life*, Cambridge, Massachusetts: MIT Press.

Rapoport, Amos (1970), *N-Person Game Theory: Concepts and Applications.* Ann Arbor: University of Michigan Press.

Ratemod (2000), Web Page: <http://www.ratemod.com/>.

Reason Foundation (1994), *Eighth Annual Report on Privatization* Los Angeles: Reason Foundation.

Rietveld, Piet (1994), 'Spatial Economic Impacts of Transport Infrastructure Supply', *Transportation Research A* 28A(4) pp. 329–341.

Robinson, Mark and Michel Van Aerde (1995), 'Examining the Delay and Environmental Impacts of Toll Plaza', *Vehicle Navigation and Information Systems Conference Proceedings - 6th International VNIS*, Seattle, WA, July,30- August 2.

Rose, A. (1953), *Historical American Highways - Public Roads of the Past*, Washington, DC: American Association of State Highway Officials.

Roth, Gabriel (1996), *Roads in a Market Economy*, Aldershot UK: Avebury Technical Press.

Rothengatter, Werner (1994), 'Do External Benefits Compensate for External Costs of Transport', *Transportation Research A* 28A(4), pp. 321–328.

Ruster, Jeff (1997), *A Retrospective on the Mexican Toll Road Program*, Private Sector Note 125, Washington, DC: World Bank Group, Finance, Private Sector, and Infrastructure Network.

Schaevitz, Robert (1991), 'Private Sector Role in US Toll Road Financing: Issues and Outlook', *Transportation Research Record,* 1197, pp. 1–8.

Sisson, Mark (1995), 'Air Quality Benefits Of Electronic Toll Collection', *Transportation Quarterly*, 49(4), pp. 93-101.

Small, Kenneth (1983), 'The Incidence of Congestion Tolls on Urban Highways', *Journal of Urban Economics*, 13(1), pp. 90–111.

Small, Kenneth and Camilla Kazimi (1995), 'On the Costs of Air Pollution from Motor Vehicles', *Journal of Transport Economics and Policy*, January, pp. 7–32.

Small, Kenneth, Clifford Winston and Carol Evans (1989), *Road Work: A New Highway Pricing and Investment Policy*, Washington, DC: Brookings Institution.

Smerk, George (1991), *The Federal Role in Urban Mass Transportation*, Bloomington, Indiana: Indiana University Press.

Smith, Adam (1776), *An Inquiry into the Nature And Causes of the Wealth of Nations, Book One of the Causes of Improvement in the Productive Powers of Labour, and of the Order according to which its Produce is Naturally Distributed among the Different Ranks of the People*, Ch. XI Part 1: <http://www.adamsmith.org.uk/smith/won-b1-c11-part-1.htm>.

Smith, Henry Ladd. (1991), *Airways: The History of Commercial Aviation in the United States*, Washington, DC: Smithsonian Institution Press.

Smith, Michael and Merritt Blakeslee (1998) The Language of Trade..
    Washington, DC: US Information Service,
    <http://www.usia.gov/usa/infousa/trade/language/language.htm>.
Spulber, Daniel (1989), *Regulation and Markets*. Cambridge,
    Massachusetts: MIT Press.
Starkie, D.N.M. and D.M. Johnson (1975), *The Economic Value of Peace
    and Quiet*, Saxon House/Lexington Books.
Stopher, Peter (1993), 'Financing Urban Rail Projects: The Case of Los
    Angeles', *Transportation,* 20(3), pp. 229–250.
Sullivan, Edward and Chaug-Ing Hsu (1988), *Accident Rates along
    Congested Freeways,* UCB-ITS-RR-88-6, Berkeley: Institute of
    Transportation Studies, University of California at Berkeley.
Taylor, Michael (1987), *The Possibility of Cooperation*, Cambridge, UK:
    Cambridge University Press.
Tiebout, Charles (1956), 'A Pure Theory of Local Expenditures', *Journal
    of Political Economy*, October, pp. 416–24.
Transportation Research Board (1985), *Highway Capacity Manual*, Special
    Report 209, Washington, DC: Transportation Research Board.
Transportation Research Board (1994), *Curbing Gridlock: Peak Period
    Fees to Relieve Traffic Congestion*, Special Report 242,
    Washington, DC: Transportation Research Board.
Train, Kenneth (1986), *Qualitative Choice Analysis*, Cambridge
    Massachusetts: MIT Press.
UK Department of Transport (1998) *Calculation of Road Traffic Noise*,
    London: Department of Transport, and Cardiff: Welsh Office.
University of Virginia Library Geospatial and Statistical Data Center,
    (1998), *1990 Census Public Use Microdata Samples Public Use
    Micro Areas -- 1% Samples,*
    <http://www.lib.virginia.edu/socsci/1pums/desc/puma.html>.
US Census Bureau (1990), *1990 Decennial Census: Population and Land
    Area by State*, Washington, DC: U.S Census Bureau.
US Census Bureau (1998), *1990 Decennial Census Public Use Microdata
    Samples (PUMS)*, generated by David Levinson using Data
    Extraction System, 1 December (1998),
    <http://www.census.gov/DES/www/welcome.html> .
US Department of Transportation (1976), *America's Highways: 1776-1976*,
    Washington, DC: Federal Highway Administration, Government
    Printing Office.
Urban Institute (1997), *Assessing The New Federalism: Project Overview*,
    <http://www.newfederalism.org>.
Verhoef, Erik (1994), 'External Effects and Social Costs of Road
    Transport', *Transportation Research A* 28A(4), pp. 273–387.

Verhoef, Erik, Peter Nijkamp and Piet Rietveld (1996), 'Second Best Congestion Pricing: The Case of an Untolled Alternative', *Journal of Urban Economics* 40 pp. 279–302.

Vickery, William (1963), 'Pricing in Urban and Suburban Transport', *American Economic Review*, 52(2), pp. 452–65.

Vickery, William (1969), 'Congestion Theory and Transport Investment', *American Economic Review,* 59, pp. 251–60.

Viton, Philip (1981), 'Optimal Tolls on the Bay Bridge', *Journal of Transport Economics and Policy*, 15, pp. 185-204.

Viton, Philip (1990), 'Private Roads', *Journal of Urban Economics*, 37, pp. 260-289.

Von Neumann, John and Oskar Morgenstern (1944), *Theory of Games and Economic Behavior*, Princeton: Princeton University Press.

Wachs, Martin (1994), 'Will Congestion Pricing Ever be Adopted?', *Access*, 4, pp. 15–19.

Walters, Alan (1961), 'The theory and measurement of private and social cost of highway congestion', *Econometrica,* 29(4), pp. 676–97.

Warner, Sam Bass (1962), *Streetcar Suburbs*, Cambridge Massachusetts: Harvard University Press.

Webb, Sidney and Beatrice Webb (1913), *English Local Government: The Story of the King's Highway*, London: Longmans, Green.

Whitt, J. Allen (1982), *Urban Elites and Mass Transportation: The Dialectics of Power*, Princeton: Princeton University Press.

Winston, Clifford (1991), 'Efficient Transportation Infrastructure Policy', *Journal of Economic Perspectives*, 5(1), pp. 113–127.

Woo, T. Hugh and Lester Hoel (1991), *'An Investigation of Toll Plaza Capacity and Level of Service'*, Virginia Transportation Research Council.

Wootton, H.J. and M. L. Poulton (1993), *Reducing Ccarbon Dioxide Emissions from Passenger Cars to 1990 Levels*, Crowthorne, Berkshire: Transportation Research Laboratory, UK Department of Transport, Environment Resource Centre.

Works Consultancy Services Ltd (1993), *Land Transport Externalities: no. 19*, Wellington, New Zealand: Transit New Zealand.

Wright, John (ed.) (1990), *Universal Almanac*, Kansas City: Andrews and McMeel.

Zarrillo, Marguerite, A. Essam Radwan, and Haitham Al-Deek (1997), 'Modeling Traffic Operations at Electronic Toll Collection and Traffic Management Systems', *Computers and Industrial Engineering*, 33(3–4), pp. 857-860.

Index